STEREOTYPE
ACCURACY

STEREOTYPE ACCURACY

TOWARD APPRECIATING GROUP DIFFERENCES

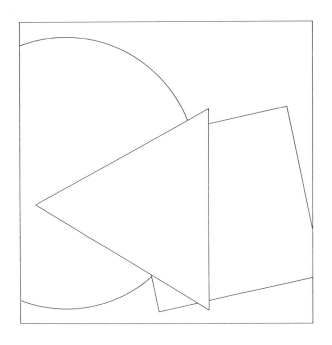

Edited by Yueh-Ting Lee, Lee J. Jussim, and Clark R. McCauley

American Psychological Association
Washington, DC

Published by the
American Psychological Association
750 First Street, NE
Washington, DC 20002

Copies may be ordered from
APA Order Department
P.O. Box 2710
Hyattsville, MD 20784

In the UK and Europe, copies may be ordered from
American Psychological Association
3 Henrietta Street
Covent Garden, London
WC2E 8LU England

Typeset in Minion by University Graphics, Inc., York, PA

Printer: Data Reproductions Corporation, Rochester Hills, MI
Cover Designer: Paul Perlow Design, New York, NY
Technical/Production Editor: Kathryn Lynch

Library of Congress Cataloging-in-Publication Data
Stereotype accuracy : toward appreciating group differences / [edited
    by] Yueh-Ting Lee, Lee Jussim, Clark McCauley.
        p.   cm.
    Papers originally presented at the Stereotype Accuracy Conference
    held at Bryn Mawr College.
    Includes bibliographical references and index.
    ISBN 1-55798-307-0
    1. Stereotype (Psychology)—Congresses.   I. Lee, Yueh-Ting.
II. Jussim, Lee.   III. McCauley, Clark R.   IV. Stereotype Accuracy
Conference (Bryn Mawr College)
BF323.S63S78   1995
303.3'85—dc20   95-16845
                                                                   CIP

British Library Cataloguing-in-Publication Data
A CIP record is available from the British Library.

Printed in the United States of America
First edition

APA Science Volumes

Taste, Experience, and Feeding: Development and Learning

Temperament: Individual Differences at the Interface of Biology and Behavior

Through the Looking Glass: Issues of Psychological Well-Being in Captive Nonhuman Primates

APA expects to publish volumes on the following conference topics:

Attribution Processes, Person Perception and Social Interaction: The Legacy of Ned Jones

Changing Ecological Approaches to Development: Organism–Environment Mutualities

Conceptual Structure and Processes: Emergence, Discovery, and Change

Converging Operations in the Study of Visual Selective Attention

Genetic, Ethological and Evolutionary Perspectives on Human Development

Global Prospects for Education: Development, Culture, and Schooling

Maintaining and Promoting Integrity in Behavioral Science Research

Marital and Family Therapy Outcome and Process Research

Measuring Changes in Patients Following Psychological and Pharmacological Interventions

Psychology of Industrial Relations

Psychophysiological Study of Attention

Stereotypes: Brain–Behavior Relationships

Work Team Dynamics and Productivity in the Context of Diversity

As part of its continuing and expanding commitment to enhance the dissemination of scientific psychological knowledge, the Science Directorate of the APA established a Scientific Conferences Program. A series of volumes resulting from these conferences is produced jointly by the Science Directorate and the Office of Communications. A call for proposals is issued twice annually by the Scientific Directorate, which, collaboratively with the APA Board of Scientific Affairs, evaluates the proposals and selects several conferences for funding. This important effort has resulted in an exceptional series of meetings and scholarly volumes, each of which has contributed to the dissemination of research and dialogue in these topical areas.

The APA Science Directorate's conferences funding program has supported 38 conferences since its inception in 1988. To date, 25 volumes resulting from conferences have been published.

WILLIAM C. HOWELL, PHD
Executive Director

VIRGINIA E. HOLT
Assistant Executive Director

Table of Contents

Contributors

Richard D. Ashmore, Livingston College, Rutgers—The State University of New Jersey

Reuben M. Baron, University of Connecticut

Monica Biernat, University of Kansas

Guillermo Duenas, Philadelphia College of Textiles and Science

Jacquelynne Eccles, University of Michigan

David C. Funder, University of California, Riverside

Lee J. Jussim, Livingston College, Rutgers—The State University of New Jersey

Yueh-Ting Lee, Westfield State College

Laura C. Longo, Livingston College, Rutgers—The State University of New Jersey

Clark R. McCauley, Bryn Mawr College

Victor Ottati, Purdue University

Carey S. Ryan, University of Pittsburgh

Charles Stangor, University of Maryland

Preface

It is not easy to do research on stereotype accuracy, for both scientific and political reasons. Many of the scientific reasons are clearly articulated in the chapters constituting this book. The political difficulties are at least as troubling. The intellectual content of this book commits multiple heresies. First, research on any type of accuracy in social perception was all but unthinkable until the 1980s. Theoretically, social psychology has been and continues to be dominated by a focus on social cognition that emphasizes error and bias; research finding evidence of accuracy runs against the theoretical zeitgeist. As Thomas Kuhn might have predicted, this is probably one of the major sources of resistance to accuracy research. Second, the idea that stereotypes may sometimes have some degree of accuracy is apparently anathema to many social scientists and laypeople. Those who document accuracy run the risk of being seen as racists, sexists, or worse.

Against such impediments, this book emerges only with the help of a great deal of teamwork. The three editors have thoroughly enjoyed working with each other and with the expert and professional colleagues who have contributed chapters to this book. In addition, we have enjoyed outstanding support from institutions and colleagues who went out of their way to help us.

Here we would like to acknowledge the institutions whose support made the book possible. First and most important is the American Psychological Association, in particular, the APA Science Directorate, which provided financial support both for the Stereotype Accuracy Conference held at Bryn Mawr College and for the development of conference contributions into this book. Second, the following institutions also provided financial and logistical support: Bryn Mawr College, Philadelphia College of Textiles and Science, Rutgers University, and Westfield State College.

We would also like to extend our thanks to the following individuals. Albert Pepitone (University of Pennsylvania) served as a discussant at the Stereotype Accuracy Conference at Bryn Mawr and offered us many helpful comments and suggestions. John Aiello (Rutgers University), Linda Albright (Westfield State College), Dana Bramel (State University of New York at Stony Brook), Tom Malloy (Rhode Island College), Melvin Manis (University of Michigan), Albert Pepitone (University of Pennsylvania), David Wilder (Rutgers University), and Arlene Walker-Andrews (Rutgers University) assisted us in reviewing our manuscripts carefully and provided us with their insightful and constructive criticisms for revising the chapters that appear in the book. Any weaknesses remaining are our own. David Kenny (University of Connecticut) and Harry Triandis (University of Illinois at Urbana-Champaign) provided us with important collaboration and encouragement. Peggy Schlegel, Kathryn Lynch, and other APA staff helped us in editing and producing this book in a meticulous and proficient way.

Finally, we are grateful to our families. Their nurturance, encouragement, and support inspired hope and optimism in us beyond what can be put into words.

Y. T. L.
L. J.
C. R. M.

PART ONE

Introduction

1

Why Study Stereotype Accuracy and Inaccuracy?

Lee J. Jussim, Clark R. McCauley, and Yueh-Ting Lee

I s this book necessary? The chapters contained each address issues of stereotype accuracy and inaccuracy. But don't we already know that stereotypes are inaccurate, exaggerated, resistant to change, ethnocentric, and harmful? Aren't only racists and sexists interested in stereotype accuracy?

Our answers are yes (a book on accuracy and inaccuracy is sorely needed), no (we do not know that stereotypes are generally inaccurate), and no (racism and sexism have no place in the study of stereotype accuracy). However, these questions highlight an important limitation and bias within the social sciences: The preponderance of scholarly theory and research on stereotypes assumes that they are bad and inaccurate. If so, then it might well be true that people interested in showing that stereotypes are accurate have hidden racist and sexist agendas. In fact, however, understanding stereotype accuracy and inaccuracy is much more interesting and complicated than simpleminded accusations of racism or sexism would seem to imply.

Correspondence concerning this chapter should be addressed to Lee J. Jussim, Department of Psychology, Rutgers University, New Brunswick, New Jersey 08903.

The idea that stereotypes are inaccurate and unjustified pervades the social sciences, many educational and business communities, and the everyday discourse of pundits and politicians. It often influences the content of programs designed to promote diversity. It is a common theme in everyday cultural discourse. Therefore, we believe that this book is potentially important for anyone interested in understanding the issues of culture, race, class, and gender that so trouble American society at the end of the twentieth century.

This book also addresses the impact of stereotyping on judgments of individual members of stereotyped groups. Thus, this book addresses issues frequently confronted by professionals responsible for evaluation of individuals in government, business, and educational institutions and organizations. These issues can be difficult. In recent years, the fairness of an individual's evaluation has not infrequently been subject to legal challenge, on grounds that amount to claiming that the evaluation was based more on group stereotypes than on individual qualifications or performance. For this reason, we believe that not only psychologists, sociologists, and other social scientists but also legal professionals, and the managers and personnel officers they serve should find this book of use. For example, issues of fairness in selection, employment, and promotion are increasingly pertinent in work settings today.

In the conclusion of this chapter, we discuss more specifically how each chapter serves these audiences. Before describing the chapters, however, we would like to concentrate on the assumption that stereotypes are bad and inaccurate. We intend to show that this assumption is conceptually problematic and empirically unjustified, and we identify both theoretical and practical reasons why the scientific study of stereotype accuracy and inaccuracy is both timely and important.

ARE STEREOTYPES NECESSARILY INACCURATE?

The answer to this question depends on whether one defines stereotypes as inaccurate beliefs about groups (see, e.g., Brigham, 1971; Mackie, 1973). If so, then, by definition, they must be inaccurate. However, defining stereotypes in this way creates serious conceptual problems. This definition would seem to require that researchers interested in stereotypes study only beliefs about groups for which invalidity has been clearly documented. For example, one could study the belief that the Jews run the banks or the belief that most African American people are on welfare. Both beliefs are demonstrably false (e.g., Marger, 1991).

Defining stereotypes as inaccurate would also appear to preclude the study of the belief that American Jews are wealthier than are most other ethnic groups or that the majority of people on welfare are minorities. Both beliefs are true (DeParle, 1994; Marger, 1991) and, therefore, would not qualify as stereotypes. This definition would also seem to preclude study of stereotypes that Germans are efficient, gay men are effeminate, or librarians are introverted. There is no evidence documenting the invalidity of these beliefs.

In fact, most reviews of stereotyping conclude that there is very little evidence regarding the validity of beliefs about groups (e.g., Brigham, 1971; Judd & Park, 1993; Jussim, 1990; McCauley, Stitt, & Segal, 1980; Ottati & Lee, chapter 2, this volume). Furthermore, it may be very difficult to obtain objective information about many attributes (such as efficiency, effeminacy, or laziness). To take seriously a definition of stereotypes as inaccurate beliefs would lead to a drastic reduction in empirical research on stereotypes. Few beliefs about groups have been empirically demonstrated to be false; therefore, few beliefs about groups would qualify as stereotypes.

Conceptually, it seems more parsimonious to leave *inaccurate* out of any definition of stereotypes (see also Ashmore & Del Boca, 1981). If someone believes that Jews are wealthier than other groups, is this not a stereotype (even if it is true)? Scientifically, is there any advantage to saying that the belief that Jews run the banks is a stereotype, but that the belief that Jews are wealthier than are other groups is not? We see no reason to assume that accurate beliefs about groups function differently than inaccurate beliefs. By definition, when people hold a belief, they think that belief is true.

We do not define stereotypes in this chapter; that task is left to the authors of the chapters that constitute this volume (see also Ashmore &

Del Boca, 1981, for a review). Regardless of differences in definition, however, all authors in this book agree that stereotypes constitute people's beliefs about groups—beliefs that may be positive or negative, accurate or inaccurate. Nonetheless, many laypeople and social scientists still seem to assume that stereotypes are inaccurate, rigid, and pernicious. In the next sections, therefore, we identify the typical accusations leveled against stereotypes and evaluate their scientific status. Are stereotypes factually incorrect? Are they rigid? Are they illogical? Do they lead people to exaggerate differences among groups?

What Is Wrong With Stereotypes?

The Classic Charges

From Katz and Braly (1933) to the present, stereotypes have been condemned as factually incorrect, illogical in origin, and irrationally resistant to new information about the stereotyped group. Each of these charges is well-founded if a stereotype is understood as an exceptionless generalization about the target group (e.g., "All Asians are smart"). However, each is baseless if a stereotype is understood as a probabilistic prediction about how the target group differs from others (McCauley et al., 1980). Below we show how few, if any, of the classic charges against stereotypes would apply to a belief that Asians are likely to do better academically than individuals from most other groups. This distinction between all-or-none beliefs and probabilistic beliefs is crucial for evaluating the validity of some of the most common charges against stereotypes.

Stereotypes are factually incorrect. This must be true if a stereotype is an all-or-none generalization about members of the stereotyped group. It cannot be the case that every German is efficient. If there is even one inefficient German, the stereotype is incorrect. Allport (1954) took this approach in distinguishing stereotypes from valid beliefs about group characteristics. For Allport, "all lawyers are crooked" is a stereotype; "lawyers are more crooked than most people" is not (p. 192).

Do people hold such all-or-none stereotypes? The research evidence

6

on this question is clear: Although people often perceive differences among groups, we are not aware of a single study identifying a single person who believed that all members of a social group had a particular stereotype attribute (see reviews by Brigham, 1971; Judd & Park, 1993; Jussim, 1990; McCauley et al., 1980).

But if stereotypes are not 100% generalizations, then it is no longer clear that they are factually incorrect. Rather, it is clear that we are in no position to evaluate the accuracy of many everyday stereotypes. Where are the data that could tell us, for instance, the percentage of Germans who are efficient or whether Germans are probabilistically more efficient than other groups?

Stereotypes are illogical in origin. It is often suggested that stereotypes are based on illogical or irrational foundations because they do not arise from personal experience. That stereotypes can be hearsay was already evident when Katz and Braly's (1933) Princeton students reported strong agreement that Turks were cruel and treacherous—even though these students also reported never having met a Turk. To accept such a pernicious group generalization on the basis of hearsay would appear to be dubious indeed.

But was it really that dubious? One must remember that in the early part of this century, Turks massacred millions of Armenians. Is it so unreasonable that college students strongly agreed about the cruelty of Turks? Would it have been unreasonable in 1950 for college students to agree on the aggressiveness of the Germans? Would it be unreasonable today for college students to agree on the cruelty of the Serbs?

But the "hearsay" charge suffers an even more serious problem: the assumption that learning about groups from other people is necessarily illogical and incorrect. We cannot help but wonder, How can any teacher suggest that only personal experience is valid learning? Must we go to the moon to learn about it? Must we go to Guatemala to learn about the rain forest? Must we go to Indonesia to learn about Indonesians?

Stereotypes are based in prejudice. This is actually a variant of the "illogical in origin" charge, and it reflects an assumption underlying much of the first 30 years of research in stereotypes (e.g., Adorno, Frenkel-

7

Brunswick, Levinson, & Sanford, 1950; Katz & Braly, 1933; LaPiere, 1936). Especially if prejudice is considered an affective predisposition to a group (an attitude of liking or disliking a social group), there is considerable historical evidence suggesting that stereotypes may sometimes serve to justify prejudice. National stereotypes, in particular, can change quickly with changing international attitudes and alliances (e.g., Americans had negative views of Germans and positive views of Russians during World War II, but positive views of Germans and negative views of Russians after World War II; see Oakes, Haslam, & Turner, 1994, for a review).

Interestingly, however, there has been little empirical study of the relation between strength or accuracy of stereotyping and attitude toward the stereotyped group. One example of this kind of inquiry is a study by Eagly and Mladinic (1989), which found that strength of gender stereotyping correlated only about .2 to .3 with attitudes toward men and women (although the study found considerably higher correlations between stereotypes of and attitudes toward Democrats and Republicans). Similarly, McCauley and Thangavelu (1991) found that strength of gender stereotyping of occupations was unrelated to attitude toward women in nontraditional occupations, although stereotype strength was positively correlated with accuracy.

On conceptual grounds, there are many stereotypes that are unlikely to be based in affect or prejudice. For example, it is hard to imagine much of a role for prejudice in the beliefs that men are taller than women, that professional basketball players are tall and athletic, or that art majors tend to be creative. Thus, the role of affect and attitude in creating stereotypes would seem to be an interesting empirical question rather than a defining component of stereotypes.

Stereotypes are irrationally resistant to new information. People rarely change their beliefs about groups when confronted with a single individual who does not fit their stereotype. Does this represent irrational resistance to new information? The answer to this is yes under only one condition: when the stereotype is an all-or-none generalization. If one meets a German who is all thumbs, never has a plan, and takes forever to accomplish anything, and still maintains a stereotype of all Germans as efficient, then one is clearly being irrational.

As noted earlier, however, we know of no research documenting the existence of people who believe all members of any stereotyped group have any particular attribute. In casual conversation, when people say things like "New Yorkers are loud and aggressive," we doubt that they mean all New Yorkers. Instead, they most likely mean that in general, or on average, New Yorkers are louder and more aggressive than most other people. Are these people being irrational if they do not change their belief when confronted with a calm, passive New Yorker? We do not think so. Should you change your belief that Alaska is colder than New York, even if we can show you evidence that one day last month, it was warmer in Alaska? Again, we do not think so. In fact, it would be irrational in a statistical sense if you did change your belief on such minimal evidence (see Tversky & Kahneman, 1971, on the "law of small numbers"). Similarly, if 12 million people live in the New York area, and if "New Yorkers are loud and aggressive," means something like "three fourths of all New Yorkers are loud and aggressive," then there are still 3 million New Yorkers who are not loud and aggressive. It would be irrational to change a belief about millions of New Yorkers on the basis of a few disconfirming individuals.

Some More Sophisticated Charges

Beginning with Campbell (1967) and LeVine and Campbell (1972), there has been a more sophisticated critique of stereotypes that goes beyond the metaphor of stereotypes as all-or-none pictures of the stereotyped group (see also Brown, 1965). LeVine and Campbell see stereotypes as probabilistic predictions that are not known to be wrong. They argued that what is wrong with stereotypes is that they are likely to be exaggerations of real group differences, that they are ethnocentric, and that they imply genetic rather than environmental causes of group differences. Again we consider these charges briefly.

Stereotypes are exaggerations of real group differences. LeVine and Campbell (1972) cite the substantial literature on contrast effects in human perception to suggest that contrast effects in perception of group differences are essentially unavoidable. As dark grey looks darker and light grey looks lighter across a contour line, so Germans should look more efficient and Italians less efficient across a group boundary. In general, if there is a real difference between two groups, the perception of that difference—the stereotype—should be incorrect at least to the extent of exaggerating the real difference.

This exaggeration hypothesis comes with impeccable credentials from sensation–perception psychology, but there is little evidence for it (Martin, 1987)—at least not when the criterion of group difference is some kind of objective measure (McCauley & Stitt, 1978; McCauley & Thangavelu, 1991; McCauley, Thangavelu, & Rozin, 1988; Swim, 1994). McCauley examines relevant research in this volume (chapter 9); here, we note only that the exaggeration hypothesis is so far only a hypothesis.

Stereotypes are ethnocentric. Brown (1965) has been perhaps the most explicit in suggesting that stereotypes are wrong because they include evaluating outgroup characteristics by ingroup standards. Certainly it is true that there is evaluation as well as description in the trait words with which stereotypes have been assessed since Katz and Braly (1933). *Efficient* is not just a summary of a behavior pattern, not just a comparison with others on a dimension of individual difference, but a positive evaluation of the upper percentiles of this dimension. Similar descriptive content, but a very different evaluation, is conveyed by traits such as *aggressive* and *assertive*. Brown objects to smuggling in an evaluative component of the stereotype as if it were as objective as the description.

Perhaps the easiest way to put the ethnocentrism charge in perspective is to recognize that personality-trait words are only one of many kinds of characteristics on which groups can be seen to differ. Perceptions of group differences may include physical appearance, behaviors, occupations, preferences, and values. At most, the charge of ethnocentrism is an argument against personality-trait stereotypes. The ethnocentrism charge has little relevance for more objective attributes. The stereotype of African Americans as having a higher percentage of female-headed families, the stereotype of women as having lower math Scholastic Achievement Test (SAT) scores, and the stereotype of business school students as less interested in taking a poetry course—these are not stereotypes that are wrong because they smuggle in an evaluation by local standards.

In addition, although stereotypes regarding personality attributes may be more subject to ethnocentrism than are more objective characteristics, there is no evidence suggesting that even stereotypes about personality attributes are *always* influenced by ethnocentrism. Like the exaggeration hypothesis, the ethnocentrism hypothesis is an interesting one. Although ethnocentrism undoubtedly *sometimes* influences evaluations (e.g., Campbell, 1967), it is premature to conclude that even stereotypes about personality *necessarily* reflect ethnocentrism.

Stereotypes imply genetic origins of group differences This charge implies that we already know that many or most group differences do not have substantial genetic foundations. The truth is, of course, that we do not know any such thing. Indeed, many have been surprised by recent evidence suggesting that even political and religious views may be more similar in separated monozygotic twins than in separated dizygotic twins (Bouchard, Lykken, McGue, Segal, et al., 1990). Although many psychologists may prefer environmental explanations to biological ones, most researchers also agree that it is exceedingly difficult to distinguish biological and environmental contributions to group differences (e.g., Gould, 1981; Mackenzie, 1984).

If we do not know the extent to which genetics causes differences among groups, we are in no position to declare that people who believe in genetic differences are inaccurate. Their beliefs may not be supported by scientific evidence, but this is because the evidence is sparse or its interpretation unclear, not because the evidence disproves genetic sources of group differences.

Even more important, this charge suffers a fundamentally flawed assumption—that people actually assume a genetic basis for group differences. We are aware of only one recent study that examined the degree to which nonpsychologists attribute group differences to biological as opposed to environmental causes (Martin & Parker, 1995; cf. Buchanan &

Cantril, 1953). This study showed that a sample of undergraduate students believed that differences in socialization and opportunities were a stronger basis for gender and race differences than were differences in biology. Whether people other than undergraduates hold similar beliefs is currently an open question.

"They all look alike to me" (outgroup homogeneity). Another more sophisticated accusation against stereotypes is that they lead people to assume that members of outgroups are more similar to one another than they really are (the outgroup is seen as more homogeneous than it really is). This is one of the few accusations against stereotypes that have received some empirical attention. Although there may be some tendency for people to see outgroups as less diverse than they really are (see Judd & Park, 1993, for a review), outgroup homogeneity is far from universal (see, e.g., Linville, Fischer, & Salovey, 1989; Simon & Pettigrew, 1990). In fact, outgroup and minority group members often see themselves as more homogeneous than they see ingroup or majority group members (Brewer, 1993; Lee, 1993; Simon & Brown, 1987). Americans and Chinese perceivers both judge Americans to be more diverse than are the Chinese—which, on many dimensions, they really are (Lee & Ottati, 1993). Like many of the other charges, outgroup homogeneity seems to be a hypothesis worth pursuing rather than an established fact.

Stereotypes' Role in Person Perception

Thus far, the charges we have reviewed all focus on stereotypes as perceptions of groups. A second set of charges focuses on the errors and biases produced by stereotypes when people interact with, perceive, or evaluate individuals from the stereotyped group. We briefly review these charges.

Stereotypes lead people to ignore individual differences. This is a variant on the "rigidity" claim: Not only is it difficult to change people's perceptions of groups, but people supposedly automatically assume that each member of a group fits the group stereotype, no matter how different any particular member may be. Before obtaining individuating information about a particular target person, perceivers often do *expect* that person to fit a stereotype of their group, but this is completely appropriate. In the absence of any other information, most people would probably expect any given day in Alaska to be colder than that day in New York, and they would expect a professional basketball player to be taller than most other people. However, we doubt that there are many perceivers who would still judge that particular day as colder in Alaska than in New York if they were also told that it was sunny, mild, and 55° F in Anchorage and cloudy, windy, and 40° F in New York. Similarly, we doubt that many people would consider Mugsy Bogues very tall if they met him; he is a professional basketball player and is listed at about 5 ft, 4 in. tall.

But do stereotypes function this way? Yes. When individuating information is ambiguous or difficult to detect (e.g., Darley & Gross, 1983; Nelson, Biernat, & Manis, 1990), people often rely on their stereotypes rather than individuating information. However, of all the studies that have manipulated both group information (e.g., ethnicity, gender, social class, and profession) and the personal characteristics of targets (e.g., job competence and academic success), we are not aware of a single one that has shown that people *ignore* individual differences (see Funder, chapter 6, this volume). Perceivers base their judgments far more on the personal characteristics of targets than on targets' gender or membership in ethnic groups (e.g., Jackson, Sullivan, & Hodge, 1993; Jussim, Coleman, & Lerch, 1987; Krueger & Rothbart, 1988; Linville & Jones, 1980; Locksley, Borgida, Brekke, & Hepburn, 1980; Rokeach & Mezei, 1966; see Jussim, 1990, for a review). Although someday some researcher may identify a condition under which stereotypes really do lead people to ignore individual differences, this hypothesis has so far only been falsified: It has been repeatedly tested, but never confirmed.

Stereotypes lead to biased perceptions of individuals. This is a weaker counterpart to the "ignore individual differences" charge. That is, although people may not *ignore* individual differences, stereotypes may still influence or bias judgments. For example, teachers may evaluate students who perform above the mean on a math test more favorably than students who score below the mean; but regardless of where students score, teachers may evaluate most boys more favorably than they deserve, and they may eval-

13

uate most girls less favorably than they deserve (see Jussim & Fleming, in press, for a detailed presentation of this argument). Undoubtedly, stereotypes do sometimes lead to these types of biases (see Jussim, 1990, 1991, for reviews). Interestingly, however, stereotypes sometimes lead to counterstereotypic judgments of individuals. Girls have been viewed as more aggressive than boys (Condry & Ross, 1985), and African American job applicants and law school candidates have been evaluated more favorably than equally qualified Whites (e.g., Jussim et al., 1987; Linville & Jones, 1980). Other studies show no evidence of stereotypes biasing judgments of individuals (e.g., Krueger & Rothbart, 1988, Study 2; Locksley et al., 1980). In general, it seems that the more information people have about individual targets, the less they rely on their social stereotypes in arriving at judgments about those individuals (Eagly, Ashmore, Makhijani, & Longo, 1991; Jussim, 1990). Although stereotypes *sometimes* lead to biased perceptions of individuals, it is a misrepresentation of the research evidence to claim or imply that stereotypes *generally* lead to biased perceptions.

Stereotypes create self-fulfilling prophecies. A self-fulfilling prophecy occurs when "an originally false definition of a situation becomes true" (Merton, 1948). For example, in the early part of this century, most unions barred African American workers from membership. Union members often claimed that African Americans were strikebreakers and could not be trusted. This severely limited African Americans' job opportunities. When faced with a strike, companies often offered jobs to all takers, and African Americans often jumped at the chance for work. Thus, the union's beliefs about African Americans were confirmed.

Undoubtedly, stereotypes are sometimes self-fulfilling (see Jussim & Fleming, in press, for a review). Often, however, the effects of expectations are small or nonexistent (see Chapman & McCauley, 1993, for a natural experiment testing the power of the expectations associated with the title, National Science Foundation graduate fellow). Furthermore, stereotypes are not necessarily inaccurate (as documented throughout this volume), and in the absence of an inaccurate expectation, a self-fulfilling prophecy cannot occur. Even inaccurate expectations do not necessarily produce self-fulfilling prophecies (Jussim, 1986, 1991).

It is worth noting that the claim that stereotypes are inaccurate contradicts the claim that stereotypes create self-fulfilling prophecies. If stereotypes create a self-fulfilling prophecy, then the stereotyped belief *becomes* true (even if it was false to begin with). For example, we know that at least part of the physical attractiveness stereotype is not self-fulfilling. That is, people believe attractive individuals are smarter than less attractive individuals, which is false (see meta-analyses by Eagly et al., 1991; Feingold, 1992). But if it is false, we know that this stereotyped belief cannot possibly be self-fulfilling. Although understanding when and how stereotypes may be self-fulfilling is an important and interesting question, it is also a misrepresentation of the research evidence to claim or imply that stereotypes *generally* lead to self-fulfilling prophecies.

WHY STUDY STEREOTYPE ACCURACY (AND INACCURACY)?

Stereotypes Have Been Stereotyped!

We have just argued that the typical charges against stereotypes are inaccurate, unjustified, exaggerated, and not based on empirical evidence. Sound familiar? However, the frequency with which these charges are repeated in the scientific literature (often without reference to empirical studies)—combined with sociopolitical factors (a desire by many social scientists to help and defend oppressed groups and to remedy injustice; a fear of being labeled *racist* or *sexist*)—has led social scientists to premature conclusions regarding stereotype accuracy and inaccuracy. If we all "know" that stereotypes are inaccurate, rigid, and ethnocentric, and that only racists and sexists say otherwise, then clearly there is no need for empirical research.

However, the current state of our scientific knowledge cannot support broad, sweeping statements about stereotypes' inaccuracy, rigidity, or irrationality. This is not because the typical charges against stereotypes are unequivocally or always false. Rather, broad generalizations are inappropriate because there is little evidence regarding many of the claims, and because when there is considerable evidence, it presents a decidedly mixed picture.

15

The Reopening of Important Research Questions

One of the main purposes of this volume is to reopen the scientific study of stereotype accuracy and inaccuracy. These issues were occasionally debated from the 1930s through the 1960s (although the debates were rarely backed by much empirical data; see Ottati & Lee, chapter 2, this volume). However, an unfortunate side effect of the cognitive revolution in social psychology of the 1970s and 1980s—with its emphasis on cognitive process, error, and bias—was that the view of stereotypes as fundamentally flawed came to dominate psychology, despite a nearly complete lack of support for any of the typical charges against stereotypes (see Funder, chapter 6, this volume; Ottati & Lee, chapter 2, this volume; Oakes et al., 1994).

So should the charges against stereotypes be dropped? We think not. Although they are inappropriate as assumptions or sweeping generalizations, they are valuable as *hypotheses*—questions for guiding future research. When are stereotypes likely to be accurate and inaccurate? To what extent do people subscribe to genetic explanations of group differences? When do stereotypes lead to self-fulfilling prophecies? These are interesting, exciting, and important questions.

Figure 1 presents a simple, two-dimensional analysis of the state of knowledge within the social sciences regarding stereotypes. One dimension is *accuracy–inaccuracy*. That is, people's beliefs about groups may range from completely accurate to completely inaccurate. As nearly all theoretical perspectives on accuracy in social perception (e.g., Funder, 1987; Judd & Park, 1993; Jussim, 1991; Kenny & Albright, 1987; Swann, 1984), our view of accuracy is as a quantitative, rather than qualitative, phenomenon. Someone who believes that most people on welfare are African American is considerably less accurate than someone who believes that about 40% of the people on welfare are African American (the U.S. census figure is 38.8%; DeParle, 1994).

The second dimension is *valence*: The content of any particular stereotype may be either positive or negative. Although valence is sometimes in the eye of the beholder, there is probably wide agreement on many attributes. For example, most of us would probably rather be wealthy, ath-

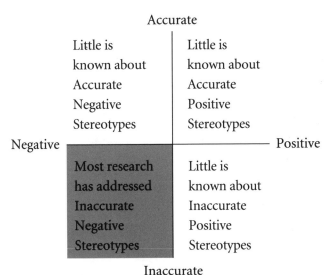

Accurate

Little is known about Accurate Negative Stereotypes	Little is known about Accurate Positive Stereotypes

Negative ———————————————— Positive

Most research has addressed Inaccurate Negative Stereotypes	Little is known about Inaccurate Positive Stereotypes

Inaccurate

Figure 1

Stereotypes may vary in accuracy and valence.

letic, intelligent, diligent, and generous than impoverished, physically weak, dumb, lazy, and cheap. Of course, sometimes essentially the same attribute may be seen in either positive or negative light (e.g., "We are thrifty; they are cheap"; see Campbell, 1967; Merton, 1948). Despite its limitations, we consider Figure 1 useful in providing a succinct overview of the current state of research on stereotypes: Most perspectives fall into the lower left-hand quadrant—emphasizing inaccuracy (e.g., error or bias) in negative stereotypes.

However, it seems to us that social scientists interested in understanding mental representations of social groups should find research in the other three quadrants to be essential. Can negative stereotypes be accurate? How about positive stereotypes? Can positive stereotypes be inaccurate? Especially in regard to both people's perceptions of groups and their perceptions of individuals belonging to salient social groups, Figure 1 raises many important research questions.

17

Understanding and Redressing Social Problems

Much of the interest in stereotypes stems from the belief that they are a major contributor to social problems such as inequalities in educational and occupational opportunities. It is somewhat surprising, therefore, to note that most recent stereotype research in social psychology has been limited to experimental laboratory studies. Whatever their value in testing possible mechanisms of error and bias, laboratory studies cannot provide direct evidence regarding the role of stereotypes in creating injustices in schools, the workplace, or the home. Such evidence can only come from study of the accuracy and impact of everyday stereotypes in the world outside the laboratory.

From a policy perspective, it is not desirable either to minimize or to maximize the contribution of stereotypes to social problems. Undoubtedly, there are inequalities between groups; undoubtedly, people hold stereotypes about groups. Does this mean that the stereotypes cause the inequality? Not necessarily. There are also differences between the quality of different restaurants, and people perceive differences in the quality of different restaurants. Does this mean that people's beliefs about the differences between two restaurants cause one restaurant to be better than the other? Inferring that stereotypes cause inequalities from the mere existence of both stereotypes and inequalities is essentially inferring causality from correlation. Perhaps group differences cause stereotypes. Perhaps other factors—such as socialization, segregation, or opportunity structure—cause both the stereotypes and the inequalities.

In the major social psychology journals, however, stereotyping and discrimination seem to be by far the most studied of potential contributors to individual injustice and group hostility. It is our impression that a count of the number of articles on different topics would suggest that individuals' stereotyping, prejudice, and discrimination are more important sources of social problems than are residential segregation patterns, crime, drug abuse, poverty, and single-parent households combined. Clearly, trivializing the role of stereotypes in injustice could exacerbate the difficulty of redressing that injustice. However, exaggerating the contribution of stereotypes to social problems may be as damaging as discounting them for two reasons: Exaggeration can lead to spending more time, energy, and money correcting stereotypes than is warranted, and the focus on stereotyping can distract attention from study of other important contributions to those same injustices.

Enhancing Intergroup Relations

From the classic view of stereotypes as negative, inaccurate, and irrational, the obvious approach to enhancing intergroup relations (e.g., reducing hostility and discrimination, increasing cooperation and harmony) is to dispel those stereotypes. Usually, this has involved encouraging direct contact with members of the disparaged group (e.g., Amir, 1969). However, such an approach fails if stereotypes are accurate. For example, if a U.S. businessman does not like dealing with Mexicans because they often show up half an hour or more after the time for which meetings have been scheduled, one cannot readily dispel the stereotype if Mexicans really do frequently show up half an hour after meetings have been scheduled (see Lee & Duenas, chapter 7, this volume, for a discussion of Mexicans' more flexible view of time).

Nonetheless, stereotype accuracy is probably crucial to enhancing intergroup relations. In fact, stereotype accuracy may be a crucial component of enhancing sensitivity to diversity and cultural awareness. If different groups are to get along with one another, they need to understand that not all groups hold the same beliefs, values, and assumptions as their own group. They need to become aware of the existence and meaning of cultural differences. From our perspective, this means enhancing the accuracy of individuals' beliefs about social groups (i.e., their stereotypes). Americans who know that Mexicans often show up 30 min or so after the meeting has been scheduled are able to prepare for it (by scheduling it earlier, by showing up after the scheduled time themselves, or by bringing other work to do). Someone who is unaware of Mexicans' greater flexibility with time is likely to feel insulted and angry. Different cultural and ethnic groups often have very different norms of nonverbal communication—norms that may often be upsetting to, or misinterpreted by, people from outside cultures (e.g., Erickson, 1979; Hall, 1959, 1966). Knowing about other cultures (developing an accurate stereotype) can help reduce intergroup friction and smooth the way for more positive interactions.

THE CHAPTERS IN THIS BOOK

Scientific research on stereotype accuracy is in its infancy. Few studies have addressed accuracy by comparing stereotypes to any sort of criterion (see Judd & Park, 1993; Jussim, 1990; Ottati & Lee, chapter 2, this volume, for reviews). As yet, there is little in the way of shared theory, questions, methods, or paradigms for investigating stereotype accuracy and inaccuracy. Nor should there be: In such an early stage, inquiry into stereotype accuracy should be open to many different approaches. We hope that this book helps initiate a revival of scientific interest in stereotype accuracy. Perhaps 15 years from now, research will have led us to better questions, improved methods, and even some unifying theories.

Although all the chapters in this book address interrelated issues of accuracy and inaccuracy in stereotypes, each is also intended to be capable of standing alone as a coherent essay. To accomplish this intent, several chapters set the context for their ideas by briefly reviewing some of the relevant research on stereotyping. Consequently, readers may find some slight redundancy in the introductory sections of some chapters.

Introduction and History

Our introduction (chapter 1) has looked back in time to trace the history of the charges against stereotypes. Broadening the historical perspective, Ottati and Lee (chapter 2) present a comprehensive review of research on stereotype accuracy and inaccuracy. These two chapters should be of value to anyone in the social sciences interested in the history of thinking about stereotypes.

Theoretical, Conceptual, and Methodological Issues

The next section offers a wide variety of perspectives in the study of stereotype accuracy. Ashmore and Longo (chapter 3) present a searching analysis of the complex issues involved in assessing stereotype accuracy and inaccuracy. They argue that assessing accuracy requires understanding the content and structure of stereotypic beliefs, clearly identifying the target group, and separating individual and group differences in stereotyping. They also address the question of where to begin the study of stereotypes (e.g., with perceivers' beliefs or with targets' attributes?) and the criterion issue (how are stereotype and group attributes assessed?).

Biernat (chapter 4) reviews her program of research showing that people use different standards in evaluating targets from different groups. This is important, because people may appear to evaluate different target individuals similarly when they use subjective scales of measurement; but differences often emerge when they evaluate targets on objective scales. Baron (chapter 5) presents an ecological/Gibsonian analysis of the nature of accuracy in social perception and then applies that analysis to understanding accuracy and inaccuracy in social stereotypes.

Funder (chapter 6) documents how, in social psychology, people are accused of error and bias when they ignore base rates (e.g., Tversky & Kahneman, 1971) and likewise are accused of error and bias when they use base rates (i.e., rely on their stereotypes when judging individuals). Funder points out the inherent contradiction of these accusations—people cannot be wrong no matter what they do—and argues that it is incorrect in principle to make judgments about accuracy from studies focusing on process. Lee and Duenas (chapter 7) focus on the role of stereotype accuracy in the management of cultural differences in organizations. They analyze several case studies of conflicts between individuals in organizations that result from misinterpretation of cultural differences. Furthermore, they argue that some forms of miscommunication, misinterpretation, and conflict may be reduced by enhancing stereotype accuracy—leading people to understand the role of culture in creating differences in perspectives, values, beliefs, and behavior among their employers, employees, and coworkers.

The chapters in this section should be of interest well beyond the field of social psychology. The methodological and conceptual issues raised by Ashmore and Longo will be relevant to anyone interested in assessing stereotypes, including commercial stereotypes of brand image or consumer image (e.g., wine drinkers vs. beer drinkers vs. nondrinkers; bottled water drinkers vs. tap water drinkers). Biernat's research showing that people use different standards when judging people from different groups is relevant to judgments made in many everyday settings, including the workplace and the classroom, and has significant implications for anyone involved in cross-cultural research or diversity training. Baron's Gibsonian perspective should be interesting to all those who seek to put cognitive psychology to work for social psychology; more abstractly, Baron's chapter is a model of the difficult art of conceptual translation between disciplines. Funder's chapter is important in raising a serious challenge to those who would rule out stereotype-based predictions as discrimination. This challenge deserves the attention of all who make or litigate personnel decisions. And finally, the chapter by Lee and Duenas offers some practical guidance to those working to prepare us for tomorrow's increasingly multicultural society: organizational psychologists, business professionals, labor relations experts, and administrators and counselors of educational institutions.

Current Evidence of Accuracy and Inaccuracy in Stereotypes

The chapters in the next section present or review recent empirical evidence regarding the accuracy of social stereotypes. Ryan (chapter 8) reviews her program of research, empirically assessing accuracy and inaccuracy in the perceptions that different groups (e.g., African Americans and Whites; Democrats and Republicans) hold of one another. Her review yields evidence of both accuracy and inaccuracy in the views that groups hold of one another. This chapter is relevant not only to social psychologists but also to political scientists and to anyone interested in race relations.

McCauley (chapter 9) reviews both classic studies and some results of his own research regarding the hypothesis that people exaggerate the differences between their own and other social groups. Although his review shows that people do sometimes exaggerate real differences among groups, it also shows that exaggeration is neither a necessary component of stereotypes nor even a common occurrence. The belief that stereotypes exaggerate real group differences is so firmly entrenched in the social sciences that this chapter should have news value for all those who are interested in intergroup relations: psychologists, anthropologists, political scientists, and sociologists.

Jussim and Eccles (chapter 10) examine whether teachers' expectations are biased by students' gender, social class, and ethnicity. Their results are surprising: Teachers' perceptions of differences between different groups of students are usually accurate. When teacher perceptions are biased, they generally favor students from stigmatized groups. In addition to addressing long-standing issues in social psychology, this chapter has obvious relevance to educators, educational psychologists, developmental psychologists, school counselors, and school psychologists.

Conclusions Old and New

In this concluding section, Stangor (chapter 11) offers a modern answer to the question, What is wrong with stereotypes? He recognizes that stereotypes are not necessarily inaccurate, but emphasizes the potential for unfairness that accompanies use of even an accurate stereotype. Finally, our conclusion (McCauley, Jussim, & Lee, chapter 12) brings together some of the implications and directions for stereotype research contained in previous chapters. We highlight our points of agreement and disagreement with those, such as Stangor, who emphasize the inaccuracy and harm that come of using stereotypes, and we suggest how and why the social sciences might profit from a renewed scientific and empirical interest in issues of stereotype accuracy and inaccuracy.

CONCLUSION

We will view this book as a success if it accomplishes two goals. The first goal is to challenge the confidence with which social science has assumed what it did not trouble to test. Specifically, we hope that the book contributes to a reduction in offhand and undocumented claims appearing in the scholarly literature that stereotypes are inaccurate, resistant to change, overgeneralized, exaggerated, and generally pernicious. The second goal is more positive. We hope that the ideas presented in this book spark a wave of empirical research on the accuracy and inaccuracy of social stereotypes. Only after extensive research that compares the content of stereotypes to relevant criterion measures will we be in a position to draw broad generalizations about the accuracy and inaccuracy of stereotypes, of the ways and extent to which they contribute to social problems and injustice, and of the ways they may contribute to the alleviation of injustice and conflict in intergroup relations.

REFERENCES

Adorno, T., Frenkel-Brunswick, E., Levinson, D., & Sanford, R. N. (1950). *The authoritarian personality.* New York: Harper.

Allport, G. (1954). *The nature of prejudice.* Cambridge, MA: Addison-Wesley.

Amir, Y. (1969). Contact hypothesis in ethnic relations. *Psychological Bulletin, 71,* 319–342.

Ashmore, R. D., & Del Boca, F. K. (1981). Conceptual approaches to stereotypes and stereotyping. In D. L. Hamilton (Ed.), *Cognitive processes in stereotyping and intergroup behavior* (pp. 1–35). Hillsdale, NJ: Erlbaum.

Bouchard, T. J., Lykken, D. T., McGue, M., Segal, N. L., et al. (1990). Sources of human psychological differences: The Minnesota study of twins reared apart. *Science, 250,* 223–228.

Brewer, M. (1993). Social identity, distinctiveness, and ingroup homogeneity. *Social Cognition, 11,* 150–164.

Brigham, J. C. (1971). Ethnic stereotypes. *Psychological Bulletin, 76,* 15–38.

Brown, R. (1965). *Social psychology.* New York: Free Press.

Buchanan, W., & Cantril, H. (1953). *How nations see each other.* Urbana: University of Illinois Press.

Campbell, D. T. (1967). Stereotypes and the perception of group differences. *American Psychologist, 22,* 817–829.

Chapman, G., & McCauley, C. (1993). Early career achievements of National Science Foundation (NSF) graduate applicants: Looking for Pygmalion and Galatea effects on NSF winners. *Journal of Applied Psychology, 78,* 815–820.

Condry, J. C., & Ross, D. F. (1985). Sex and aggression: The influence of gender label on the perception of aggression in children. *Child Development, 56,* 225–233.

Darley, J. M., & Gross, P. H. (1983). A hypothesis-confirming bias in labelling effects. *Journal of Personality and Social Psychology, 44,* 20–33.

DeParle, J. (1994, June 19). Welfare as we've known it. *The New York Times* ("The Week in Review"), p. 4.

Eagly, A. H., Ashmore, R. D., Makhijani, M. G., & Longo, L. (1991). What is beautiful is good, but . . . : A meta-analytic review of research on the physical attractiveness stereotype. *Psychological Bulletin, 110,* 109–128.

Eagly, A. H., & Mladinic, A. (1989). Gender stereotypes and attitudes toward men and women. *Personality and Social Psychology Bulletin, 15,* 543–558.

Erickson, F. (1979). Talking down: Some cultural sources of miscommunication in interracial interviews. In A. Wolfgang (Ed.), *Nonverbal behavior* (pp. 99–126). San Diego, CA: Academic Press.

Feingold, A. (1992). Good-looking people are not what we think. *Psychological Bulletin, 111,* 304–341.

Funder, D. C. (1987). Errors and mistakes: Evaluating the accuracy of social judgment. *Psychological Bulletin, 101,* 75–90.

Gould, S. J. (1981). *The mismeasure of man.* New York: Norton.

Hall, E. T. (1959). *The silent language.* Greenwich, CT: Fawcett Publications.

Hall, E.T. (1966). *The hidden dimension.* Garden City, NY: Doubleday.

Jackson, L. A., Sullivan, L. A., & Hodge, C. N. (1993). Stereotype effects on attributions, predictions, and evaluations: No two social judgments are quite alike. *Journal of Personality and Social Psychology, 65,* 69–84.

Judd, C. M., & Park, B. (1993). Definition and assessment of accuracy in social stereotypes. *Psychological Review, 100,* 109–128.

Jussim, L. (1986). Self-fulfilling prophecies: A theoretical and integrative review. *Psychological Review, 93,* 429–445.

Jussim, L. (1990). Social reality and social problems: The role of expectancies. *Journal of Social Issues, 46,* 9–34.

Jussim, L. (1991). Social perception and social reality: A reflection–construction model. *Psychological Review, 98,* 54–73.

Jussim, L., Coleman, L., & Lerch, L. (1987). The nature of stereotypes: A comparison and integration of three theories. *Journal of Personality and Social Psychology, 52,* 536–546.

Jussim, L., & Fleming, C. (in press). Self-fulfilling prophecies and the maintenance of social stereotypes. In N. Macrae, M. Hewstone, & C. Stangor (Eds.), *The foundations of stereotypes and stereotyping*. New York: Guilford Press.

Katz, D., & Braly, K. (1933). Racial stereotypes of one hundred college students. *Journal of Abnormal and Social Psychology, 28*, 280–290.

Kenny, D. A., & Albright, L. (1987). Accuracy in interpersonal perception: A social relations analysis. *Psychological Bulletin, 102*, 390–402.

Krueger, J., & Rothbart, M. (1988). Use of categorical and individuating information in making inferences about personality. *Journal of Personality and Social Psychology, 55*, 187–195.

LaPiere, R. T. (1936). Type-rationalizations of group antipathy. *Social Forces, 15*, 232–237.

Lee, Y. (1993). Ingroup preference and homogeneity among African American and Chinese American students. *Journal of Social Psychology, 133*, 225–235.

Lee, Y., & Ottati, V. (1993). Determinants of in-group and out-group perceptions of heterogeneity: An investigation of Sino-American stereotypes. *Journal of Cross-Cultural Psychology, 24*, 298–318.

LeVine, R. A., & Campbell, D. T. (1972). *Ethnocentrism: Theories of conflict, ethnic attitudes, and group behavior*. New York: Wiley.

Linville, P. W., Fischer, G. W., & Salovey, P. (1989). Perceived distributions of the characteristics of in-group and out-group members: Empirical evidence and a computer simulation. *Journal of Personality and Social Psychology, 57*, 165–188.

Linville, P. W., & Jones, E. E. (1980). Polarized appraisal of out-group members. *Journal of Personality and Social Psychology, 38*, 689–703.

Locksley, A., Borgida, E., Brekke, N., & Hepburn, C. (1980). Sex stereotypes and social judgment. *Journal of Personality and Social Psychology, 39*, 821–831.

Mackenzie, B. (1984). Explaining race differences in IQ: The logic, the methodology, and the evidence. *American Psychologist, 39*, 1214–1233.

Mackie, M. (1973). Arriving at "truth" by definition: The case of stereotype inaccuracy. *Social Problems, 20*, 431–447.

Marger, M. N. (1991). *Race and ethnic relations*. Belmont, CA: Wadsworth.

Martin, C. (1987). A ratio measure of sex stereotyping. *Journal of Personality and Social Psychology, 52*, 489–499.

Martin, C. L., & Parker, S. (1995). Folk theories about sex and race differences. *Personality and Social Psychology Bulletin, 21*, 45–57.

McCauley, C., & Stitt, C. L. (1978). An individual and quantitative measure of stereotypes. *Journal of Personality and Social Psychology, 36,* 929–940.

McCauley, C., Stitt, C. L., & Segal, M. (1980). Stereotyping: From prejudice to prediction. *Psychological Bulletin, 87,* 195–208.

McCauley, C. R., & Thangavelu, K. (1991). Individual differences in sex stereotyping of occupations and personality traits. *Social Psychology Quarterly, 54,* 267–279.

McCauley, C., Thangavelu, K., & Rozin, P. (1988). Sex stereotyping of occupations in relation to television representations and census facts. *Basic and Applied Social Psychology, 9,* 197–212.

Merton, R. K. (1948). The self-fulfilling prophecy. *Antioch Review, 8,* 193–210.

Nelson, T. E., Biernat, M. R., & Manis, M. (1990). Everyday base rates (sex stereotypes): Potent and resilient. *Journal of Personality and Social Psychology, 59,* 664–675.

Oakes, P. J., Haslam, S. A., & Turner, J. C. (1994). *Stereotyping and social reality.* Cambridge, MA: Basil Blackwell.

Rokeach, M., & Mezei, L. (1966). Race and shared belief as factors in social choice. *Science, 151,* 167–172.

Simon, B., & Brown, R. J. (1987). Perceived intragroup homogeneity in minority–majority contexts. *Journal of Personality and Social Psychology, 53,* 703–711.

Simon, B., & Pettigrew, T. F. (1990). Social identity and perceived group homogeneity: Evidence for the ingroup homogeneity effect. *European Journal of Social Psychology, 20,* 269–286.

Swann, W. B. (1984). Quest for accuracy in person perception: A matter of pragmatics. *Psychological Review, 91,* 457–477.

Swim, J. K. (1994). Perceived versus meta-analytic effect sizes: An assessment of the accuracy of gender stereotypes. *Journal of Personality and Social Psychology, 66,* 21–36.

Tversky, A., & Kahneman, D. (1971). Belief in the law of small numbers. *Psychological Bulletin, 2,* 105–110.

2

Accuracy: A Neglected Component of Stereotype Research

Victor Ottati and Yueh-Ting Lee

Silent False Assumption No. 5:
"The stereotypes concerning characteristics of cultural
and racial groups are entirely false."
Suggested Correction No. 5:
"The stereotypes concerning characteristics of cultural and racial
groups are a combination of truth and falsehood."

(Gustav Ichheiser, 1970, p. 76)

In the past quarter century, research in cognitive and social psychology has focused largely on perceptual error and bias (e.g., Bar-Tal, Graumann, Kruglanski, & Stroebe, 1989; Fiske & Taylor, 1991; Hamilton, 1981; Higgins & Bargh, 1987; Kahneman, Slovic, & Tversky, 1982; Miller & Turn-

We would like to thank Linda Albright, Dana Bramel, Marilynn Brewer, David Funder, Lee Jussim, Jim Hassell, Russ Kleinbach, Saul Lassoff, Clark McCauley, Albert Pepitone, and Harry Triandis for their helpful comments on drafts of this chapter.

Correspondence concerning this chapter can be addressed either to Yueh-Ting Lee, Department of Psychology, Westfield State College, Westfield, Massachusetts 01086 (Y_LEE@FOMA.WSC.MASS.EDU), or to Victor Ottati, Department of Psychological Sciences, Purdue University, West Lafayette, Indiana 47907-1364.

bull, 1986; Nisbett & Ross, 1980; Zanna & Olson, 1994).[1] The stereotyping literature is no exception. Numerous cognitive social psychologists have lamented that people are guilty of being psychologically naive, oblivious, and insensitive. Ross and Nisbett (1991), for example, emphasized that human perceptions and judgments are characterized by "ignorance" (p. 69), "dramatic overconfidence," general misperceptions, and other biases (p. 86). Even when researchers do address the accuracy issue (e.g., Judd & Park, 1993), inaccuracies in stereotype content are the predominant focus of attention. Though evidence of perceptual accuracy, including the "kernel-of-truth" component of stereotypes, does exist (see Berry, 1991; Biernat & Manis, 1994; Bramel, 1992; Fiske, 1993a; Funder, 1987, 1992; Funder & Sneed, 1993; Jussim, 1991, 1993; Kenny, 1994; Kenny & Albright, 1987; Lee & Ottati, 1995; McCauley & Thangavelu, 1991; Swim, 1994), accuracy research is the clear underdog amidst this popular social and cognitive trend.[2]

The current chapter, while acknowledging that stereotypes can possess a component of bias or inaccuracy, sounds a call for a renewed investigation into the accuracy component of stereotypes. In doing so, we address four interrelated issues. First, we consider the definition of the stereotype construct and provide a brief history of stereotyping research. Next, we review extant research that suggests that stereotypes do indeed possess an accuracy component. We then consider a variety of theoretical models that provide an explanatory basis for stereotype accuracy. We conclude by discussing social and academic forces that have impeded research on stereotype accuracy.

DEFINITION AND HISTORY OF THE STEREOTYPE CONCEPT

Although no single definition of *stereotype* is unanimously accepted, most researchers agree that stereotypes involve ascribing characteristics to so-

---

[1]In her recent work, Fiske (1993a, 1993b) addressed the accuracy issue.

[2]Note that the terms *accuracy* and *kernel of truth* are used in this article interchangeably in regard to stereotypes. To us, the kernel of truth has little to do with perceptual exaggeration; it relates to veridical differences between social and cultural groups.

cial groups or segments of society (Lee & Ottati, 1995; D. Mackie & Hamilton, 1993; Oakes, Haslam, & Turner, 1994; Zanna & Olson, 1994). These characteristics may include traits (e.g., *industrious*), physical attributes, societal role (e.g., occupation), or even specific behaviors. Stereotypic characterizations of a social group are implicitly comparative. For example, the belief that the "Chinese are industrious" implies that the Chinese are more industrious than most other ethnic groups. Many scholars make a distinction between the mean and variance of each dimension composing a stereotype. For example, an individual may believe that the average basketball player is extremely tall but also recognize that there is considerable variability among basketball players along this dimension. A stereotype may be accurate or inaccurate in either of these respects.

Formal analysis of stereotyping began with Lippmann's (1922/1965) seminal book, entitled *Public Opinion*.[3] Lippmann stressed that stereotypic representations of social groups were both incomplete and biased. Moreover, he emphasized that stereotypes were insensitive to individual variability within social groups and persisted even in the face of contradictory evidence. At the same time, Lippmann acknowledged that stereotypes serve a basic and necessary function: economization of cognitive resources. Katz and Braly (1933) performed one of the earliest empirical investigations of social stereotyping. In their study, subjects were given a list of 84 psychological trait adjectives (e.g., *sly, alert, aggressive, superstitious,* and *quiet*) and were asked to "characterize . . . ten racial and national groups" (Katz & Braly, 1933, p. 282). The stereotype of each group was defined as the set of traits most frequently assigned to the group. For instance, the Chinese stereotype included *superstitious* (35%), *conservative* (30%), and *industrious* (19%). Katz and Braly (1933) were primarily interested in the link between stereotypes and prejudice. Stereotypes, in their view, were public fictions with little factual basis. These public fictions served to justify unwarranted negative emotional reactions toward social groups.

---

[3]According to Rudmin (1989), James Morier was the first person who discussed stereotypes, in his book, *The Adventure of Hajji Baba of Ispahan,* which was published in 1824. This book was almost 100 years earlier than Lippmann's. Lippmann was even aware of it. Originally, for Morier, a stereotype or stereotyped behavior did not necessarily mean something inaccurate or negative but "indicate[d] common ancestry and intercultural affiliation" (see Rudmin, 1989, p. 10).

From about 1940 to 1970, debate concerning the accuracy of stereo-types became prevalent. Some researchers argued that stereotypes existed without any realistic basis or kernel of truth (Fishman, 1956; Klineberg, 1954; LaPiere, 1936; Schoenfeld, 1942).[4] It was noted that certain social stereotypes directly contradicted more objective social observations. For example, Armenian laborers residing in southern California were stereotyped as dishonest, deceitful liars and troublemakers during the 1920s. In fact, LaPiere (1936) found that Armenians in this locale appeared less often in legal cases and possessed credit ratings that rivaled those of other ethnic groups. Other psychologists (Campbell, 1967; Ichheiser, 1943, 1970; Schuman, 1966; Triandis & Vassiliou, 1967; Vinacke, 1956) argued that stereotypes possess a kernel of truth. Vinacke (1956), for example, postulated that it would be ridiculous to assert that groups of a given national or cultural origin do not have certain general characteristics that differentiate them from groups of different origin. Triandis and Vassiliou (1967) empirically demonstrated that Greek and American stereotypes possess a substantial component of veridicality, especially when they are elicited from people who have firsthand knowledge of the group being stereotyped.

Unfortunately, more recent research in social psychology has not been characterized by this healthy form of debate. This is due, in part, to the fact that recent research has focused almost exclusively on the cognitive process of stereotyping. This focus on process, which is by no means without value, has failed to address the question of whether stereotypes possess accurate content in real-world contexts. To the contrary, this research agenda has focused on laboratory conditions that promote biased, inaccurate, and irrational stereo-typic inferences (for a review, see Fiske, 1993a, 1993b; Funder, 1987, 1991; Jussim, 1991; Kenny, 1991; Kenny & Albright, 1987; Kruglanski, 1989).

IS EVERY STEREOTYPE INACCURATE?

A few years ago, one author of this paper received a letter that stated the following: "Heaven is a place with an American house, Chinese food,

---

[4]Like Lippmann (1922/1965), Klineberg (1954) at times held that a stereotype was a faithful representation of reality (cited in Abate & Berrien, 1967; also see Curtis, 1991).

British police, a German car, and French art. Hell is a place with a Japanese house, Chinese police, British food, German art, and a French car." These stereotypic judgments may simply reflect overgeneralization, misperception, rigidity, simplification, or incorrect learning. On the other hand, these judgments may also possess a component of accuracy. As Bertrand Russell (1974) noted, "If everyday experience is not to be wholly illusory, there must be some relation between appearance and the reality behind it" (p. 65). Similarly, even Lippmann (1922/1965), who described stereotypes as "pictures in our heads" (p. 3), acknowledged the following:

> The myth is not necessarily false. It might happen to be wholly true. It may happen to be partly true. If it has affected human conduct a long time, it is almost certain to contain much that is profoundly and importantly true. (p. 80)

It may be true, for example, that American housing is more spacious than Japanese housing, on the average. To the extent that this is so, these stereotypic judgments function as thought-saving ways of analyzing the sociocultural environment (G. W. Allport, 1954; Triandis & Vassiliou, 1967). Below, we review past evidence concerning the veridicality of stereotypes.

EVIDENCE OF STEREOTYPE ACCURACY

The tendency for stereotypes to possess a "kernel" (G. W. Allport, 1954) or "grain" (Campbell, 1967) of truth is implicit in both anthropological and sociological analyses of social behavior:

> The prediction that the greater a difference between groups, the more likely that difference will appear in the stereotypes they hold of each other, seems obvious when one starts from the anthropological position that groups, cultures, etc., do in fact differ, and asks then the questions as to how these differences will be treated in mutual imagery. Sociology also provides an expectation of a grain of truth in stereotypes, in descriptions of social class differences and the tendency for ethnic groups to become concentrated in one social class. (Campbell, 1967, p. 823)

Mead (1956), an anthropologist of great stature, contended that groups of different national or cultural origin have certain general characteristics that make them distinctive from other groups. According to her, the general characteristics that make up stereotypes are incomplete, but partially accurate, descriptions of different cultural groups. In a sociological review article, M. Mackie (1973) proposed that research on accuracy and validity should not be neglected and that *stereotype* and *prejudice* are not synonymous terms. According to M. Mackie, numerous studies (e.g., Akers, 1968; Rosen, 1959) have established that ethnic categories possess characteristics that are in keeping with folk impressions of different cultural groups.

There is no cardinal measure of perceptual accuracy. Nevertheless, accuracy is implied by a variety of patterns of convergence (see Bruner & Tagiuri, 1954; Cronbach, 1955; Funder, 1987; Judd & Park, 1993; Kenny, 1994; Malloy & Janowski, 1992; Tagiuri, 1969). One involves intersubjective agreement. That is, different perceivers may share a consensual perception of a target stimulus. When this convergence cannot be attributed to imitation or contagion, accuracy is implied. In some cases, a relatively objective accuracy criterion exists (e.g., per capita murder rate in Philadelphia). Convergence between perceptions and objective indicators of this type strongly implies accuracy. Accuracy can also be viewed in terms of prediction. In this case, accurate judgments are simply those judgments that correctly predict behaviors. Another definition of accuracy is more pragmatic or meaning oriented in nature. In this case, accurate judgments are defined either as those judgments that enable people to solve real-world problems in an adaptive manner (Baron, chapter 5, this volume; James, 1907; Swann, 1984) or as those judgments involving how perceivers and targets understand the meanings of the world (Ashmore & Longo, chapter 3, this volume; Biernat, chapter 4, this volume; Lee & Duenas, chapter 7, this volume).

When focusing on stereotype accuracy, it is useful to distinguish *heterostereotypes* from *autostereotypes*. A heterostereotype is simply one group's stereotype of another group. An autostereotype is defined as a group's stereotype of its own group members: a kind of self-image defined at the group level. Empirical studies that specifically focus on stereotype accuracy can be divided into four groups, each reflecting a distinct method of assessing accuracy: (a) studies in which accuracy is implied by convergence across different heterostereotypes of the same target group, (b) studies in which accuracy is implied by convergence between an autostereotype and heterostereotype of the same target group, (c) studies in which accuracy is implied by correspondence between stereotypic beliefs and more objective indicators of target group characteristics, and (d) studies that view accuracy in terms of perceptual sensitivity to intra-group variation. We summarize each in turn.

Accuracy as Convergence Across Heterostereotypes

As noted previously, a heterostereotype is simply one group's stereotype of another group. In many cases, different perceiver groups share a similar heterostereotype of a particular target group. This pattern of perceptual convergence is consistent with the notion that stereotypes can accurately reflect the target group's objective characteristics. According to G. W. Allport's (1954) "earned reputation theory," this form of convergence may be especially prevalent when perceivers have had the experience of interacting directly with the target group.

Vinacke (1949) examined the stereotypes of eight interacting groups at the University of Hawaii. These were Japanese, Chinese, White, Korean, Filipino, Hawaiian, Samoan, and Black students. Vinacke reported that the different subject groups agreed on essential aspects of group images. For example, there was strong agreement that Hawaiians are musical, easygoing, and friendly. Analogous findings were obtained by Prothro and Melikian (1954, 1955). They found convergence in stereotypes held by Arab and American students with reference to Germans, Blacks, and Jews.

Accuracy as Convergence Between a Heterostereotype and an Autostereotype

In some cases, heterostereotypes of a target group correspond to the target group's self-image, or autostereotype. Vinacke (1949), in addition to finding convergence across heterostereotypes, obtained convergence between heterostereotypes and the autostereotype of the target group. For example, in keeping with the image held by other groups, Hawaiian students perceived themselves as musical, easygoing, and friendly. Almost two decades later, Schuman (1966) reported similar findings when investigating stereotype accuracy in Bangladesh (previously East Pakistan). In this study, East Pakistani students were asked to describe the general characteristics of people in four districts (i.e., Noakhali, Comila, Barisal, and Mymensingh). One third of the student sample characterized the people of Noakhali as *pious, shrewd,* and *money loving.* More important, the Noakhali agreed with the perceivers of the other three districts (i.e., Comila, Barisal, and Mymensingh). That is, the Noakhali, who were perceived by the other three groups as *pious, shrewd,* and *money loving,* perceived themselves to be more religious and more concerned with job payment and advancement.

Abate and Berrien (1967) used 15 behavioral orientations (e.g., *achievement, deference, order, exhibition,* and *autonomy*) from the Edwards Personal Preference Schedule to study stereotypes between Americans and Japanese. They found relatively high agreement between self-stereotypes and those provided by the opposite cultures. For example, both the subjects at Rutgers University and the subjects at universities in Tokyo reported that Japanese people are more likely to follow orders and to be less autonomy oriented than Americans. In a study of Greek and American stereotypes, Triandis and Vassiliou (1967) demonstrated that this form of perceptual convergence can increase when members of the two groups experience firsthand contact with each other.

Almost two decades later, Bond (1986) examined the mutual stereotypes of two interacting groups at the Chinese University of Hong Kong. American exchange students and local Chinese undergraduates were asked to rate a typical ingroup member (autostereotype) and a typical outgroup member (heterostereotype) on 30 bipolar trait scales. He reported that both groups agreed that the typical Chinese student is more emotionally controlled, but less open and extraverted, than the typical American exchange student (also see Bond, 1986, p. 239). Convergence among Sino-American autostereotypes has also been reported along other dimensions

(Lee, 1995; Triandis, 1990). For example, Lee (1995) reported that both American and Chinese individuals perceive the government of the United States of America as more democratic and open to critical opinion than the government of the People's Republic of China.

Accuracy as Convergence Between Stereotypes and More Objective Indicators

In some cases, it is possible to compare stereotypic perceptions of a social group with more objective indicators of that group's characteristics (e.g., McCauley, Thangavelu, & Rozin, 1988). When these correspond, it is extremely difficult to argue that stereotypes are bereft of an accuracy component. Evidence of this nature occurs in a variety of domains. These include occupational stereotypes, gender stereotypes, and stereotypes based on physical appearance (e.g., the physical attractiveness stereotype).

In 1965, Balk examined occupational stereotypes of engineers. At that time, it was generally believed that engineers are exceptionally competent in technical work, but incompetent in social leadership roles (Balk, 1965). A comparison of engineering and liberal arts students' personality assessment profiles indicated that as a group, engineering students showed less tolerance and sensitivity for social ambiguity than did liberal arts students. If tolerance and sensitivity for social ambiguity are important components of leadership ability, then the commonly held stereotype of engineers appears to contain a component of accuracy.

A number of studies suggest that gender stereotypes possess a veridical component. In keeping with popular gender role stereotypes, girls have been found to excel in verbal ability, whereas boys excel in visual–spatial and mathematical ability (Maccoby & Jacklin, 1974). Girls show greater proficiency in reading during the elementary school years (Feshbach, Adelman, & Fuller, 1977). Their superiority on tasks involving reading, composition, and complex verbal tasks (e.g., analogies) becomes even more apparent during the junior and high school years.

In two recent studies on emotional openness, Jussim and his colleagues (Jussim, Milburn, & Nelson, 1991) predicted and found a kernel of truth in gender role stereotypes. Women, generally perceived to be more willing to express their feelings than men, were (on average) more likely to do so. Other research on gender roles appears to support this finding (Ashmore & Del Boca, 1981, Broverman, Vogel, Broverman, Clarkson, & Rosenkrantz, 1972; Maccoby & Jacklin, 1974).

With regard to human aggression, it is generally believed that men are more aggressive than women (Broverman et al., 1972; Maccoby & Jacklin, 1974). On the basis of a meta-analysis of 63 studies, Eagly and Steffen (1986) concluded that males do in fact behave more aggressively than females. Furthermore, the Federal Bureau of Investigation (cited in Aronson, 1992) reports that men are arrested for violent crimes more frequently than women. A similar gender difference is characteristic of other cultures (Jussim, 1990).

Experimental findings also suggest that the physical attractiveness stereotype may contain a kernel of truth. In an experiment by Goldman and Lewis (1977), subjects were asked to interact with opposite-sex partners whom they could not see. Each subject engaged in three telephone conversations and rated their telephone partners with regard to social skills, anxiety, liking, and desirability for future interaction. The results indicated that physically attractive partners were rated as more socially skillful and more likable than less attractive partners. Goldman and Lewis (1977) concluded that the physical attractiveness stereotype possesses a kernel of truth.

In a series of facial studies, Berry and her colleagues (Berry, 1990, 1991; Berry & Wero, 1993) reported that subjects were capable of accurately predicting a target's psychological traits or dimensions (e.g., *dominance, warmth,* and *honesty*) from facial photographs. For example, Berry (1990) asked college students in her seminar to rate one another with regard to *honesty, warmth,* and *dominance* during the 1st, 5th, and 9th weeks of the semester. Another group of students (i.e., judges) who knew nothing about those seminar participants made judgments of the latter on the basis of photographs of their faces. Appearance-based impressions predicted ratings that had been provided by classmates along each dimension. This provides us with further evidence of the kernel of truth in psychological perceptions.

Table 1

**Mean Perceived Heterogeneity as a Function of Target Group for
Chinese and American Perceivers**

	Perceiver	
Target	American	Chinese
American	21.92	22.35
Chinese	17.92	17.13

NOTE: Higher scores indicate more heterogeneity.

Accuracy as Sensitivity to Intragroup Variation

As noted previously, many scholars assume that stereotypic images of a
social group contain a representation of both the group mean and variance along each attribute dimension. Most of the previously cited studies
suggest that representations of the target group mean possess an accuracy
component. Lee and Ottati (1993) have recently presented evidence that
indicates that stereotypic representations of target group variability also
possess an accuracy component.

Lee and Ottati (1993) began by citing a wide range of anthropological studies that suggest that Chinese people are, objectively speaking, more
homogeneous than American people. In keeping with the kernel-of-truth
hypothesis, Lee and Ottati (1993) reported that both Chinese and American subjects perceived Chinese people to be more homogeneous than
Americans.[5] Mean perceptions of ingroup and outgroup homogeneity are
shown in Table 1 for both the Chinese and the American sample. In accordance with the kernel-of-truth hypothesis, both samples agreed that
Americans are more heterogeneous than Chinese. This suggests that both
groups were capable of accurately perceiving the amount of intragroup
variation within both cultures.

---

[5]Homogeneity was measured when both samples were asked to report on the degree of the within-
culture similarity. For example, mainland Chinese and American subjects were asked to indicate how similar the Chinese (or Americans) are to each other with regard to their behavior, physical appearance (e.g.,
style of clothes and skin color), and language.

Lee and Ottati's (1993) findings suggest that stereotypic perceptions are sensitive to the actual amount of variability within the target group. Much earlier research suggests that individuals can also accurately discriminate target group members who fall at the low end of the distribution from target group members who fall at the high end of the distribution. Specifically, Clarke and Campbell (1955) found that perceptions of the intelligence (i.e., grade estimates) of Black individuals were significantly correlated with their level of academic performance regardless of whether the perceiver was White ($r = .56$) or Black ($r = .47$).

WHY STEREOTYPES CONTAIN A KERNEL OF TRUTH: SOME THEORETICAL EXPLANATIONS

The previously cited work provides rather convincing evidence of the fact that many stereotypes possess a component of accuracy. We now outline a number of theoretical perspectives that can accommodate the view that stereotypes contain an accuracy component.

Stereotypes as Rational Categories

If social perceivers were to perceive each person as an individual, they would face the difficulty of considering "an enormous amount of information that could quickly overload cognitive processing and storage capacities" (Hamilton & Trolier, 1986, p. 128). When confronted with too much information, the individual must group or categorize this information on the basis of underlying commonalities or shared properties:

> Categorization serves several useful functions for us. Most obviously, we can simplify our environment by categorizing objects. Second, categorization enables us to generate expectations about the properties of those objects. These expectations, in turn, guide our behavior toward the objects. A third consequence of categorization is that it permits us to consider a greater amount of information at any one time. (Wilder, 1981, p. 213)

Put simply, individuals need categorization to understand and make sense of their environment, both physical and social (Asch, 1952; Brewer, 1979;

Curtis, 1991; Heider, 1958; Tajfel, 1981). Social categorization or stereotyping, according to this view, is a cognitive necessity.

According to Allport, a rational category "starts to grow up from a kernel of truth" (G. W. Allport, 1954, p. 22) and enlarges and solidifies itself through the increment of relevant experience. Regarding the accuracy of rational categories and stereotypes, Allport continues as follows:

> Scientific laws are examples of rational categories. They are backed up by experience. Every event to which they pertain turns out in a certain way. Even if the laws are not 100% perfect, we consider them rational if they have a high probability of predicting a happening. (p. 22)

To the extent that stereotypes reflect rational categories, they enable one to make reasonable inferences. It is probable, for example, that a native-born American speaks better English than a Chinese immigrant. A stereotype that captures this group difference is, therefore, quite rational. G. W. Allport (1954) argued that many stereotypes have a kernel of truth because they are, explicitly or implicitly, based on rational categories or on the categorical ideas we form about groups (p. 125).[6]

Probabilistic Models

Many researchers (e.g., Fishbein & Ajzen, 1975; McGuire, 1981; Wyer & Goldberg, 1970) have argued that subjective probability estimates follow the laws of objective probability. On the basis of Bayes theorem, McCauley and his colleagues (McCauley & Stitt, 1978; McCauley, Stitt, & Segal, 1980; McCauley et al., 1988) suggested that stereotypes are generalizations about a class of people that distinguish that class from others. In their own words, stereotyping is regarded as "differential trait attribution or differential prediction based on group membership information," and "we conceive of stereotype prediction as probabilistic rather than all-or-none" (McCauley et al., 1980, p. 197).

---

[6]Two things should be made clear here. First, regarding categories and stereotypes, Allport (1954) was somewhat inconsistent. On the one hand, for him, a stereotype was not identical to a category but was "a fixed idea that accompanies the category" (p. 191). On the other hand, both stereotypes and categories start from a kernel of truth. Second, although he did allude to the probabilistic nature of stereotypes, he did not explicitly address it in the manner described by the probabilistic models that follow.

Thus, one can predict the subjective probability that a Chinese person is inhibited, with the following Bayesian formula:

$$p(I/C) = p(I) \times [p(C/I)/p(C)],$$

where I is the trait *inhibited* and C stands for the social category *Chinese*. Essentially, this formula indicates that the probability of inferring that a Chinese person is inhibited can be predicted on the basis of the base-rate probability that anyone is inhibited $[p(I)]$ multiplied by a ratio that takes into account that the target person is Chinese. There are, of course, numerous reasons why the inferred subjective probability may diverge from the actual objective probability. The beliefs that underlie this inference (the subjective probabilities on the right side of the equation) may themselves diverge from the correct objective probabilities. Alternatively, hedonic consistency pressures (e.g., balance) may lead the individual to adjust the inferred probability upward or downward. Yet, as noted previously, it is unlikely that the underlying subjective beliefs will be completely insensitive to objective constraints. Furthermore, adjustments due to hedonic consistency do not occur in an informational vacuum. To the contrary, these adjustments are made from a starting point that is, usually in part, rooted in the probability predicted from the Bayesian model. In summary, although the inferred stereotypic belief may contain a component of bias, it also contains a component of veridicality.

Ecological (and Evolutionary) Models

McArthur and Baron (1983) proposed an ecological theory of social perception. Their model assumes that perception serves an adaptive function and that the external world must, therefore, provide information to guide biologically and socially functional behaviors. That is, by informing action, perception is assumed to promote individual goal attainment as well as species survival (also see Baron, chapter 5, this volume; Berry & Wero, 1993). The information available in the environment specifies, among other things, *environmental affordance*, which involves the opportunities for acting or being acted on that are provided by environmental entities

(McArthur & Baron, 1983, p. 216). Gibson (1979) used vivid examples to describe affordance: "Each thing says what it is. . . a fruit says 'eat me'; water says 'drink me'; and thunder says 'fear me' " (p. 138).

Evolutionarily, stereotypes are necessary in the course of human development and survival. Fox (1992) posited that "the essence of stereotypical thinking is that it is fast and gives us a basis for immediate action in uncertain circumstances" (p. 140). For example, we would act quickly (in terms of stereotypes) if making decisions under stress or emergency. This is because "our brains developed to achieve just such thought-action in the struggle for survival" (Fox, 1992, p. 140).

In keeping with the Bayesian approach, the ecological (and evolutionary) theory suggests that judgments and perceptions are relatively accurate reflections of our physical and social environment. Perceptions of environmental affordance must be accurate if they are to function as an adaptive guide for the behavioral realization of need fulfillment and goal attainment. Total inaccuracy would preclude the survival of the human species.

The Reflection–Construction Model

According to Jussim's (1991) reflection–construction model, our perceptions not only create and construct social reality but also accurately reflect social reality. The model basically describes relations among perceivers' beliefs (e.g., expectations, stereotypes, and schemata) with respect to particular targets and their characteristics and behaviors. The model starts with *background information*, which refers to any input used as a basis for forming a belief (e.g., direct observation of targets, targets' past behavior, sociocultural context, age, group membership, personality, humor, and hearsay).

It is assumed that a perceiver's judgment is based on the target person's individuating attributes and behavior as well as the perceiver's cognitive expectancies and assumptions (e.g., stereotype-based expectancies). In addition, the perceiver's beliefs and expectancies exert an influence on the target person's behavior. This interplay between the perceiver's construal of reality and the target person's manifest behavior promotes an interactive psychobehavioral system in which perception serves both a reflective and a constructive function. The constructive aspect of social cognition is not limited to going beyond the information given. To the contrary, social cognition actually "creates reality" by exerting a tangible influence on the target person's behavior. As a result, perception of the individual target person contains a veridical component for two reasons. First, these perceptions are assumed, in part, to accurately reflect the target person's individuating behavior. Second, the perceiver's social beliefs and stereotypes are assumed to partially determine the target person's manifest behavior. As a result, expectancy-driven perceptions often coincide with the target person's overt behavior (see Jussim, 1993).

Information-Processing Models

Information-processing models of social judgment suggest that an individual engages in a number of psychological steps en route to formulating a stereotypic judgment (Crocker, 1981; Wyer & Srull, 1989). (a) The individual must sample cases from the population of cases existing in the objective social category. Insofar as the individual cannot be exposed to the full universe of cases, this initial sampling stage is inherently incomplete or selective. (b) The individual must encode or interpret the specific case information and represent it in long-term memory. (c) The individual must retrieve the specific case information from long-term memory and estimate the frequency of cases that confirm or disconfirm the stereotypic judgment. (d) The individual must use this estimate as a basis for reporting an overt stereotypic judgment.

Information-processing research strongly suggests that each of these stages is susceptible to bias and error. Insofar as selective exposure is not random, the individual may selectively sample a biased set of instances from the objective social category (Iyengar & Ottati, 1994; Ottati & Wyer, 1990). Encoding is often selective, and as such, the encoded set of cases may not reflect an unbiased sample of the set of cases presented to the individual. Ambiguous case information may be interpreted in a biased manner that is consistent with prior expectancies. Information retrieval, which is also selective, may produce a biased set of instances that does not coincide with the mix of confirming and disconfirming instances represented in memory. Finally, the weight ascribed to the retrieved instances may be biased (e.g., increased weight ascribed to negatively evaluated instances). All of these processes, then, are in accordance with the view that stereotypic judgments are biased, inaccurate, or unfounded.

On the other hand, a half-empty glass is also half-full. Information-processing theorists often forget to mention that each of these stages is, to some degree, constrained by the objective nature of the data at hand. Selective sampling of population cases is constrained by the set of instances that compose the larger social category. It is not possible, for example, to selectively sample female players of the National Football League (NFL). Interpretation is also, to some degree, constrained by the nature of the datum observed. It is difficult to interpret a linebacker's behavior as nonaggressive. Last, selective retrieval is constrained by the set of instances represented in memory. One cannot selectively retrieve female players of the NFL from memory. As a consequence, social stereotypes (e.g., "NFL linebackers play aggressively and are male") often possess a component of veridicality.

The information-processing approach possesses a theoretical foundation in J. S. Bruner's (1992) "new look" in perception. The new look in perception basically assumes that one goes beyond the information given. In current information-processing terminology, perceivers often ascribe stereotypic default values to specific cases, when provided with incomplete individuating information about a member of a social category. Thus, one may assume that a particular linebacker plays aggressively in the absence of having ever seen him perform on the field.

Unfortunately, Bruner's famous dictum has often been misinterpreted to mean that people disregard the information given or that people see things that are not there (Fiske & Neuberg, 1990; Hamilton & Sherman, 1989; Higgins & Bargh, 1987; Jones, 1986; Markus & Zajonc, 1985; Sherman, Judd, & Park, 1989; Snyder, 1984). In fact, perceivers rarely completely disregard individuating information about a social category member. Furthermore, going beyond the information given need not produce inaccurate social inferences. To the contrary, stereotype-based inferences are often accurate to some degree:

What we generally mean when we speak of representation or veridicality is that perception is predictive in varying degrees. . . . The categorical placement of the object leads to appropriate consequences in terms of later behavior directed toward the perceived object. (J. S. Bruner, 1973, p. 8)

J. S. Bruner assumed that perceptions and inferences, including those that are based on social categories, are responsive to the objective world. To go beyond the information given need not imply a distortion of reality. In the absence of individuating information about a specific Democratic candidate, for example, a perceiver may infer that the candidate favors a decrease in military spending. In most cases, this stereotype-based inference will be correct.

Motivational Models

Early models of stereotyping often assumed that stereotypic beliefs are motivationally driven (Dollard, Doob, Miller, Mowrer, & Sears, 1939; Katz & Braly, 1933). *Prejudice*, an unjustified negative emotional reaction to a target group, was assumed to result from displacement of hostility and frustration toward convenient scapegoats. Stereotypic beliefs about the target group, according to this view, are inaccurate rationalizations that function to reinforce unjustified hatred toward the outgroup.

It is undoubtedly true that stereotypic beliefs about outgroups are commonly more negative than those regarding the ingroup. In some cases, this discrepancy may result from the dynamic just described. However, even when motivationally driven, stereotypic beliefs can possess an accuracy component. A good example of this tendency was demonstrated long ago by E. M. Bruner (1956). In an anthropological investigation, E. M. Bruner examined stereotypic perceptions between Hidatsa Indians and local ranchers of European extraction (i.e., the Yankees) in the Dakotas. According to Campbell (1967), the moral requirement of immediate sharing was fully imperative for the Hidatsa Indians, as was the imperative of thrift and providence among the Yankees. Both groups accurately perceived these cultural differences but used different labels to describe them. That is, the Hidatsa Indians regarded their own behavior as *generous* and *un-*

selfish while regarding the Yankees as *stingy* and *selfish*. On the other hand, the Yankees considered their own behavior as *thrifty* and *provident* while considering the Hidatsa Indians as *profligate* and *improvident*. These labels, though indicative of ingroup favoritism, are also consistent with the kernel-of-truth hypothesis.

WHY IS RESEARCH ON STEREOTYPE ACCURACY SO RARE?

Thus far, we have presented evidence of accuracy in stereotyping and discussed a number of theoretical models that can accommodate this form of accuracy. Yet, despite compelling empirical and theoretical reasons for doing so, few contemporary social scientists explicitly emphasize the accuracy of social stereotypes. Why is this the case? We consider two plausible explanations: adherence to psychological tradition and avoidance of social retribution.

Scarcity of research on the accuracy of stereotypes has a long history and tradition. Historically, this tendency may be dated back to Freudian psychoanalytic theory. Freud (1953) held that our personality structure contains an *id* (unconscious biological instincts or libido), an *ego* (cognitive responses to objective reality), and a *superego* (internalized social and moral codes). Traditional psychoanalytic theory emphasized the role of the id in determining social judgments and behavior. As such, social cognition and behavior were assumed to be the result of irrational and unconscious psychological forces.

Following this tradition, many social psychologists (see critiques in Ashmore & Del Boca, 1981; Bramel, 1992; Brigham, 1971; Ehrlich, 1973) considered stereotypes as faulty generalizations or productions of inaccurate imagination. In many cases (e.g., F. H. Allport, 1933; Katz & Braly, 1933; Horowitz, 1936; Lippmann, 1922/1965), stereotypes were depicted as psychological projections rather than rationally derived categories used to organize and simplify the social world. As a consequence, stereotypes were assumed to reflect cognitive distortion, misunderstanding, and miscommunication (Bramel, 1992).

Adherence to psychological tradition is not the only force that has impeded research on stereotype accuracy. Another involves the avoidance of social retribution. Scientists, including psychologists, are social animals who cannot perform their research in a social vacuum.[7] They cannot engage in research without being influenced by social changes and political movements. As Szwed (1972), a Black anthropologist cogently stated, "Interracial politics are intertwined with social science such that current changes in political strategy and style instantly reverberate through social science" (p. 169). Most social scientists tend to exaggerate the similarities between racial and cultural groups while discounting or denying real cultural differences and identities. Thus, little attention has been paid to research on multiculturalism, real cultural differences, and the accuracy of stereotypes.

Why is this the case? As Kristol (1991) noted, it is difficult, and even dangerous, to talk candidly about group differences in the present social climate. Such candor is bound to provoke accusations of insensitivity or even racism (see Stangor, chapter 11, this volume). Emphasis on the veridical component of stereotypes engenders these accusations because people associate stereotyping with pejorative forms of prejudice. To evade these accusations and to be politically correct, social scientists avoid a frank discussion of significant cultural differences. This form of denial, often engendered by a legitimate commitment to eradicate racism and prejudice, may actually promote discrimination against minority groups. By neglecting the unique characteristics of minority groups (Lee, 1993), we may promote a social climate that forces minority group members to be unwillingly assimilated into the mainstream culture.

CONCLUSION

The Dancing Bear

According to Funder (1987), an *error* is quite different from a *mistake*. An error is "a judgment of a laboratory stimulus that deviates from a model

---

[7]In psychology, for example, most of the subjects have been White and middle class (Graham, 1992). According to Graham, this occurs partly because psychologists have "fears associated with conducting socially sensitive research" (p. 637).

of how that judgment should be made" (p. 76). A mistake is "an incorrect judgment in the real world" (p. 76). It is common, for example, for laboratory studies to manipulate stereotypic cues and individuating information about a target person independently. Under these conditions, the effect of the stereotype on perceivers' judgments can produce errors, wherein judgments are at odds with the implications of relevant individuating information. Yet, insofar as stereotypes possess a kernel of truth, real-world judgments that are based on social stereotypes will often produce judgments similar to those that would have been arrived at on the basis of individuating considerations. Thus, the same psychological process that produces an error in the laboratory may not produce a mistake in the real world.

Moreover, laboratory research on error has often been misinterpreted and overstressed in psychology (see Friend, Rafferty, & Bramel, 1990). For example, in his well-known conformity study, Asch (1952) found that about two thirds (62.2%) of the responses were accurate and independent of the majority trend; the remaining one third (36.2%) of the responses yielded errors (i.e., identical with or conforming to those of the erroneous majority; see Asch, 1952, p. 457). Unfortunately, when citing or referring to Asch's research, most scholars mention only the errors (see Friend et al., 1990).

Are human perceptions and judgments completely veridical? Obviously not. Yet, the fact that human perceptions and judgments are accurate to any degree should not be overlooked or disvalued. To borrow Funder's (1989) analogy, "what makes a dancing bear so impressive is not that it dances well, but that it dances at all" (p. 212). Human perceptions and judgments are not perfect, but "in the face of enormous difficulties, it seems remarkable they manage to have any accuracy at all" (p. 212).

Cautionary Notes and Implications

Any discussion of accuracy in social stereotyping is likely to invite misinterpretation. Some cautionary notes and concluding clarifications are therefore essential. First, to suggest that stereotypes possess a kernel of truth in no way implies that all stereotypes are "good." Because accuracy and evaluation are two separate dimensions (see Jussim, McCauley, & Lee, chapter 1, this volume), accurate stereotypes may be positive or negative. Moreover, accurate stereotypes may be harmful, regardless of whether they are positive or negative (see Stangor, chapter 11, this volume). This chapter has simply argued that human perceptions, including stereotypes, possess a kernel of truth (e.g., Albright, Kenny, & Malloy, 1988; Ashmore & Del Boca, 1981; Berry, 1990; Brigham, 1971; Fox, 1992; Funder, 1987; Jussim, 1991, 1993).

Second, subjective confidence regarding stereotype accuracy should not be confused with genuine stereotype accuracy. To the contrary, such confidence may sometimes reflect an attempt to justify hostility against victimized groups. According to Tajfel (1969), people who are prejudiced think of themselves as being fairly efficient in recognizing members of groups they dislike. For example, Lindzey and Rogolsky (1950) reported that prejudiced subjects were more confident in their judgments, and Cooper (1958) found that his subjects "claimed relatively high ability in recognizing members of those groups toward which they held antipathetic attitudes, and relatively low ability in recognizing members of those groups toward which they held affinitive attitudes" (p. 23). Furthermore, people who are highly authoritarian display an eager readiness to assign ethnic labels (Siegel, 1954). In brief, we must distinguish an individual's confidence in being accurate from an individual's actual level of accuracy. Undue confidence in the kernel-of-truth notion may serve to justify deep-seated prejudice, bias, and discrimination against victimized groups. As social scientists and as citizens, we must be alert to this possibility.

Third, we have emphasized the veridical component of stereotypes to complement the current emphasis on bias and error in stereotyping. We do not suggest that these other approaches to stereotyping are without value. We simply stress that stereotypes can have a kernel of truth and that this component should not be neglected in psychological science.

Finally and most important, we believe that the study of accuracy in social stereotyping can enhance awareness of multiculturalism and, as such, reduce an ethnocentric social perspective. Stereotypes can accurately reflect real differences and identities between cultures or social groups. Accepting these cultural differences and identities may promote greater understanding among cultures. Furthermore, the recognition of real cultural differences may further enable us to understand and resolve realistic conflicts among groups. Only when we understand intergroup differences objectively and accurately can we change or minimize intergroup conflict. According to realistic group conflict theory (LeVine & Campbell, 1972), group conflicts "are rational in the sense that groups do have incompatible goals and are in competition for scarce resources" (p. 29). To deny that real differences exist among groups does little to resolve the problem. Stereotypes provide a starting point from which we can proceed toward understanding real cultural differences:

> A stereotype, as we have seen, is not necessarily a source of error. Knowledge of the generalized other is often helpful. To know universal or group norms is a good starting point—and especially so if the other is typical of his culture or class, that is to say, if his pattern of qualities approaches the "basic personality" of his group. (G. W. Allport, 1963, p. 514)

REFERENCES

Abate, M., & Berrien, F. K. (1967). Validations of stereotypes: Japanese versus American students. *Journal of Personality and Social Psychology, 7,* 435–438.

Akers, F. C. (1968). Negro and White automobile-buying behavior: New evidence. *Journal of Marketing Research, 5,* 283–290.

Albright, L., Kenny, D., & Malloy, T. (1988). Consensus in personality judgments at zero acquaintance. *Journal of Personality and Social Psychology, 55,* 387–395.

Allport, F. H. (1933). *Institutional behavior: Toward a reinterpretation of contemporary social organizations.* Chapel Hill: University of North Carolina Press.

Allport, G. W. (1954). *The nature of prejudice.* Reading, MA: Addison-Wesley.

Allport, G. W. (1963). *Pattern and growth in personality.* New York: Holt, Rinehart & Winston.

Aronson, E. (1992). *Social animal.* New York: W. H. Freeman.

Asch, S. E. (1952). *Social psychology.* Englewood Cliffs, NJ: Prentice Hall.

Ashmore, R. D., & Del Boca, F. K. (1981). Conceptual approaches to stereotypes and stereotyping. In D. L. Hamilton (Ed.), *Cognitive processes in stereotyping and intergroup behavior* (pp. 1–35). Hillsdale, NJ: Erlbaum.

Balk, W. L. (1965). The destructive stereotype. *Journal of Industrial Engineering, 16*, 208–211.

Bar-Tal, D., Graumann, C. F., Kruglanski, A. W., & Stroebe, W. (Eds.). (1989). *Stereotyping and prejudice: Changing conceptions.* New York: Springer-Verlag.

Berry, D. S. (1990). Taking people at face value: Evidence for the kernel of truth hypothesis. *Social Cognition, 8*, 343–361.

Berry, D. S. (1991). Accuracy in social perception: Contribution of facial and vocal information. *Journal of Personality and Social Psychology, 61*, 298–307.

Berry, D. S., & Wero, J. L. F. (1993). Accuracy in face perception: A view from ecological psychology. *Journal of Personality, 61*, 497–520.

Biernat, M., & Manis, M. (1994). Shifting standards and stereotype-based judgments. *Journal of Personality and Social Psychology, 66*, 5–20.

Bond, M. H. (1986). *The psychology of the Chinese people.* London: Oxford University Press.

Bramel, D. (1992, August). *On bringing intergroup conflict back into the study of prejudice.* Paper presented at the 100th Annual Convention of the American Psychological Association, Washington, DC.

Brewer, M. B. (1979). Ingroup bias in the minimal intergroup situation: A cognitive–motivational analysis. *Psychological Bulletin, 86*, 307–324.

Brigham, J. C. (1971). Ethnic stereotypes. *Psychological Bulletin, 76*, 15–38.

Broverman, I. K., Vogel, S. R., Broverman, D. M., Clarkson, F. E., & Rosenkrantz, P. S. (1972). Sex-role stereotypes: A current appraisal. *Journal of Social Issues, 28*, 59–78.

Bruner, E. M. (1956). Primary group experience and the process of acculturation. *American Anthropologist, 58*, 605–623.

Bruner, J. S. (1973). *Beyond the information given.* New York: Norton.

Bruner, J. S. (1992). Another look at New Look 1. *American Psychologist, 47*, 780–783.

Bruner, J. S., & Tagiuri, R. (1954). The perception of people. In G. Lindzey (Ed.), *The handbook of social psychology* (Vol. 2, pp. 634–654). Cambridge, MA: Addison-Wesley.

Campbell, D. T. (1967). Stereotypes and the perception of group differences. *American Psychologist, 22*, 817–829.

Campbell, D. T., & LeVine, R. A. (1961). A proposal for cooperative cross-cultural research on ethnocentrism. *Journal of Conflict Resolution, 5*, 82–108.

Clarke, R. B., & Campbell, D. T. (1955). A demonstration of bias in estimates of Negro ability. *Journal of Abnormal and Social Psychology, 51,* 585–588.

Cooper, J. B. (1958). Prejudicial attitudes and the identification of their stimulus objects: A phenomenological approach. *Journal of Social Psychology, 48,* 15–23.

Crocker, J. (1981). Judgment of covariation by social perceivers. *Psychological Bulletin, 90,* 272–292.

Cronbach, L. J. (1955). Processes affecting scores on "understanding of others" and "assumed similarity." *Psychological Bulletin, 52,* 177–193.

Curtis, M. (1991). Walter Lippmann reconsidered. *Society, 28,* 23–31.

Dollard, J., Doob, L. W., Miller, N. E., Mowrer, O. H., & Sears, R. R. (1939). *Frustration and aggression.* New Haven, CT: Yale University Press.

Eagly, A. H., & Steffen, V. J. (1986). Gender and aggressive behavior: A meta-analysis review of the social psychological literature. *Psychological Bulletin, 100,* 309–330.

Ehrlich, H. J. (1973). *The social psychology of prejudice.* New York: Wiley.

Feshbach, S., Adelman, H., & Fuller, W. (1977). The prediction of reading and related academic problems. *Journal of Educational Psychology, 69,* 299–308.

Fishbein, M., & Ajzen, I. (1975). *Belief, attitude, intention and behavior: An introduction to theory and research.* Reading, MA: Addison-Wesley.

Fishman, J. A. (1956). An examination of the process and function of social stereotyping. *Journal of Social Psychology, 43,* 26–64.

Fiske, S. T. (1993a). Social cognition and social perception. *Annual Review of Psychology, 44,* 155–194.

Fiske, S. T. (1993b). Thinking is for doing: Portrait of social cognition from daguerreotype to laserphoto. *Journal of Personality and Social Psychology, 63,* 877–889.

Fiske, S. T., & Neuberg, S. L. (1990). A continuum of impression formation, from category-based to individuating processes: Influences of information and motivation on attention and interpretation. In M. P. Zanna (Ed.), *Advances in experimental social psychology* (Vol. 23, pp. 1–74). San Diego, CA: Academic Press.

Fiske, S. T., & Taylor, S. E. (1991). *Social cognition* (2nd ed.). New York: McGraw-Hill.

Fox, R. (1992). Prejudice and the unfinished mind: A new look at an old failing. *Psychological Inquiry, 3,* 137–152.

Freud, S. (1953). *The standard edition of the complete psychological works* (J. Strachey, Ed. and Trans.). London: Hogarth Press.

Friend, R., Rafferty, Y., & Bramel, D. (1990). A puzzling misinterpretation of the Asch "conformity" study. *European Journal of Social Psychology, 20,* 29–44.

Funder, D. C. (1987). Errors and mistakes: Evaluating the accuracy of social judgment. *Psychological Bulletin, 101,* 75–90.

Funder, D. C. (1989). Accuracy in personality judgment and the dancing bear. In D. M. Buss & N. Canter (Eds.), *Personality psychology: Recent trends and emerging directions* (pp. 210–223). New York: Springer-Verlag.

Funder, D. C. (1991). Judgments of personality: A new approach to the accuracy issue. In R. Hogan (Series Ed.), *Perspectives in personality: Part B. A research annual: Vol. 3. Approaches to understanding lives* (pp. 107–132). London: Jessica Kingsley.

Funder, D. C. (1992). Everything you know is wrong. *Contemporary Psychology, 37,* 319–320.

Funder, D. C., & Sneed, C. D. (1993). Behavioral manifestation of personality: An ecological approach to judgmental accuracy. *Journal of Personality and Social Psychology, 64,* 479–490.

Gibson, J. H. (1979). *The ecological approach to visual perception.* Boston: Houghton Mifflin.

Goldman, W., & Lewis, P. (1977). Beautiful is good: Evidence that the physically attractive are more socially skillful. *Journal of Experimental Social Psychology, 13,* 125–130.

Graham, S. (1992). Most of the subjects were White and middle class: Trends in published research on African Americans in selected APA journals, 1970–1989. *American Psychologist, 47,* 629–639.

Hamilton, D. L. (Ed.). (1981). *Cognitive processes in stereotyping and intergroup behavior.* Hillsdale, NJ: Erlbaum.

Hamilton, D. L., & Sherman, S. J. (1989). Illusory correlation: Implications for stereotype theory and research. In D. Bar-Tal, C. Graumann, A. Kruglanski, & W. Stroebe (Eds.), *Stereotyping and prejudice: Changing concepts* (pp. 59–82). London: Springer-Verlag.

Hamilton, D. L., & Trolier, T. K. (1986). Stereotypes and stereotyping: An overview of the cognitive approach. In J. F. Dovidio & S. L. Gaertner (Eds.), *Prejudice, discrimination and racism* (pp. 127–163). San Diego, CA: Academic Press.

Heider, F. (1958). *The psychology of interpersonal relations.* New York: Wiley.

Higgins, E. T., & Bargh, J. A. (1987). Social cognition and social perception. *Annual Review of Psychology, 38,* 369–425.

Horowitz, E. L. (1936). The development of attitude toward the negro. *Archives of Psychology*, 194.

Ichheiser, G. (1943). Why psychologists tend to overlook certain "obvious" facts. *Philosophy of Science, 10*, 204–207.

Ichheiser, G. (1970). *Appearances and realities: Misunderstanding in human relations.* San Francisco: Jossey-Bass.

Iyengar, S., & Ottati, V. (1994). Cognitive perspective in political psychology. In R. S. Wyer & T. K. Srull (Eds.), *Handbook of social cognition* (Vol. 2, pp. 143–187). Hillsdale, NJ: Erlbaum.

James, W. (1907). *Pragmatism*. New York: Longmans-Green

Jones, E. (1986). Interpreting interpersonal behavior: The effect of expectancies. *Science, 234*, 41–46.

Judd, C. M., & Park, B. (1993). Definition and assessment of accuracy in social stereotypes. *Psychological Review, 100*, 109–128.

Jussim, L. (1990). Social reality and social problems: The role of expectancies. *Journal of Social Issues, 46*, 9–34.

Jussim, L. (1991). Social perception and social reality: A reflection and construction model. *Psychological Review, 98*, 54–73.

Jussim, L. (1993). Accuracy in interpersonal expectations: A reflection–construction analysis of current and classic research. *Journal of Personality, 61*, 638–668.

Jussim, L., Milburn, M., & Nelson, W. (1991). Emotional openness: Sex-role stereotypes and self-perceptions. *Representative Research in Social Psychology, 19*, 3–20.

Kahneman, D., Slovic, P., & Tversky, A. (1982). *Judgments under uncertainty: Heuristics and biases.* Cambridge, England: Cambridge University Press.

Katz, D., & Braly, K. (1933). Racial stereotypes of one hundred college students. *Journal of Abnormal and Social Psychology, 28*, 280–290.

Kenny, D. (1991). A general model of consensus and accuracy in interpersonal perception. *Psychological Review, 98*, 155–163.

Kenny, D. (1994). *Interpersonal perception: A social relations analysis.* New York: Guilford Press.

Kenny, D., & Albright, L. (1987). Accuracy in interpersonal perception: A social relations analysis. *Psychological Bulletin, 102*, 390–402.

Klineberg, O. (1954). *Social psychology.* New York: Holt.

Kristol, I. (1991, July). The tragedy of multiculturalism. *The Wall Street Journal*, A10.

Kruglanski, A. W. (1989). The psychology of being "right": The problem of accuracy in social perception and cognition. *Psychological Bulletin, 106*, 395–409.

LaPiere, R. T. (1936). Type-rationalizations of group antiplay. *Social Forces, 15,* 232–237.

Lee, Y. T. (1993). Ingroup preference and homogeneity among African American and Chinese American students. *Journal of Social Psychology, 132,* 225–235.

Lee, Y. T. (1995). A comparison of politics and personality in China and in the U.S.: Testify a "kernel of truth" hypothesis. *Journal of Contemporary China, 9,* 56–68.

Lee, Y. T., & Ottati, V. (1993). Determinants of ingroup and outgroup perceptions of heterogeneity: An investigation of Sino-American stereotypes. *Journal of Cross-Cultural Psychology, 24,* 298–318.

Lee, Y. T., & Ottati, V. (1995). Perceived ingroup homogeneity as a function of group membership salience and stereotype threat. *Personality and Social Psychology Bulletin, 21,* 610–619.

LeVine, R. A., & Campbell, D. T. (1972). *Ethnocentrism.* New York: Wiley.

Lindzey, G., & Rogolsky, S. (1950). Prejudice and identification of minority group membership. *Journal of Abnormal and Social Psychology, 45,* 37–53.

Lippmann, W. (1965). *Public opinion.* New York: Free Press.

Maccoby, E. E., & Jacklin, C. N. (1974). *The psychology of sex differences.* Stanford, CA: Stanford University Press.

Mackie, D., & Hamilton, D. (1993). *Affect, cognition and stereotyping: Interactive processes in group perception.* San Diego, CA: Academic Press.

Mackie, M. (1973). Arriving at "truth" by definition: The case of stereotype inaccuracy. *Social Problems, 20,* 431–447.

Malloy, T., & Janowski, C. (1992). Perceptions and metaperceptions of leadership: Components, accuracy, and dispositional correlations. *Personality and Social Psychology Bulletin, 18,* 700–708.

Markus, H., & Zajonc, R. B. (1985). The cognitive perspective in social psychology. In G. Lindzey & E. Aronson (Eds.), *The handbook of social psychology* (3rd ed., pp. 137–230). New York: Random House.

McArthur, L. Z., & Baron, R. M. (1983). Toward an ecological theory of social perception. *Psychological Review, 90,* 215–238.

McCauley, C., & Stitt, C. L. (1978). An individual and quantitative measure of stereotype. *Journal of Personality and Social Psychology, 36,* 929–940.

McCauley, C., Stitt, C. L., & Segal, M. (1980). Stereotyping: From prejudice to prediction. *Psychological Bulletin, 87,* 195–208.

McCauley, C., & Thangavelu, K. (1991). Individual differences in sex stereotyping of occupations and personality traits. *Social Psychology Quarterly, 54,* 267–279.

McCauley, C., Thangavelu, K., & Rozin, P. (1988). Sex stereotyping of occupations in relation to television representation and census facts. *Basic and Applied Social Psychology, 9,* 197–212.

McGuire, W. J. (1981). The probabilogical model of cognitive structure and attitude change. In R. E. Petty, T. M. Ostrom, & T. C. Brock (Eds.), *Cognitive responses in persuasion* (pp. 291–307). Hillsdale, NJ: Erlbaum.

Mead, M. (1956). The cross-cultural approach to the study of personality. In J. L. McCary (Ed.), *Psychology of personality* (pp. 201–252). New York: Grove Press.

Miller, D. T., & Turnbull, W. (1986). Expectancies and interpersonal processes. *Annual Review of Psychology, 37,* 233–256.

Nisbett, R., & Ross, L. (1980). *Human inference: Strategies and shortcomings of social judgment.* Englewood Cliffs, NJ: Prentice Hall.

Oakes, P. J., Haslam, S. A., & Turner, J. C. (1994). *Stereotyping and social reality.* Cambridge, MA: Basil Blackwell.

Ottati, V. (1990). Determinants of political judgments: The joint influence of normative and heuristic rules of inference. *Political Behavior, 12,* 159–179.

Ottati, V., & Wyer, R. S., Jr. (1990). The cognitive mediators of political choice: Toward a comprehensive model of political information processing. In J. A. Ferejohn & J. H. Kuklinski (Eds.), *Information and democratic process* (pp. 186–216). Urbana: University of Illinois Press.

Prothro, E. T., & Melikian, L. H. (1954). Studies in stereotypes: III. Arab students in the Near East. *Journal of Social Psychology, 40,* 237–243.

Prothro, E. T., & Melikian, L. H. (1955). Studies in stereotypes: V. Familiarity and the kernel of truth hypothesis. *Journal of Social Psychology, 41,* 3–10.

Rosen, B. C. (1959). Race, ethnicity and the achievement syndrome. *American Sociological Review, 24,* 47–60.

Ross, L., & Nisbett, R. E. (1991). *The person and the situation: Perspectives of social psychology.* New York: McGraw-Hill.

Rudmin, F. W. (1989). The pleasure of serendipity in historical research: On finding "stereotype" in Morier's (1824) Hajji Baba. *Cross-Cultural Psychology Bulletin, 23,* 8–11.

Russell, B. (1974). A skeptical view of mysticism. In W. P. Alston & R. B. Brandt (Eds.), *The problems of philosophy* (2nd ed., pp. 62–66). Boston: Allyn & Bacon.

Schoenfeld, N. (1942). An experimental study of some problems relating to stereotypes. *Archives of Psychology, 38*(No. 270).

Schuman, H. (1966). Social change and the validity of regional stereotypes in East Pakistan. *Sociometry, 29,* 428–440.

Sherman, S. J., Judd, C. M., & Park, B. (1989). Social cognition. *Annual Review of Psychology, 40,* 281–326.

Siegel, S. (1954). Certain determinants and correlates of authoritarianism. *Genetical Psychology: Monograph, 49,* 187–229.

Snyder, M. (1984). When belief creates reality. In L. Berkowitz (Ed.), *Advances in experimental social psychology* (Vol. 18, pp. 247–305). San Diego, CA: Academic Press.

Swann, W. B. (1984). Quest for accuracy in person perception: A matter of pragmatics. *Psychological Review, 91,* 457–477.

Swim, J. (1994). Perceived versus meta-analytic effect sizes: An assessment of accuracy of gender stereotypes. *Journal of Personality and Social Psychology, 66,* 21–36.

Szwed, J. F. (1972). An American anthropological dilemma: The politics of Afro-American culture. In B. Hymes (Ed.), *Reinventing anthropology* (pp. 153–181). New York: Random House.

Tagiuri, R. (1969). Person perception. In G. Lindzey & E. Aronson (Eds.), *The handbook of social psychology* (Vol. 3, pp. 395–449). Reading, MA: Addison-Wesley.

Tajfel, H. (1969). Social and cultural factors in perception. In G. Lindzey & E. Aronson (Eds.), *The handbook of social psychology* (Vol. 3, 2nd ed., pp. 315–394). Reading, MA: Addison-Wesley.

Tajfel, H. (1981). *Human groups and social categories.* Cambridge, England: Cambridge University Press.

Triandis, H. C. (1990). Cross-cultural studies of individualism and collectivism. In J. Berman (Ed.), *Nebraska Symposium on Motivation: Vol. 37. Cross-cultural perspectives. Current theory and research in motivation* (pp. 41–133). Lincoln: University of Nebraska Press.

Triandis, H. C., & Vassiliou, V. (1967). Frequency of contact and stereotyping. *Journal of Personality and Social Psychology, 7,* 316–328.

Tversky, A., & Kahneman, D. (1982). Availability: A heuristic for judging frequency and probability. In D. Kahneman, P. Slovic, & A. Tversky (Eds.), *Judgment under uncertainty: Heuristics and biases* (pp. 163–178). Cambridge, England: Cambridge University Press.

Vinacke, W. E. (1949). Stereotyping among national–racial groups in Hawaii: A study in ethnocentrisim. *Journal of Social Psychology, 30,* 265–291.

Vinacke, W. E. (1956). Exploration in the dynamic process of stereotyping. *Journal of Social Psychology, 43,* 105–132.

Wilder, D. A. (1981). Perceiving persons as a group: Categorization and intergroup relations. In D. L. Hamilton (Ed.), *Cognitive processes in stereotyping and intergroup behavior* (pp. 213–257). Hillsdale, NJ: Erlbaum.

Wyer, R., & Goldberg, L. (1970). A probabilistic analysis of the relations among beliefs and attitudes. *Psychological Review, 22,* 100–120.

Wyer, R. S., Jr., & Ottati, V. (in press). Political information processing. In S. Iyengar & J. McGuire (Eds.), *Current approaches in political psychology.* Durham, NC: Duke University Press.

Wyer, R. S., & Srull, T. K. (1989). *Memory and cognition in its social context.* Hillsdale, NJ: Erlbaum.

Zanna, M. P., & Olson, J. M. (Eds.). (1994). *The psychology of prejudice: The Ontario symposium* (Vol. 7). Hillsdale, NJ: Erlbaum.

PART TWO

Theory, Concepts, and Methodology

3

Accuracy of Stereotypes: What Research on Physical Attractiveness Can Teach Us

Richard D. Ashmore and Laura C. Longo

The folk wisdom injunction, "Don't judge a book by its cover," suggests that stereotypes based on observed physical characteristics may not be accurate. With regard to physical attractiveness in particular, this stance is evident in the notion that "beauty is only skin deep." At the same time, there is no reason to assume that stereotypes are by definition inaccurate (Ashmore & Del Boca, 1981), and there are conceptual (e.g., Campbell, 1967) and empirical (e.g., McCauley & Stitt, 1978) reasons to think that stereotypes might reflect actual group characteristics. Our view is that the accuracy–inaccuracy of stereotypes depends on several factors. We, thus, join a tradition of social scientists concerned with identifying the conceptual and empirical issues involved in determining the accuracy of social perception.

Cronbach (1955) distinguished four components of global accuracy scores in person perception research (i.e., elevation, differential elevation,

A preliminary and partial version of this chapter was presented at the Conference on Stereotype Accuracy, Bryn Mawr, Pennsylvania, June 10–11, 1994. The research reported in this chapter was supported by National Science Foundation Grant BNS-8616149. We thank the foundation for its financial assistance and also express our gratitude to Marc Beebe, who helped in preparing this chapter.

Correspondence concerning this chapter should be addressed to Richard D. Ashmore, Department of Psychology, Tillett Hall, Livingston Campus, Rutgers University, New Brunswick, New Jersey 08903.

stereotype accuracy, and differential accuracy). More recently, Jussim (1991) provided a conceptual framework for work on the accuracy of social perception, and several others have provided more specific models for the study and assessment of accuracy. These include Kenny and Albright's (1987) social relations model analysis of interpersonal perception accuracy; Kenny's (1991) identification of six factors determining consensus in personality ratings; Funder's (1987) distinction between "errors" and "mistakes" in social judgments; and Bernieri, Zuckerman, Koestner, and Rosenthal's (1994) use of four different approaches to assessing moderators of person perception accuracy. Most pertinent to the present chapter, Judd and Park (1993) identified three components of stereotype accuracy (i.e., stereotypic inaccuracy, valence inaccuracy, and dispersion inaccuracy).

In this chapter, we use the physical attractiveness literature to identify and describe five major issues that we feel are important for addressing the accuracy of stereotypes. Some of the considerations we propose represent original ways of approaching this topic; others are refinements of ideas suggested by others in this line of work concerned with identifying the conditions under which social perception in general, and stereotypes in particular, are relatively accurate or relatively inaccurate.

The chapter is organized as follows. First, we provide working answers to the questions, What is a stereotype, and what is stereotype accuracy? Next, we take up, in turn, five factors that we feel must be considered in studying stereotype accuracy–inaccuracy.

WHAT IS A STEREOTYPE?

Ashmore and Del Boca (1981) suggested the following core definition of *stereotype*: "A set of beliefs about the personal attributes of a group of people" (p. 16). To this these authors added the notion of cognitive structure and rephrased this core definition in terms of the person perception construct, implicit personality theory (Rosenberg, Nelson, & Vivekananthan, 1968), as follows: A stereotype is a hypothetical cognitive construct that comprises the structured set of inferential relations that link personal attributes to a social category (see also Ashmore, 1981; Ashmore & Del Boca, 1979; Ashmore, Del Boca, & Wohlers, 1986).

WHAT IS STEREOTYPE ACCURACY?

Accuracy is the question of how closely the set of inferential relations in the mind of a perceiver matches the objectively measured ("real") qualities of the group (social category) in question (see Funder, 1987, and Assessment of Stereotype and Objective Group Attributes and Determination of Degree of Stereotype–Reality Fit, below). Judd and Park (1993) addressed the accuracy issue by identifying three distinct components in assessing stereotype–actual group qualities matches: the mean, variance, and evaluative tone of stereotypic inferences (on the multiple components of social perception accuracy, see also Bernieri et al., 1994; Cronbach, 1955).

Our analysis complements Judd and Park's (1993) by raising five questions involved in conceptualizing stereotypes and their degree of fit to actual group qualities: (a) What is the content and structure of stereotypic beliefs? (b) What is the stereotype target? (c) In whose head is the stereotype? (d) In studying stereotype accuracy, does one begin with the stereotype, with objective group characteristics, or with both simultaneously? (e) How are the stereotype and actual group attributes assessed and the degree of stereotype–reality fit determined? The first three questions concern the stereotype; the fourth and fifth involve studying the stereotype–reality covariation.

CONSIDERATIONS IN STEREOTYPE ACCURACY

We take up each of the five questions in turn and use the literature on physical attractiveness to illustrate the implications of each for the general issue of when stereotypes are accurate or inaccurate.

What Is the Content and Structure of Stereotypic Beliefs?

The accuracy of social stereotypes depends on which stereotypic beliefs are considered. The elements of stereotypes are not homogeneous in terms of content and are not either/or in terms of the mental linkage of personal qualities to the social category. Instead, each stereotype contains multiple elements (the issue of content), and these vary in how closely they are cognitively associated with the social category in question (the issue of structure). We begin with the latter issue.

Although most stereotype accuracy work tests whether the items that are in the stereotype fit actual qualities of the group, we suggest that the elements of a stereotype vary in the degree to which they are mentally linked to the social category in question. That is, stereotypes are graded cognitive structures with some elements seen as very closely associated, and others only very loosely associated, with the social category.[1] If we are right, this makes the accuracy issue even more complicated than the task that Judd and Park (1993) described as "fraught with perils and far from simple" (p. 127). For a stereotype to be judged as accurate, how exactly should actual group differences fit the graded nature of stereotypic beliefs?

Turning to the issue of content, stereotypic beliefs can be categorized in many different ways. Two are noted here: (a) type of attribute and (b) meaning of attribute.

Concerning the former, Judd and Park (1993) distinguished "questions of fact," "questions of belief or attitude," and "personality attributes" (pp. 113–114). Ashmore and Del Boca (1979) noted that most gender stereotype work assesses personality traits. Deaux and Lewis (1984) suggested that in addition to traits, the following components of gender stereotypes should be considered: physical features, role behaviors, sexual preference, and occupations. The same tendency for researchers to focus on personality traits has been true not just of gender stereotype assessment but also of gender role identity measures (e.g., Bem Sex-Role In-

---

[1]Others have made related points about the variable linkage of personal attributes in social stereotypes. In assessing the shared stereotypes of a group of perceivers, some stereotype elements are endorsed by a large proportion of perceivers, whereas others are endorsed by a smaller percentage of subjects. For example, in a study by Williams and Bennett (1975), those traits assigned by at least 75% of the respondents to males or females were termed *focused sex stereotypes*, whereas those characteristics seen as stereotypic of men or women by 60% to 75% of the subjects were termed *expanded sex stereotypes*. McCauley and Stitt (1978) asked participants to estimate the percentage of target group members who had each of a set of attributes and found that these percentages varied considerably across a set of potentially stereotypic elements. Thus, some attributes were perceived to be true of a relatively high percentage of the target group, whereas other qualities were seen as true of a much lower proportion of the group under consideration.

ventory [BSRI; Bem, 1974]). Building on and extending Huston's (1983) analysis, Ashmore (1990) suggested that gender identity includes the following types of personal attributes: (a) biological–physical–material (my body and what I do to it and put on it); (b) social relationships (me with other people); (c) interests and abilities (what I am good at and what I like to do); (d) stylistic behavior (how I walk, talk, and interact); (e) personal–social attributes (what I am like on the inside; this includes, but is not restricted to, personality traits).

Although Ashmore (1990) did not investigate stereotypes, his review of meta-analyses of actual gender differences indicated that the largest objectively assessed male–female differences were for stylistic (especially nonverbal) behaviors and biological–physical–material variables (especially those involving athletic skill). To date, there has not been much work on *perceptions* of female–male differences on biological–physical–material and stylistic behaviors. Swim (1994) recently assessed perceived gender differences on one biological–physical–material attribute and two stylistic behaviors. In terms of physical characteristics, she found that perceivers underestimated gender differences in height. Regarding stylistic behaviors, she found that perceivers were accurate in terms of gender differences in the tendency to appear involved in conversations, but that they underestimated the extent to which women gazed during conversations. (Both of these effects, however, depended on how stereotypic beliefs were assessed.) With the exception of these three characteristics, little is known about gender stereotypes in these two broad categories of personal attributes and whether such stereotypes match actual group differences.

It is also possible to partition the contents of stereotypes on the basis of the meaning of stereotypic beliefs. Osgood, Suci, and Tannenbaum (1957) identified three dimensions of connotative meaning: evaluation, potency, and activity. Judd and Park (1993) included evaluation in their analysis of stereotype accuracy. We believe that their argument can be taken further. Rosenberg (1977) added denotative meaning to the semantic differential system by partitioning the evaluative continuum into multiple content-specific types of goodness (e.g., good in social activities, good in intellectual activities, mature, and honest). Our work with gender stereotypes shows that people think men and women are good in different ways: Men are stereotyped as good in intellectual activities and leadership roles, whereas women are stereotyped as good in social activities (cf. Ashmore et al., 1986; see also Eagly, Mladinic, & Otto, 1991).

Eagly, Ashmore, Makhijani, and Longo (1991) used Rosenberg's system of partitioning evaluation, together with the notion of differentially associated stereotype elements, to assess people's multifaceted stereotypes about physical attractiveness. On the basis of direct observation and media portrayals of how attractive people behave and are treated by others, Eagly, Ashmore, et al. hypothesized that good-looking people would be strongly stereotyped as good in social competence and achievement, moderately stereotyped as strong and well-adjusted, more weakly assumed to be good in intellectual activities, and not stereotyped in terms of honesty and concern for others.

Dion, Berscheid, and Walster (1972) demonstrated that attractive individuals are perceived to possess a wide variety of positive personal qualities. Their experiment served as a model for many more studies, and the resulting body of research established what has been termed the *beauty-is-good* stereotype. Eagly, Ashmore, et al. (1991) used meta-analysis to quantitatively summarize the accumulated research and to test their predictions about how beliefs about physical attractiveness vary with type of evaluative content.

As is reported in the left-hand side of Exhibit 1, the effect sizes for the attractive–unattractive comparison varied greatly as a function of type of dependent variable. The results were almost exactly as predicted. Social competence had the largest effect size, and it was larger in magnitude than that of adjustment, potency, and intellectual competence (though not significantly so from the first two), which do not differ from one another, but which are larger in size than integrity and concern for others, neither of which differs significantly from zero.

Feingold (1992) reported an independent replication of this analysis. Although his sample of studies is not identical and he used a different way to categorize dependent variables, his findings were remarkably similar to those of Eagly and her coworkers. When his categories are organized as

<table>
<tr><td colspan="4" align="center">Exhibit 1</td></tr>
</table>

Exhibit 1
Mean Weighted Effect Size by Attribute Content in Two Meta-Analyses of the Physical Attractiveness Stereotype

Eagly, Ashmore, Makhijani, & Longo, 1991		Feingold, 1992	
Attribution	d	Attribution	d
Social Competence	.68	Social Skills	.88
		Sexual Warmth	.78
		Sociability	.46
		Social Competence	.71
Adjustment	.52	General Mental Health	.50
Potency	.49	Dominance	.54
Intellectual Competence	.46	Intelligence	.31
Integrity	.13	Character	−.04
Concern for Others	.01	Modesty	.34

NOTE: Data from "What Is Beautiful Is Good, But . . . : A Meta-Analytic Review of Research on the Physical Attractiveness Stereotype" by A. H. Eagly, R. D. Ashmore, M. G. Makhijani, and L. C. Longo, *Psychological Bulletin*, 1991, Vol. 110, pp. 109–128; and from "Good-Looking People Are Not What We Think" by A. Feingold, *Psychological Bulletin*, 1992, Vol. 111, pp. 304–341.

per those used by Eagly, Ashmore, et al., it can be seen that the results are strikingly similar (see the right-hand side of Exhibit 1).

In summary, as Dion et al. (1972) suggested, in people's stereotypic thinking, "what is beautiful is good," but this varies considerably by type of evaluation. Social goodness is the heart of the physical attractiveness stereotype; adjustment, potency, and intellectual competence are moderately inferred on the basis of looks; integrity and concern for others are believed to be unrelated to good looks.

How do the objective personal qualities of attractive people map onto this multifaceted, differentially linked stereotype? Feingold (1992) compared two meta-analyses, one assessing attractiveness stereotypes and the other measuring the objective link between looks and personal attributes.

Table 1

Mean Weighted Correlations by Attribute Type in Feingold's (1992)
Meta-Analyses of the Physical Attractiveness Stereotype and of
Actual Attractive–Unattractive Differences

| | Average correlation of attractive–unattractive difference | |
Research domain	Stereotype	Actual
Social Skills	.40	.23
Sociability	.22	.04
General Mental Health	.24	.05
Dominance	.26	.07
Intelligence	.15	−.04
Character	−.02	−.01

NOTE: Data from "Good-Looking People Are Not What We Think" by A. Feingold, *Psychological Bulletin*, 1992, Vol. 111, pp. 304–341, Table 10, p. 331.

He concluded that attractiveness stereotypes are not accurate; hence, his title, "Good-Looking People Are Not What We Think."

Feingold (1992) identified six variables that he judged to be similar enough in the stereotype and actual differences literatures to allow their comparison. Table 1 reports the correlations for both the perceived (stereotypic) and actual attractive–unattractive difference. As can be seen, only for social skills is a sizable stereotypic correlation matched by a relatively large actual attractive–unattractive difference. For sociability, general mental health, and dominance, there are small-to-moderate stereotypic relationships (.22 to .26), but the point-biserial correlations for actual attractive–unattractive comparisons are negligible (.04 to .07). Feingold emphasized this lack of stereotype–reality fit to conclude that the beauty stereotype is not valid.

At the same time, Table 1 may indicate more accuracy than Feingold acknowledged. It is not just that one variable of six shows some stereotype–objective reality fit. Instead, reality seems to match stereotypic perception for the content area most strongly linked in people's minds with good versus bad looks. This suggests that accuracy may be expected primarily for core, or central, attributes of social stereotypes.[2] This may be because people are able to see clear real differences. It has been suggested that person perception accuracy may be influenced by the degree that a given trait is observable (Bernieri et al., 1994, p. 376), and observers may regard such visible attributes as "easy to judge" (Funder & Dobroth, 1987). Or stereotype–reality convergence might be highest for core stereotype elements because self-fulfilling prophecies (based on widely held cultural stereotypes) create individuals whose attributes fit those expected based on their attractiveness level.[3] Most likely, core elements of stereotypes fit objective group qualities because of some combination of these and other factors. Whatever the fate of our conjecture that reality–stereotype fit might be greatest for central stereotype elements, conceiving of stereotypes as multifaceted and differentially linked mental structures raises important issues for accuracy research.

---

[2]The core elements of a stereotype are those personal qualities that are most closely mentally associated with the social category in question. Conceptually, centrality of stereotype elements is analogous to attitude strength (Olson & Zanna, 1993, p. 123). Empirically, there are multiple operationalizations that potentially tap this construct. We have used multidimensional scaling to uncover gender stereotypes, and those traits having the most extreme projections onto the fitted male–female (target) axis are considered to be the elements with the closest inferential relation to the categories of male and female. They are, hence, the core elements of the gender stereotypes. In studies of the physical attractiveness stereotype, where perceivers ascribe traits and other qualities to attractive versus unattractive targets, core elements of the beauty stereotype are those items with the largest attractive–unattractive mean differences. These operationalizations of core stereotype elements may be correlated with percentage-of-target-group-members measures, but it is more likely that core stereotype elements will have high diagnostic ratio scores (e.g., McCauley & Stitt, 1978). These various indexes all concern the *size* of the perceived association between a social category and a personal attribute (or the size of the difference between the mental links of an attribute with two contrast categories [e.g., the link of sociability to attractive people vs. that to unattractive targets]). It is also possible that core stereotype elements might be measured by asking respondents how *certain* they are of the perceived association between a personal quality and a social category. Research is needed to determine how these different measures interrelate and how they covary with actual group qualities.

[3]In his review of the relations between social perception and social reality, Jussim (1991) concluded that "even meta-analyses that have addressed conditions under which self-fulfilling prophecy effects are most powerful have found small effects" (p. 70). We suggest that consideration of the content and structure of stereotypes, especially the notion that stereotypes are multifaceted with elements varying in how closely they are mentally linked with the category in question, might improve understanding of when and how social perception shapes social reality.

What Is the Stereotype Target?

Just as stereotype content is not homogeneous, so, too, the targets of stereotypic thinking are not singular. Most stereotype research has been done on shared beliefs about superordinate categories (e.g., *Russians* or *men*). Over the past decade and a half, however, considerable evidence has accumulated that perceivers can and do distinguish subtypes within the overarching social categories determined by race (e.g., Devine & Baker, 1991), age (e.g., Brewer, Dull, & Lui, 1981), and gender (e.g., Clifton, McGrath, & Wick, 1976). Furthermore, not all subtypes fit neatly under their superordinate category. That is, beliefs about some subtypes are not consistent with stereotypic conceptions of the overarching category (e.g., the view of a "wimp" as a weak and ineffectual type of man contrasts sharply with the stereotype of men as strong and agentic). This inconsistency between stereotypes about some subtypes and beliefs about their superordinate category considerably complicates the issue of determining whether stereotypes are accurate.

Together with Solomon, we have conducted two studies designed to uncover content-specific types of physical attractiveness. One study assessed the views of editors at major fashion magazines, people who are experts in beauty perception (Solomon, Ashmore, & Longo, 1995); the other used nonexpert subjects, a sample of introductory psychology students (Ashmore, Solomon, & Longo, 1995). In both studies, respondents were asked to free sort 96 photographs of female professional fashion models (all of whom are beautiful for a living). The sorting data were used to compute psychological distance scores between each pair of photographs, and these were inputted into a *multidimensional scaling* algorithm. Multidimensional scaling is an analytic procedure that uncovers cognitive structure by representing the objects under study (here, photos of attractive females) as points in an *n*-dimensional euclidian space. Thus, scaling produced a mental map depicting people's thinking about female beauty. In both studies, a three-dimensional scaling solution was optimal, and it was possible to identify specific looks discriminated by the perceivers (i.e., the psychological North–South and East–West of these mental maps of attractiveness). As predicted, these included: *cute* (a youthful form of female good looks), *sexy* (an overtly sexual variety of beauty), and *trendy* (an up-to-date, in-fashion type of physical attractiveness).

Ashmore et al. (1995) also used an independent sample of respondents to assess perceptions of the personality and ability of the models. This allowed us to measure stereotypic expectations associated with the uncovered attractiveness subtypes. For both male and female college students, their stereotypes about the *cute* subtype were consistent with the overall beauty-is-good, especially in social activities, stereotype documented in the meta-analyses by Eagly, Ashmore, et al. (1991) and Feingold (1992). However, beliefs about other beauty types did not fit so neatly with the stereotype of the superordinate category (physically attractive people). Sexy beauties were stereotyped by men as neither low nor high on sociability and related attributes and by women as slightly not good in social activities.

It is possible to imagine types of female beauty that are even more inconsistent with stereotypes about the superordinate category. The core of the beauty-is-good stereotype is social competence and achievement, but the "ice queen" subtype is defined not just by her Nordic good looks, but also by her cold and unsociable demeanor. Also, the overall attractive people category is moderately mentally linked to intellectual competence, but the stereotype of the "dumb blonde" seems widely shared in American culture.

Are these instances of subtype stereotypes that are inconsistent with superordinate category stereotypes simply isolated examples? We think not. Ashmore, Del Boca, and Titus (1984), and others have suggested that in part, subtypes develop because perceivers are exposed to individuals who do not fit a superordinate category stereotype. In this regard, Taylor (1981) and others refer to subtyping as serving a *boundary maintenance* function. The perceiver retains the superordinate category stereotype and creates a new category, the subtype, to account for the exception. Assuming that there are a sufficient number of exceptions, that these exceptions share identifiable features, and that perceivers can see these exceptions (directly or through the media), it is likely that most social stereotypes will have at least some associated subcategory stereotypes that conflict with beliefs about the superordinate category.

Why exactly does this create a problem for those interested in the accuracy issue? If two stereotypes, both of which appear to apply to the same target, do not agree with one another, how is one to determine whether real differences fit stereotypic beliefs? From our work on types of good looks, should a sexy female be high in social attributes (from the superordinate category stereotype), neither low nor high in social competence (males' stereotype of the sexy subtype), or somewhat low in social qualities (females' stereotype of the sexy subtype)? This leads directly to the third issue to be considered: Not only may the content of stereotypes vary as a function of the target, it may also vary as a function of the perceiver. Thus, we ask . . .

In Whose Head Is the Stereotype?

Although researchers and laypersons often speak of the male stereotype or the Black stereotype, there is, in fact, no single stereotype of any target group. Ashmore and Del Boca (1981) distinguish *cultural* from *personal* stereotypes, which parallels the distinction made by McCauley, Stitt, and Segal (1980) between social and individual stereotypes. A cultural (social) stereotype is a set of beliefs about a social category that is widely shared in a particular society. Personal (individual) stereotypes are the beliefs about a social group held by a particular individual.[4] In addition, it is likely that there are *subcultural* stereotypes: structured sets of beliefs about a social category that are widely held by an identifiable subset of perceivers in a particular society. For example, Black Americans may hold a somewhat different set of beliefs about their own group than do Whites or Hispanics or Asian Americans (see Judd & Park, 1993, on ingroup–outgroup differences and the stereotype accuracy issue). The possibility of subcultural stereotypes is related to what Kenny (1991) termed *shared meaning systems*, in his model of consensus and accuracy in interpersonal perception. Just as members of a subculture are likely to share beliefs about social categories, they are also likely to have similar ways of interpreting, or giving meaning to, the social behaviors they observe.

---

[4]Judd and Park (1993) phrased the stereotype accuracy issue in terms of the beliefs of individuals, but the work they reviewed emphasized shared, not personal, stereotypic conceptions.

With regard to physical attractiveness, it is certainly possible that good-looking people differ from those average or below average in appearance in what they think beautiful and ugly people are like. Although the ingroup–outgroup notion has not yet been systematically applied to understanding attractiveness stereotypes, the small amount of available work suggests that it is a fruitful topic to pursue. For example, on the basis of his replication of Dion et al.'s (1972) research, Dermer (1973/1974) concluded the following: "Attributions made by unattractive participants did not generally conform with the [what is beautiful is good] stereotype: these participants did not reliably consider attractive targets to have any more socially desirable personalities than unattractive targets" (p. 1).

Another possibility is that individuals who differ in expertise about looks also have different stereotypes about beauty (see Fiske & Taylor, 1991, regarding expertise and its implications for social cognition). As noted above, Solomon et al. (1992) asked editors of fashion magazines to free sort 96 photos of fashion models. The editors are experts in beauty perception; they regularly judge the looks of beautiful women, and success in their profession depends, in part, on how good they are at making such judgments. Did their perceptual skill influence how they thought about beauty? In many ways, the beauty experts (editors) and novices (college students) had similar implicit theories of beauty. Perhaps most important, both distinguished cute, sexy, and trendy types of female good looks.

At the same time, however, there were some dramatic disagreements. The most striking was how the "sex kitten" models (dressed in bikinis with cheesecake poses) were stereotyped. The experts viewed these as, among other things, examples of *not* a good fashion model. Male college students had a completely different perspective, viewing these same models as extremely good fashion models. Similarly, female college students saw stiffly posed models wearing elegant evening clothes as good fashion models, whereas experts viewed these same models as not good fashion models.

These contrasting stereotypes in the heads of different perceivers create complexity for the accuracy researcher. If we were to collect objective evidence about being a good fashion model (e.g., money earned), for one group (male or female college students) to have an accurate stereotype, the other perceiver group (fashion experts) would have to have a very inaccurate stereotype. In the present case, we would expect that the experts would be more accurate, because they are more knowledgeable about, and more concerned with, the phenomenon in question. However, experts may not always be more accurate than novices. The more general point is that different perceiver groups (based on sharing an ethnic subculture, leisure activities, and the like, as well as occupationally based perceptual skills) may have different stereotypes about a particular social group, and these stereotypic beliefs may not be in agreement (see Lee & Duenas, chapter 7, this volume). As a consequence, accuracy researchers may find that some perceivers' stereotypes better fit reality than do the pictures in the heads of other perceivers.

In Studying Stereotype Accuracy, Does One Begin With the Stereotype, With Objective Group Characteristics, or With Both Simultaneously?

Three basic approaches to conducting stereotype accuracy research can be identified: (a) Begin with objectively determined group characteristics, (b) identify variables that have both stereotype and actual group-differences measures, and (c) begin with the documented stereotype. Although one of the earliest accuracy studies (LaPiere, 1936) took the third approach, recent accuracy researchers have emphasized the first two approaches. Empirically determined stereotype accuracy may vary with type of sequential approach, and each strategy has both strengths and weaknesses.

Some accuracy researchers first identify objective and quantitative indexes of group characteristics, especially those that differentiate logical contrast categories, and then ask a sample of people to estimate these indexes. For example, McCauley and Stitt (1978), in their investigation of the accuracy of racial stereotypes, began by finding census data on demographic variables for Black Americans and White Americans (e.g., welfare rate and percentage unemployed) and then asked subjects to estimate these rates. They found that stereotypic perceptions matched reality fairly well, but underestimated actual racial differences. This research certainly showed that people seem relatively knowledgeable about some aspects of publicly available data about societally important behaviors. But did it show that racial stereotypes are accurate (albeit conservative) representations of reality? Do the social perception indexes that McCauley and Stitt used constitute a good operationalization of the structured sets of beliefs that Americans have about Whites and Blacks? In some ways, the answer seems obviously yes, because the measured variables included welfare rate (Blacks are often stereotyped as lazy and dependent on welfare) and percentage who were high school graduates (a long-standing feature of Whites' beliefs about Blacks is that they are not intelligent). At the same time, census data were not available for other facets of shared beliefs about Black Americans (e.g., the stereotype that Blacks are musical), and as a consequence, the accuracy of these stereotypic conceptions was not investigated.

A second concern about the reality-back-to-stereotype approach is what to do about objective and publicly available data that do not appear to be part of the dominant cultural stereotype of a particular group? For example, it would be possible to use resolved cases of employment or housing discrimination to assess whether Black Americans are more often the victims of racial discrimination than are White Americans.[5] For most Black Americans, this would be considered a widely known fact; for most White Americans, it would probably be a disputed point. (At least some White males feel that they are more commonly discriminated against than are ethnic minorities and women.)

Other accuracy researchers do not begin with objectively assessed group differences, but instead consider the stereotype and reality simultaneously. They do this by capitalizing on shared content in two related literatures: one on stereotypes and the other on group differences. Because race and gender are topics that have caught the attention of both social psychologists concerned with stereotypes and differential psychologists

---

[5]Furthermore, objective measures of discrimination may miss the many small, yet crucial, everyday ways in which Whites put Blacks at a disadvantage (e.g., the routine stopping by police of Black male motorists in White neighborhoods; cf. Cose, 1993).

concerned with group differences, there are considerable data available on both actual and perceived racial and gender differences. Where these literatures have similar variables, it is possible to assess the degree to which they agree. Swim (1994) did this recently with gender stereotypes.

This was also the approach of Feingold (1992) regarding attractiveness stereotypes. As can be seen in Table 1, he was able to find apparent objective-difference-measure analogues of several major aspects of beliefs about good-looking people. But there were not measures of actual attractive versus unattractive differences for all aspects of cultural stereotypes about beauty. For example, it has been suggested that "what is beautiful is self-centered" (Cash & Janda, 1984, p. 52), and Feingold's (1992) meta-analysis showed a significant (negative) effect size for stereotypes about Modesty (see Exhibit 1). However, he was not able to find analogues of Modesty in work on actual attractive versus not attractive individuals. Similarly, it has been argued that "what is beautiful is sex-typed" (i.e., attractive males are stereotyped as highly masculine in personality, interests, and the like, and attractive females as very feminine, when compared with their less attractive counterparts [Cash, 1981; Cash & Smith, 1982]), but Feingold (1992) did not assess the accuracy of this aspect of beliefs about looks, apparently because data were not available on the reality side.

The third and final approach to studying stereotype accuracy is to begin with the stereotype in question and then collect the real group-differences data necessary to ascertain how accurate these beliefs are. Longo and Ashmore (1990) did just this. We began with the content and structure of the beauty-is-good stereotype as documented by the Eagly, Ashmore, et al. (1991) study described earlier. Specifically, we noted that in people's minds, social competence and achievement are strongly linked, intellectual competence and achievement are moderately related, and concern for others is not associated with physical attractiveness. We then administered a personality inventory (the Jackson Personality Inventory [Jackson, 1976]), which was specifically selected because it contained scales that are adequate operationalizations of each of these personality domains. As expected, attractive versus unattractive individuals did differ on the social competence scale, but not on the concern for others scale. (Contrary to prediction, there was no difference for the intellectual competence scale.) The stereotype–reality match for social competence was partially inconsistent with Feingold's (1992) finding that stereotypes and actual behavior coincided for social skills, but not for sociability. It may be that the stereotype-to-reality strategy is better at detecting consistency, because the actual behavior measures selected are based on a clear and specific conceptualization of the stereotype and not simply an attempt to find a stereotype and an objective measure that are similar enough. This leads directly to the fifth and final issue we discuss.

Assessment of Stereotype and Objective Group Attributes and Determination of Degree of Stereotype–Reality Fit

The research task is relatively straightforward if one begins by identifying available objective measures, because the stereotype measure can then be designed so that it very closely approximates the index of real group qualities.

The task is more difficult if either of the other two approaches is used. To illustrate, we focus on Feingold's (1992) finding that although attractive people are stereotyped as high in sociability, there was no significant difference between people rated as very attractive and people rated as not attractive, on objective measures of sociability. If, as Eagly, Ashmore, et al. (1991) and Feingold (1992) have found, social competence and achievement are the core of the consensual beauty stereotype, it would seem that attractive people should also score as relatively sociable. It is certainly possible that Feingold's negative finding means that the stereotype is inaccurate. Another possibility is that the lack of agreement stems, at least in part, from how stereotypes and actual sociability were measured in the studies quantitatively summarized by Feingold. Most stereotype measures are simple and direct trait inferences. For example, perceivers are asked to rate attractive and unattractive individuals on scales such as sociable–unsociable. Objective sociability, on the other hand, is most often measured by asking subjects to complete a personality scale in which sociability is based on subjects' judgments of multiple items as true or not true of self. Although some of these items may approximate the direct sociability rating used to assess stereotypic perceptions, other items inquire about behavior patterns and motivations. The following are two examples: "I would prefer a quiet evening at home to attending a social event" (from the Jackson Personality Inventory [1976], a widely used instrument); "Do you like to mix socially with people?" (from the Eysenck Personality Inventory [Eysenck & Eysenck, 1968], which is also widely used and cited by Feingold [1992] as "typical" [p. 311] of the sociability measures included in his meta-analysis). This difference in how beliefs about, and actual group differences in, personality are assessed could account for the lack of stereotype–reality agreement. By analogy with Ajzen and Fishbein's (1977) notion of attitude–behavior correspondence, it is possible that stereotypes are not predictive of reality when stereotype and actual group attributes measures do not correspond with one another.[6]

The issue of correspondence particularly complicates the question of stereotype accuracy when the apparently same content may not mean the same thing to actor and perceiver. Continuing with the same example of sociability, some people may see themselves as sociable even if they agree with statements such as "I would prefer a quiet evening at home to attending a social event." Reis et al. (1982) found that highly attractive females were relatively passive in interpersonal relations. Beautiful women often get invited to social events, and in fact, they probably need to develop strategies for reducing social engagements (see, e.g., Garcia, Stinson, Ickes, Bissonnette, & Briggs, 1991, pp. 44 & 46). Thus, attractive females may not want or prefer social events. As a consequence, they might not score particularly high on indexes of sociability that involve items about motivation to approach social activities. At the same time, these same at-

---

[6]Furthermore, people may lack access to relevant information about self or may be unwilling to reveal this to researchers (Judd & Park, 1993). If so, the reliability and validity of objective reality measures is undermined, and the fit of stereotype to actual group qualities is spuriously reduced. The more general point is that "actual group qualities" is a hypothetical construct (just as is "stereotype"), which requires care and precision in conceptualization (e.g., is the actual group quality under consideration a personality trait, ability, or interest [all of which are internal and only linked to publicly observable action by a cross-situation pattern of behavior] or a behavior [and if so, a single act or a pattern of behavior]?) and in measurement (e.g., if the group quality of interest is a personality trait, then a single behavioral indicator will not be a valid index of this quality).

tractive women might regard themselves as sociable, because they are often at social events and because they seem to be successful at such events. Outside observers may also regard beautiful women as sociable because they, too, use the same public information to arrive at this conclusion.

The possibility of different interpretations of the apparently same content has other implications for the stereotype accuracy issue. For example, what about stereotypes and reality concerning beauty and interpersonal influence? On the subjective or stereotype side, when people are asked, "How good are physically attractive people at getting others to do what they want?" what social influence scenarios do respondents have in mind? Do they think of compliance situations where a simple and noncostly request is made of another person, or do they call to mind a person delivering a persuasive speech to a dubious audience? On the objective-differences, or reality, side, what types of influence situations have been studied, and what has been found?

Longo and Ashmore (1994) found that college students have a relatively strong and broad stereotype that "what is beautiful is powerful." In an experiment modeled after Dion et al. (1972), we asked subjects to judge the overall influence ability, as well as the persuasiveness, compliance-attaining, and conformity-obtaining ability of targets who were high or low in physical attractiveness. On all four types of dependent variables, good-looking individuals were assumed to be better than were their more homely counterparts, and this was true across gender of perceiver and gender of target. This robust beauty-is-powerful stereotype does not fit well with the findings of studies that have assessed actual attractive–unattractive differences in interpersonal power. Only in terms of compliance is there relatively clear evidence that good-looking people are particularly successful at getting others to do what they want. Even here the picture is not simple. Six of nine studies on beauty and compliance have involved having an attractive (vs. not attractive) female ask a favor of a male and produced a significant effect of agent physical attractiveness (Longo, 1990). Thus, it does seem that a female's attractiveness enhances her ability to get a male to comply with a simple request, but the published literature does not indicate how general this phenomenon is. Perhaps when people are asked about interpersonal power, they have in mind cross-gender compliance settings and not persuasion or conformity paradigms involving same-gender, as well as cross-gender, interactions. Whatever we learn about how people construe interpersonal power, the point for accuracy researchers is that seemingly unitary personal attributes (e.g., sociability and social influence ability) are multifaceted, and how these facets are measured on both the stereotype and actual-differences sides can influence how closely stereotypes match real group qualities.

CONCLUSION

The issue of stereotype accuracy–inaccuracy seems simple: Does the stereotype of a group match the actual qualities of that group? We have argued that this simplicity is deceptive, and we posed and discussed five questions to illustrate the complexities involved. Three of these concern the stereotype side of the overall issue: (a) What is the content and structure of stereotypic beliefs? (b) what is the stereotype target? and (c) in whose head is the stereotype? In each case, we emphasized that stereotypes are not simple, unitary, or singular. Rather, stereotypes contain multiple contents that vary in how closely mentally linked they are to the social category in question; stereotypes of superordinate categories and subcategories do not always agree; different perceiver groups may have different and contrasting stereotypes of the same target group.

The next two topics we covered involve how one studies stereotype–reality covariation: (d) In studying stereotype accuracy, does one begin with the stereotype, with objective group characteristics, or with both simultaneously? and (e) how are the stereotype and actual group attributes assessed and the degree of stereotype–reality fit determined? Again, where one begins the research process and how one operationalizes variables are not simple and easy decisions, and what one does decide can influence the degree of stereotype–reality match demonstrated.

The overall message we want to communicate is that the study of stereotype accuracy–inaccuracy is complicated and complex. This is much the same message that Cronbach (1955) wanted to convey four decades ago.

Most researchers interpreted Cronbach as suggesting that studying social perception accuracy is too complicated, and thus, they abandoned this topic. We do not feel that the issue of stereotype accuracy, even with the complexities that we and others have noted, is too difficult and messy to be scientifically feasible and fruitful. In fact, our view is quite the reverse. As the question researchers ask shifts from, "Are stereotypes accurate?" to "Under what conditions are stereotypes relatively more accurate versus inaccurate?", not only will we learn more about this basic and important question but also we will uncover much of scientific and practical value about stereotypes and about the realities of actual group differences.

REFERENCES

Ajzen, I., & Fishbein, M. (1977). Attitude–behavior relations: A theoretical analysis and review of empirical research. *Psychological Bulletin, 84,* 888–918.

Ashmore, R. D. (1981). Sex stereotypes and implicit personality theory. In D. L. Hamilton (Ed.), *Cognitive processes in stereotyping and intergroup behavior* (pp. 37–81). Hillsdale, NJ: Erlbaum.

Ashmore, R. D. (1990). Sex, gender, and the individual. In L. A. Pervin (Ed.), *Handbook of personality: Theory and research* (pp. 486–526). New York: Guilford Press.

Ashmore, R. D., & Del Boca, F. K. (1979). Sex stereotypes and implicit personality theory: Toward a cognitive–social psychological conceptualization. *Sex Roles, 5,* 219–248.

Ashmore, R. D., & Del Boca, F. K. (1981). Conceptual approaches to stereotypes and stereotyping. In D. L. Hamilton (Ed.), *Cognitive processes in stereotyping and intergroup behavior* (pp. 1–35). Hillsdale, NJ: Erlbaum.

Ashmore, R. D., Del Boca, F. K., & Titus, D. (1984, August). *Types of women and men: Yours, mine and ours.* Paper presented at the 92nd Annual Convention of the American Psychological Association, Toronto.

Ashmore, R. D., Del Boca, F. K., & Wohlers, A. J. (1986). Gender stereotypes. In R. D. Ashmore & F. K. Del Boca (Eds.), *The social psychology of female–male relations: A critical analysis of central concepts* (pp. 69–119). Orlando, FL: Academic Press.

Ashmore, R. D., Solomon, M. R., & Longo, L. C. (1995). *Thinking about beauty: A multidimensional approach to the structure of perceived physical attractiveness.* Manuscript under review.

Bem, S. L. (1974). The measurement of psychological androgyny. *Journal of Consulting and Clinical Psychology, 42,* 165–172.

Bernieri, F. J., Zuckerman, M., Koestner, R., & Rosenthal, R. (1994). Measuring person perception accuracy: Another look at self–other agreement. *Personality and Social Psychology Bulletin, 20,* 367–378.

Brewer, M. B., Dull, V., & Lui, L. (1981). Perceptions of the elderly: Stereotypes as prototypes. *Journal of Personality and Social Psychology, 41,* 656–670.

Campbell, D. T. (1967). Stereotypes and the perception of group differences. *American Psychologist, 22,* 817–829.

Cash, T. F. (1981). Physical attractiveness: An annotated bibliography of theory and research in the behavioral sciences. *Psychological Documents, 11,* 83. (Ms. No. 2370)

Cash, T. F., & Janda, L. H. (1984, December). The eye of the beholder. *Psychology Today,* pp. 46–52.

Cash, T. F., & Smith, E. (1982). Physical attractiveness and personality among American college students. *The Journal of Psychology, 111,* 183–191.

Clifton, A. K., McGrath, D., & Wick, B. (1976). Stereotypes of woman: A single category? *Sex Roles, 2,* 135–148.

Cose, E. (1993). *The rage of a privileged class.* New York: Harper Collins.

Cronbach, L. J. (1955). Processes affecting scores on "Understanding of others" and "Assumed similarity." *Psychological Bulletin, 52,* 177–193.

Deaux, K., & Lewis, L. L. (1984). Structure of gender stereotypes: Interrelationships among components and gender label. *Journal of Personality and Social Psychology, 46,* 991–1004.

Dermer, M. (1974). When beauty fails (Doctoral dissertation, University of Minnesota, 1973). *Dissertation Abstracts International, 34,* 4402A.

Devine, P. G., & Baker, S. M. (1991). Measurement of racial stereotype subtyping. *Personality and Social Psychology Bulletin, 17,* 44–50.

Dion, K. K., Berscheid, E., & Walster, E. (1972). What is beautiful is good. *Journal of Personality and Social Psychology, 24,* 285–290.

Eagly, A. H., Ashmore, R. D., Makhijani, M. G., & Longo, L. C. (1991). What is beautiful is good, but . . . : A meta-analytic review of research on the physical attractiveness stereotype. *Psychological Bulletin, 110,* 109–128.

Eagly, A. H., Mladinic, A., & Otto, S. (1991). Are women evaluated more favorably than men? An analysis of attitudes, beliefs, and emotions. *Psychology of Women Quarterly, 15,* 203–216.

Eysenck, H. J., & Eysenck, S. B. G. (1968). *Manual for the Eysenck Personality Inventory.* San Diego, CA: Educational and Industrial Testing Service.

Feingold, A. (1992). Good-looking people are not what we think. *Psychological Bulletin, 111,* 304–341.

Fiske, S. T., & Taylor, S. E. (1991). *Social cognition* (2nd ed.). New York: McGraw-Hill.

Funder, D. C. (1987). Errors and mistakes: Evaluating the accuracy of social judgment. *Psychological Bulletin, 101,* 75–90.

Funder, D. C., & Dobroth, K. M. (1987). Differences between traits: Properties associated with interjudge agreement. *Journal of Personality and Social Psychology, 52,* 409–418.

Garcia, S., Stinson, L., Ickes, W., Bissonnette, V., & Briggs, S. R. (1991). Shyness and physical attractiveness in mixed-sex dyads. *Journal of Personality and Social Psychology, 61,* 35–49.

Huston, A. C. (1983). Sex-typing. In E. M. Hetherington (Vol. Ed.), *Handbook of child psychology: Vol. 4. Socialization, personality and social development* (4th ed., pp. 387–467). New York: Wiley.

Jackson, D. N. (1976). *Jackson Personality Inventory.* Port Huron, MI: Research Psychologists Press.

Judd, C. M., & Park, B. (1993). Definition and assessment of accuracy in social stereotypes. *Psychological Review, 100,* 109–128.

Jussim, L. (1991). Social perception and social reality: A reflection–construction model. *Psychological Review, 98,* 54–73.

Kenny, D. A. (1991). A general model of consensus and accuracy in interpersonal perception. *Psychological Review, 98,* 155–163.

Kenny, D. A., & Albright, L. (1987). Accuracy in interpersonal perception: A social relations analysis. *Psychological Bulletin, 102,* 390–402.

LaPiere, R. T. (1936). Type-rationalizations of group antipathy. *Social Forces, 15,* 232–237.

Longo, L. C. (1990). *Physical attractiveness and social influence: A critical review with an eye toward sex differences.* Unpublished manuscript, Rutgers University, New Brunswick, NJ.

Longo, L. C., & Ashmore, R. D. (1990, August). *The relationship between looks and personality: Strong and general or content specific?* Paper presented at the 98th Annual Convention of the American Psychological Association, Boston.

Longo, L. C., & Ashmore, R. D. (1994). *What is beautiful is powerful.* Unpublished manuscript under editorial review, New Brunswick, NJ.

McCauley, C., & Stitt, C. L. (1978). An individual and quantitative measure of stereotype. *Journal of Personality and Social Psychology, 36,* 929–940.

McCauley, C., Stitt, C. L., & Segal, M. (1980). Stereotyping: From prejudice to prediction. *Psychological Bulletin, 87,* 195–208.

Olson, J. M., & Zanna, M. P. (1993). Attitudes and attitude change. *Annual Review of Psychology, 44,* 117–154.

Osgood, C. E., Suci, G. J., & Tannenbaum, P. H. (1957). *The measurement of meaning.* Urbana: University of Illinois Press.

Reis, H., Wheeler, L., Spiegel, N., Kernis, M. H., Nezlek, J., & Perri, M. (1982). Physical attractiveness in social interaction: II. Why does appearance affect social experience? *Journal of Personality and Social Psychology, 43,* 979–996.

Rosenberg, S. (1977). New approaches to the analysis of personal constructs in person perception. In A. L. Land & J. K. Cole (Eds.), *Nebraska Symposium on Motivation* (Vol. 24, pp. 179–242). Lincoln: University of Nebraska Press.

Rosenberg, S., Nelson, C., & Vivekananthan, P. S. (1968). A multidimensional approach to the structure of personality impressions. *Journal of Personality and Social Psychology, 9,* 283–294.

Solomon, M. R., Ashmore, R. D., & Longo, L. C. (1992). The beauty match-up hypothesis: Congruence between types of beauty and product images in advertising. *Journal of Advertising, 21,* 23–34.

Swim, J. (1994). Perceived versus meta-analytic effect sizes: An assessment of accuracy of gender stereotypes. *Journal of Personality and Social Psychology, 66,* 21–36.

Taylor, S. E. (1981). A categorization approach to stereotyping. In D. L. Hamilton (Ed.), *Cognitive processes in stereotyping and intergroup behavior* (pp. 88–114). Hillsdale, NJ: Erlbaum.

Williams, J. E., & Bennett, S. M. (1975). The definition of sex stereotypes via the Adjective Check List. *Sex Roles, 1,* 327–337.

4

The Shifting Standards Model: Implications of Stereotype Accuracy for Social Judgment

Monica Biernat

This volume is designed to open the question of stereotype accuracy to scientific scrutiny and discussion. The perspectives described here largely focus either on accuracy of *content* (e.g., do the stereotypes that perceivers hold meet some external criteria of accuracy?) or of *process* (e.g., regardless of the accuracy or inaccuracy of stereotypes, are these constructs used in a reasonable manner, relative to other information, in the judgment of specific members of stereotyped groups?). This chapter generally fits under the "process" rubric, but asks a slightly different set of questions about accuracy, which arises out of a recently developed perspective on stereotype-based judgment: the *shifting standards model* (Biernat & Manis, 1994; Biernat, Manis, & Nelson, 1991). In general, the model suggests that when perceivers make judgments about members of social categories on stereotype-relevant dimensions, they do so by calling to mind a within-group standard of comparison (e.g., male targets are judged relative to a male standard, and female targets relative to a female standard). This shifting or adjustment of standards may mean that judgmental labels applied to targets from different social groups are

Correspondence concerning this chapter should be addressed to Monica Biernat, Department of Psychology, 426 Fraser Hall, University of Kansas, Lawrence, Kansas 66045-2160.

not directly comparable—their meaning is specific and relative to the category membership of the target being judged.

This model, which will be outlined more fully below, raises several questions relevant to the accuracy issue: (a) Is there a way to avoid the contamination of target judgments that result from stereotype-based standard shifts; that is, can judgment be measured in a way that captures perceivers' "true" mental representations of targets, (b) to what extent does the accuracy of a stereotype affect the degree to which judgment standards shift based on targets' category membership, and (c) what are the implications of standard shifts for real-world judgments, where, for the judgment recipient, accuracy and fairness matter most? The goal of this chapter is to provide a general overview of the shifting standards model and then to examine each of these accuracy-related questions in turn. Whereas the model has generated a considerable amount of data relevant to the first two issues, reflection on the third question will be more speculative and less data bound.

THE SHIFTING STANDARDS MODEL

The basic assumption of this approach is that concurrent with holding a stereotype of a group, one calls to mind a particular standard of judgment against which members of that group are evaluated on the stereotyped dimension. Before going further, both the terms *stereotype* and *standard* should be defined. I generally accept Ashmore and Del Boca's (1981) broad definition of a stereotype as a "set of beliefs about the personal attributes of a group of people" (p. 16), a definition that makes no assumptions about the goodness or accuracy of a stereotyped belief and allows one to incorporate a variety of group-based beliefs under the same rubric. For example, in the shifting standards work, the belief that "men are taller than women" is described as a stereotype, as is the belief that "Whites are more verbally able than Blacks." Although these beliefs may differ along a number of dimensions (including their accuracy and verifiability), the assumption in this work is that both are structurally similar in that they provide cognitive representations of group characteristics. The conception of stereotypes used here is also solidly based in the assumption that stereotypes implicitly (or explicitly) involve perceived between-group differences (e.g., men are tall *in comparison with* women; see McCauley & Stitt, 1978; McCauley, Stitt, & Segal, 1980; Tajfel, 1969).

A *standard* is comparable to an *expectation,* but incorporates not just a discrete judgment point or mean (e.g., the expectation that a man will be tall), but also a range of likely outcomes or behaviors anticipated from members of the target group (e.g., most men will probably range from about 5 ft, 7 in. to 6 ft, 2 in.). Yet a standard does invoke a *threshold,* that is, a criterion against which dichotomous judgments are made (see Dunning & Cohen, 1992). For example, I may set a higher threshold for judging whether a person is "tall" if that person is a man rather than a woman. A *stereotype-based standard* is, therefore, an expectation about the likely mean and range of group members on the attribute in question. This idea is rooted in the literature suggesting that stereotypes involve both mean level and variability representations (Judd & Park, 1988, 1993; Park & Judd, 1990).

The shifting standards model suggests that stereotypes lead the perceiver to shift or adjust his or her standards of judgment depending on a target's social category. Men, for example, are expected to be more aggressive than women. When judging how aggressive a particular man or woman is, perceivers' standards are likely to shift in accordance with this expectation (e.g., an aggressive behavior is likely to be perceived as more aggressive in a woman than in a man, because this behavior is more likely to surpass the perceiver's expectations for the typical aggressiveness of women than of men).[1]

In most social judgment research, and perhaps in most real-world interactions, individuals make judgments of targets using *subjective* language. For example, a subject might judge a female target as *very aggres-*

---

[1]Note that in this example, and in virtually all of the work that has thus far been conducted on the shifting standards model, the focus has been on *quantitative* differences in judgment standards. However, some standard shifts may also be *qualitative* in nature (e.g., the meaning of aggression for a male may include conceptions of physical aggression; for females it may not). This aspect of standard shifts awaits further elaboration and empirical work.

sive, perhaps a 7 on a 1–7 rating scale. Similarly, a perceiver might comment that he met a *really tall* woman. One question that the shifting standards model raises is what people mean when they use terms like *very* or *really*, or *aggressive* or *tall?* In everyday-language use, such words are understood to have different referents, depending on the object being described. So, for example, we expect that a large cat will still comfortably fit in a small house. It is obvious in cases like this that we routinely shift judgment standards as we move from one category of referents (cats) to another (houses). Similarly, with regard to social categories, we may implicitly understand that an aggressive woman may be less *objectively* aggressive than an aggressive man. This should be true, of course, only among perceivers who believe that men, as a group, are more aggressive than women.

What this means for social judgment in the laboratory and in the real world is that verbal assessments of targets from different social groups (men vs. women or Blacks vs. Whites) may not be *directly* comparable. That is, the label *very tall* applied to a woman communicates a different meaning than does that same label applied to a man. Looked at another way, a man and a woman of the same objective height (e.g., 5 ft, 9 in.) are likely to prompt different labeling (*quite tall* for a woman; *about average* for a man). We seem to implicitly accept this shifting of meaning in some judgment domains, such as height; but in others, we may not. For example, in most person perception experiments in which perceivers provide subjective trait ratings of targets, researchers tend to take these judgments at face value: If a male and a female target receive comparable aggressiveness ratings, we assume this means that subjects actually perceive the targets as equal in aggressiveness and that stereotypes are inoperative (see Locksley, Borgida, Brekke, & Hepburn, 1980; Locksley, Hepburn, & Ortiz, 1982). However, one suggestion that arises from the shifting standards model is that findings of this sort are open to another interpretation: that stereotypes *do* exert an influence on judgment, in that they affect the standard of comparison brought to mind. In other words, stereotypes may be operating even when it appears that they are not.

In general, the shifting standards model assumes that when a subject or judge is provided with a subjective response scale on which to evaluate a group of targets (such as women), the end-anchors of the rating scale are shifted so as to maximize expected differentiation among group members. This idea is not new to the judgment literature. Volkmann's (1951) "rubber band" model assumes that subjects set the endpoints of their rating scales to match what they think will be the endpoints of the stimulus range to which they are exposed. The subjective meaning of various response categories changes as a stimulus range extends or retracts (see also Postman & Miller, 1945). Parducci's "range" and "frequency" principles make similar predictions concerning how judges assign stimuli to appropriate rating categories (Parducci, 1963, 1965; Parducci & Perrett, 1971). Upshaw's (1962, 1969) variable perspective model also suggests that judgments are based on where stimuli (e.g., attitudinal stimuli) fall within an individual's subjective frame of reference, or perspective. These shifts or adjustments in the anchoring and extension of response scales lead to differential labeling and evaluation of comparable targets, who happen to belong to different social categories.

Assuming that people do indeed routinely shift or adjust judgment standards depending on the category membership of the targets being judged, it becomes difficult to know precisely what a judge means when he or she uses a particular evaluative label. For example, how should a researcher interpret the fact that a Black law school applicant with strong credentials is rated a 10 on a scale of overall quality, whereas a comparable White law student is rated an 8 (see Linville & Jones, 1980)? How can the researcher tap into the perceiver's true mental representations of these targets? The shifting standards model offers some answers to these questions.

THE ACCURATE "CAPTURE" OF MENTAL REPRESENTATIONS

The phenomenon of standard shifts in judgment and the interpretational problems it invites become moot if judgments are made on *objective*, or *externally anchored*, response scales. For example, even though a 5 ft, 9 in.

woman might be subjectively perceived as *quite tall* and a 5 ft, 9 in. man as *average*, perceivers would readily agree that these targets are objectively the same. And, if asked to judge height in feet and inches, the perceiver cannot adjust the meaning of rating points for male and female targets: An inch is an inch, regardless of who or what is being measured with that unit. A basic prediction of the shifting standards model, then, is that subjective ratings scales will reveal evidence of standard shifts, whereas objective scales will not. Instead, the latter will provide a more accurate reflection of a perceiver's mental representations of targets. To extend the height example above, subjective height judgments would suggest that the perceiver sees the female target as taller than the male; objective height judgments would suggest that the two are perceived as equal in height—an accurate judgment in this instance.

Defining "Subjective" and "Objective" Scales

Because this distinction between subjective and objective response scales is a central methodological and theoretical aspect of the shifting standards model, a clear articulation of what is meant by these types of scales is in order. Any judgment can presumably be made in either subjective or objective measurement units; for example, one can judge height using a response language that ranges from *very short* to *very tall* (subjective) or using feet and inches as a metric (objective). More generally, by a *subjective* scale, I refer to any rating format in which the subject is free to impose his or her own meaning on the scale points; that is, the meaning of a unit of measurement can be adjusted to accommodate the object or target being judged. This is most typically seen in scales using a Likert-type or semantic-differential format. For example, endorsing a 5 on a Likert scale, or checking a response option labeled *very competent*, are subjective judgments: The meaning of a 5 or of a *very competent* can shift, depending on the nature of the object being so described.

It is somewhat more difficult to articulate what is meant by an *objective* scale. In the most straightforward sense, an objective scale is one in which the measurement units have the same meaning, regardless of the category to which the rated object belongs. Obviously, judgment units such as feet and inches, pounds, or dollars earned are objective in nature: A dollar is a dollar, regardless of who is earning it. In this sense, one might refer to such rating scales as *common-rule* or *externally anchored* scales.

But because I am interested in stereotype-based standards, and because most stereotypes focus on traits or other attributes that one is less able to directly, objectively measure, I include under the rubric of *objective* scales such indicators as assigned letter grades or Scholastic Aptitude Test (SAT) scores (for assessing competence of a target), explicit behaviors, and rank orderings of targets on a dimension of interest. A letter grade is not as clearly objective as an inch, but there is general agreement in our culture that a letter grade should be based on meeting some unwavering criteria for performance and that an A means an A, regardless of who has received it.[2] SAT scores come closer to meeting the common-rule criterion; that is, scores are based not on the social category membership of the student, but on a count of correct answers. To interpret the degree of performance indicated by an SAT score, one need not be told the social category membership of the test taker.

Similarly, I would describe a ranking procedure as an objective judgment indicator because it forces explicit comparison of targets on the dimension of interest. In general, then, the term *objective* refers, in this research, to response formats as diverse as feet and inches, letter grades, and rank orderings. What these scales have in common is the constant meaning of their measurement units, regardless of the social category membership of the targets being judged. According to the model, such scales differ from subjective scales in that they do not allow for category-based shifts in the meaning of response options.

Research on Response Scale Effects

As an initial test of our model, we relied on a height judgment paradigm; subjects were asked to estimate the heights of male and female targets in either subjective or objective units. The domain of height provided an ap-

---

[2]As teachers, of course, most of us will admit that grades are not as firmly based on objective performance as we would like to think; however, a survey of students at the University of Florida revealed that they did, indeed, perceive letter grades to be objective in nature.

pealing starting point for several reasons. First, in earlier research (Nelson, Biernat, & Manis, 1990), we documented that the belief that men are taller than women is a very powerful one: It influences judgments of individual targets even under conditions designed to strongly discourage its use. For example, even when told that a sample of male and female targets was matched for height (i.e., that the sex stereotype did not apply) and when offered money for accurate judgment, subjects continued to judge men as taller than women. In short, we have little doubt that virtually all adults accept and are influenced by the stereotype that men are taller than women (children's beliefs are another matter; Biernat, 1993). Furthermore, beliefs about gender and height are presumably grounded in everyday experience, are relatively affect free, and are accurate (within limits). The latter quality allows us to easily compare judgments to social reality, in a manner that is typically not possible in stereotype research. And finally, height judgment is particularly appealing from a shifting standards standpoint because it is directly associated with an objective response scale: feet and inches.

In our first test of the shifting standards perspective, subjects viewed a series of 40 full-body photographs of male and female targets, whose true heights were known to us (Biernat et al., 1991, Study 1). Although concealed from the subjects, the male and female targets had been matched for height, that is, for every female of a certain height there was a corresponding male in the stimulus set. One third of the subjects were asked to judge height in feet and inches (objective condition), and the other two thirds judged height using subjective—*short* (1) to *tall* (7)—response scales. Of the subjective-judgment group, half were asked to judge the heights of the targets compared with the height of the average person (*average-person condition*), and half made height judgments in relation to the targets' sex category, that is, compared with the height of the average man or woman (*average-for-sex condition*).

The shifting standards predictions were that *objective* height judgments would clearly reveal the operation of the sex stereotype (male targets judged taller than female targets), *average-person* judgments would reduce this difference (because subjects were being evaluated in relation to a common standard), and *average-for-sex* judgments would completely eliminate this judged sex difference (because targets were compared only with same-sex others). This was precisely the pattern we found: In feet and inches, the perceived male–female height differential was about 1.0 standardized units; in average-person units, this difference dropped to 0.2; and in average-for-sex units, it was reduced to 0.0.

Given that this volume concerns accuracy, the reader should note the difficulty of drawing conclusions about accurate judgment in these data. Subjects in the objective condition did show evidence of their (accurate) belief that men are taller than women. However, in this particular set of targets, there was no sex difference in height, and therefore the judgment was inaccurate. By this latter standard, subjects in the average-for-sex condition appeared to be more accurate: Their height ratings did not differ for women and men. On the other hand, if these subjects were responsive to height cues and truly used within-sex height standards, they should have judged the women as taller than the men: In this sample, the female targets were taller than the average female, and the male targets shorter than the average male. This example serves to point out the difficulty of setting an accuracy criterion and of making confident statements about judgmental accuracy. The main point of the shifting standards model in this regard is that whether individual judgments are accurate or not, objective rating scales will be more likely than are subjective ratings to reflect perceivers' mental representations with reasonable fidelity. In this case, we know that people believe that men are taller than women, and the objective height judgments reflect that.

In a second study testing this perspective, we extended our analysis to other sex-relevant beliefs that are also accurate and clearly associated with objective indexes of measurement. Along with height judgments, our subjects were asked to judge a different sample of 40 male and female targets on the dimensions of weight, income, and age (Biernat et al., 1991, Study 2). Half of the subjects used objective rating units (feet and inches, pounds, dollars, and years), and half used subjective units, comparing the targets to the average person (short–tall, light–heavy, financially unsuccessful–financially successful, and young–old). This study also allowed us to test an important aspect of the shifting standards model—namely, that standard shifts should occur only on stereotyped judgment dimensions. Sex is clearly differentially associated with height, weight, and income, but not with age that is, there is no stereotype that says "men and women differ, on average, in age." Therefore, different judgment scales should produce different male–female judgment patterns only on the first three dimensions, but not with regard to age.

Again, this is precisely the pattern we found. For height, weight, and income judgments, objective ratings revealed stereotype-consistent judgment effects: Male targets were judged as taller, heavier, and richer than female targets. Subjective ratings, however, generally showed reductions of these effects, and in the case of financial judgments, a reversal: Although men were perceived as earning more money than women, the women were judged as more financially successful than the men. In contrast, for age judgments (the non–sex-linked attribute), the comparable effect was not significant.

In looking at these data using "target" as the unit of analysis, we discovered some evidence that the cognitive process described earlier in this chapter may indeed have been contributing to subjects' judgments. Specifically, we noted that female and male targets who were rated the same in subjective units were nonetheless seen to differ substantially in objective units. For example, a female target rated a "4" on the subjective scale of financial success was objectively rated as earning about $23,000 a year. In comparison, a male target, also subjectively rated a "4," was perceived to earn about $40,000 a year (see Biernat et al., 1991, Figure 7). Clearly, subjects used their subjective rating scales differentially to judge women and men on stereotype-relevant attributes; they did not do this on judgments irrelevant to gender (i.e., age). Other work has also replicated this latter effect by demonstrating that standard shifts did not occur on judgment dimensions for which subjects reported holding no sex stereotypes (e.g., hours of studying or number of movies seen; see Biernat et al., 1991, Study 3).

Summary

In answer, then, to the first accuracy question—is there a way to avoid the contamination of target judgments that result from stereotype-based standard shifts—the shifting standards model suggests that researchers, and perhaps individuals interacting in the real world, may avoid or overcome the possible meaning confusion that results from the use of differential judgment standards by relying on more objective, externally anchored, or common-rule judgments. These may more faithfully capture perceivers' true mental representations of targets. Thus far, however, this phenomenon has been demonstrated in a rather restricted range of judgment domains. To bolster the argument further, the next section describes a series of studies regarding standard shifts that focus on judgments more traditionally considered to be meaningful social stereotypes. These include the beliefs that men are more competent than women, Whites are more verbally able than Blacks, women are more verbally able than men, Blacks are more athletic than Whites, and men are more aggressive than women. In turning to these judgment domains, I also turn to the second accuracy-related question raised by the shifting standards model: To what extent does the accuracy of a stereotype affect the degree to which judgment standards shift based on targets' category membership?

SHIFTING STANDARDS BASED ON STEREOTYPES OF UNKNOWN ACCURACY OR INACCURACY[3]

Beliefs about height, weight, and income are not the most provocative of social stereotypes. For this reason, we sought to establish the validity of the shifting standards model in judgment domains that lie closer to those stereotypes about which there is more scientific and social concern. In making the move from judgments of height to judgments of competence, for example, one consequently moves from a focus on accurate beliefs that virtually everyone endorses, to beliefs of unknown accuracy that vary in strength from individual to individual. To what extent is the phenomenon of shifting standards dependent on the accuracy or verifiability of the relevant stereotype?

---

[3]Of course, the accuracy of each of the other stereotypes we examine in this chapter could be tested by choosing appropriate criteria (e.g., see McCauley & Thangavelu, 1991). However, as content accuracy per se is not a key concern of the shifting standards model, we simply note that gender-based beliefs about height, weight, and income are clearly accurate, whereas by comparison, the accuracy of the other stereotypes is either less clear, unknown, or at least contested by some.

An easy, perhaps too glib, answer to this question is "not at all." In a series of studies examining the various social stereotypes mentioned briefly above, we found effects quite comparable to those described for the height, weight, and income studies. That is, objective scales revealed evidence of stereotype operation, whereas subjective scales did not. These findings are elaborated below, after which I turn to a more complex answer to the question posed above.

Objective Versus Subjective Judgments in More Provocative Stereotype Domains

"Men Are More Competent Than Women"

Building on the work of Goldberg (1968), in which female subjects judged pieces of written work more negatively when they were attributed to a female (Joan McKay) than a male (John McKay) author, we sought to examine, from a shifting standards perspective, the operation of the very general gender stereotype that men are more competent than women (Biernat & Manis, 1994, Study 1). Although the Goldberg (1968) study prompted a flurry of research activity, a closer look reveals that the gender effect he described was actually quite weak; indeed, a meta-analytical review published 20 years later reached the same conclusion (Swim, Borgida, Maruyama, & Myers, 1989). From a shifting standards perspective, we noticed, however, that virtually all of the judgment studies using the Joan McKay–John McKay paradigm relied on subjective response scales, which, we have argued, are subject to standard shifts. These scales may, therefore, mask the fact that subjects are indeed guided by this gender belief. In our research, we predicted that target gender differences in judgment *would* be apparent on objective rather than subjective-judgment indexes and that the gender typing of the article would affect the direction of that effect. Rather than endorsing an overarching stereotype that men are more competent than women, we thought that subjects might subscribe to the beliefs that "men are better than women at writing about masculine topics" and "women are better than men at writing about feminine topics." Given the reasoning of the shifting standards model, objective judgments should reveal the operation of these representations; subjective scales should not.

In our research, subjects read a one-page article, attributed to either Joan or John McKay, that focused on either a masculine (e.g., bass fishing), feminine (e.g., cooking nutritious meals), or gender-neutral topic (e.g., the mind–body problem). The articles were judged on three dimensions: overall quality, monetary worth, and interest value for readers. Half of the subjects made these judgments in objective units (e.g., how much money [in dollars] would you pay the author if you were an editor?), and half in subjective units (e.g., *very little money* to *lots of money*).

The data were consistent with the pattern predicted above. Among subjects in the objective-judgment condition, feminine articles were judged more positively when written by Joan than by John (i.e., Joan was paid an average of $246, and John was paid $83), and masculine articles were judged more positively when written by John than by Joan ($248 and $176 for John and Joan, respectively). Subjects in the subjective-judgment condition did not differentially judge male and female authors by topic, and neutral articles were similarly unaffected by gender and scale effects.

In an analogous study, subjects were asked to pretend they were employers and to consider either "Katherine" or "Kenneth" Anderson for either a "masculine" (chief of staff) or "feminine" (secretary) position in their company (see Biernat & Kobrynowicz, 1995). The targets had mediocre qualifications, reflected in a resumé, and the job description was equivalent across the masculine–feminine conditions—only the title was changed. Similar to the magazine article study described above, objective judgments revealed that Katherine was evaluated more positively than Kenneth for the secretarial position, but Kenneth was evaluated more positively than Katherine for the chief of staff position. Subjective evaluations showed reversals of these effects. Both of these studies again suggest that objective response scales reveal what we believe to be subjects' true mental representations of male and female targets' context-specific competence, whereas subjective scales, presumably because of their shift in meaning on the basis of gender category, do not.

"Whites Are More Verbally Able Than Blacks; Women Are More Verbally Able Than Men"

In a study designed to assess the operation of these two social stereotypes simultaneously, we asked subjects to make judgments of the verbal ability of a series of 40 Black and White, male and female targets. To ensure that subjects had some legitimate basis on which to make their judgments, two vocabulary definitions that the high-school-age targets had supposedly offered in an oral test were provided along with each photograph (see Biernat & Manis, 1994, Study 2). Once again, we expected that objective ratings (in this case, predicted letter grades—A to E) would reveal evidence of stereotype operation and that subjective ratings—*low verbal ability* (1) to *high verbal ability* (5)—would indicate reductions or reversals of these effects.

This prediction was supported for both the racial and gender stereotypes. On objective scales, White targets were judged more verbally able than Black targets; on subjective scales, this difference was significantly reduced. Independent of this race effect, female targets were judged more verbally able than male targets in objective units, and this effect was nonsignificantly reversed among subjects in the subjective-rating condition. Once again, in a substantively different judgment domain, using a different methodology, the shifting standards model was supported. Objective ratings remained more true than did subjective ratings to what we believe to be subjects' underlying representations of Black and White, male and female targets. Furthermore, these data demonstrated the phenomenon in a case where the stereotype favors a typically disadvantaged group: women.

"Blacks Are More Athletic Than Whites"

Continuing this latter theme, we examined the operation of a positive stereotype of Blacks by having subjects judge the athleticism of 10 Black and White male targets from photographs (Biernat & Manis, 1994, Study 3). All subjects made subjective judgments of these targets, on scales ranging from *unathletic* (1) to *athletic* (7) rating scales and then performed an objective-rating task: They rank ordered the 10 targets on an athleticism continuum. Because this study used a within-subject manipulation of response scale, we were able to compare the number of times Black targets were subjectively *rated* as more athletic than White targets with the number of times these Black targets were *ranked* as more athletic than White targets. In keeping with the shifting standards perspective and relying on a very different conception of objective responding, we found that Black targets were more often *ranked* than rated as more athletic than White targets. Furthermore, "ties" in subjective-rating units (e.g., a Black and a White target each rated a "5") were likely to be "resolved" by ranking the Black more athletic than the White.

"Men Are More Aggressive Than Women"

Because we had difficulty coming up with a way of objectively measuring aggression, we relied on a rather different methodology to tap into how this stereotype might affect standard shifts. If a perceiver believes that men are more aggressive than women, he or she might be expected to set different thresholds to diagnose aggression in male and female targets. Specifically, one should set a lower threshold to diagnose aggression for women than for men. The converse of this stereotype, that men are less passive than women, should operate comparably. That is, given that women are expected to be more passive than men, a lower threshold should be set for diagnosing passivity in men than in women.

In a study designed to test these predictions, subjects were asked to think of either a male or a female target (Larry or Linda) and then to consider, in turn, two lists of 20 behaviors that this target may have engaged in (Biernat & Manis, 1994, Study 4). One list contained 20 behaviors that were rated as very assertive, and the other list contained 20 behaviors rated as very passive by the pilot-test judges in Locksley et al.'s (1980, 1982) research. The subjects' task in this study was simply to consider each behavior and to indicate "if you think that by engaging in this behavior, Linda/Larry has provided you with evidence that she/he is an aggressive/passive person." In keeping with the earlier predictions, in 14 of 20 cases, behaviors were judged to be more diagnostic of aggressiveness if Linda rather than Larry engaged in them, and in 16 of 20 cases, behaviors were judged to be more diagnostic of unassertiveness (passivity) when engaged in by Larry rather than Linda (ps < .05). Sex of the target affected the diagnostic criteria for these gender-relevant dimensions.

Summary

Across these very different judgment domains, we continued to find support for the main premise of the shifting standards model—that objective judgments would be more likely than subjective judgments to provide evidence that stereotypes were operative. More generally, we believe that objective ratings, because they do not change in meaning when applied to targets from different social categories, more accurately reflect subjects' stereotype-based mental representations. Although these study designs and methods were quite different from those used in the height, weight, and income judgment studies, the fundamental finding was unchanged. This, then, leads to the straightforward conclusion that the accuracy of the stereotype has little effect on the basic operation of the shifting standards model.

Some Caveats

A few qualifications to this conclusion may be in order. The underlying, content-based accuracy of a stereotype may matter to the shifting standards model to the extent that (a) accurate stereotypes are more likely to "automatically" invite the use of different judgment standards, (b) accurate stereotypes are less subject to social desirability concerns that could affect judges' willingness to differentially use judgment standards (or to be highly affected by them), and (c) accurate stereotypes are less likely to differ in strength from individual to individual, whereas individual differences are more likely to play a role in the case of less accurate stereotypes.

Thus far, the shifting standards model has generated only minimal evidence relevant to the "automaticity" point. It is unlikely that the use of shifting standards represents an absolute or pure form of automaticity; rather, the phenomenon may fall under the rubric of what Bargh (1989) refers to as "goal dependent" (p. 19) automaticity. This involves awareness of an instigating stimulus (e.g., the category member), a processing goal (e.g., to make a judgment), and allocation of focal attention to the process.

However, automatic standard shifts should require no intention that the effect occur and no conscious guidance to completion (see Bargh, 1989, p. 10). Our research on height judgments has provided some indication that even when asked to use a common standard of judgment (Biernat et al., 1991, Study 1), subjects still continue to use different height referents for men and women (their perceived male–female difference lies between that for the objective [absolute common referent] and average-for-sex conditions). This suggests that it may be difficult to "let go" of the within-category referent, at least in a domain such as height, where the underlying gender-based belief is so strong (Nelson et al., 1990).

However, we also used an experimental manipulation of judgmental standards in the race and athleticism study described above. We reasoned that if individuals accept the stereotype that Blacks are more athletic than Whites, Black males should represent the highest or harshest standard of athleticism, whereas a group such as "women" might represent a relatively weak athletic standard. Judgments of the athleticism of all targets, Black and White, should therefore be lowered when perceivers are explicitly asked to use "Black male" as the judgment standard and heightened when that standard is "women." However, if Blacks are automatically judged in relation to Blacks, and Whites to Whites, instructional sets may not overcome these tendencies. In our research, subjective athleticism ratings of both Black and White targets were highly responsive to the manipulated comparison standards, suggesting, perhaps, that athleticism judgments are less likely to automatically invoke stereotype-based standard shifts than are height judgments. Clearly, more work is needed to test for the automaticity of the shifting standards process and to outline the dimensions of stereotypes (including their accuracy) that are likely to contribute to this automaticity.

Other research from the shifting standards perspective speaks to the individual-differences issue (point c, above). An explicit assumption of the shifting standards model is that people will use different standards to evaluate targets from divergent social categories to the extent that they personally endorse the relevant stereotypes. Just as standards apparently do not shift on judgment dimensions that are unrelated to stereotypes (see

Biernat et al., 1991), they also should not shift among individuals who do not adopt the stereotypes. This plays into the accuracy question in that there is likely to be very little variability in the acceptance of accurate stereotypes (e.g., all adults will agree that men are generally taller than women). Furthermore, there are likely to be fewer social desirability concerns, that is, less reticence about expressing stereotype-based judgments, when accurate stereotypes are involved (point b above). For stereotypes of unknown accuracy, however, individuals are more likely to vary in their degree or confidence of endorsement.

In several of the studies described above, we included individual-difference measures that we thought were relevant to the stereotypes in question. For example, in the Joan McKay–John McKay research, we measured subjects' Attitudes Toward Women (Spence & Helmreich, 1972); in the verbal ability and athleticism studies, we included measures of modern racism (McConahay, Hardee, & Batts, 1981) and base-rate perceptions of verbal ability and athleticism across gender and race groups (see Biernat & Manis, 1994). In each case, we predicted that individuals who endorsed the relevant attitude or stereotype most strongly would be most likely to show evidence of the shifting standards effect. Although there were some inconsistencies across studies, there was general support for the prediction that individuals who rejected gender or racial stereotypes did *not* shift their standards when evaluating members of these different groups.

Again, it is likely that the endorsement of accurate stereotypes may be more widespread (and less culture specific) than that of stereotypes of unknown accuracy. The consequence is that evidence of standard shifts may appear to be more robust in the former case, where individual differences are fewer. As is true of the automaticity and social desirability points raised above, this issue can best be considered by conducting research in which stereotypes that vary in accuracy are directly compared.

IMPLICATIONS OF STANDARD SHIFTS FOR REAL-WORLD JUDGMENTS

A third question raised by the shifting standards model concerns the implications of the phenomenon for real-world judgment situations. Decisions such as hirings, promotions, school acceptances, and performance evaluations, for example, may be affected by standard shifts, such that individuals from different social categories are judged with different referents in mind. Here, I will touch on two relevant issues to which the shifting standards model speaks. One involves a consideration of both expectancy-based (assimilative) and shifting standard (contrastive) processes in real-world judgment, and the other focuses on perceivers' understanding of subjective evaluations.

Expectancy-Guided Bias and Shifting Standards

One issue to which we have begun to turn our attention concerns the fact that the shifting standards model makes predictions that run counter to research on expectancy-guided encoding and behavioral perception (Neuberg, 1994; Snyder, 1992). The latter body of work suggests that holding a stereotype of a group will lead perceivers to judge the behavior of target group members in a stereotype-consistent (assimilative) manner. The shifting standards model suggests, however, that within-category comparison standards can result in a stereotyped group member being evaluated inconsistently with the stereotype (a contrastive pattern).

A sociological version of the expectancy-guided bias literature, known as "expectation states" and "status characteristics" theory (Berger, Fisek, Norman, & Zelditch, 1977; Berger, Rosenholtz, & Zelditch, 1980; Berger, Wagner, & Zelditch, 1985; Webster & Foschi, 1988), explicitly plays out a series of predictions regarding double standards used in gender-based judgments of competence. This model suggests that standards of ability are stricter (i.e., require more evidence of ability) for women than for men and, simultaneously, that standards for lack of ability are lower (i.e., require less evidence of lack of ability) for women than for men (Foddy & Smithson, 1989; Foschi, 1992). Thus, a woman might be required to "jump through more hoops" to prove her competence than a man. In contrast, under the logic described in the diagnosticity-of-aggression study described above (Biernat & Manis, 1994, Study 4), the shifting standards model predicts that if perceivers believe men are more competent than women, they will set *lower* standards for women than for men. In other words, judges may accept an objectively lower level of competence as evidence of "meeting standards" in a woman.

This raises questions concerning the relative likelihood that judgment will be guided by expectations or affected by standard shifts. For example, when choosing between two objectively equal job applicants, one male and one female, will an employer who accepts traditional gender stereotypes be affected by his pro-male bias and hire the male, or will he be impressed that this particular woman has surpassed his (low) expectations for female competence and hire her? One factor that may determine which phenomenon occurs is the type of judgment being made. The status characteristics model focuses specifically on how target gender affects judges' tendency to make an inference or attribution of *ability*. The shifting standards model, on the other hand, has more to do with meeting minimum requirements or thresholds to qualify for a position or category label. Thus, the sexist employer might be more impressed by the female candidate, who has surprisingly exceeded his low expectations (a contrast), but may nonetheless be unlikely to make the attribution that her success is due to her ability. To illustrate this point, in the Kenneth/Katherine study described earlier, in which job candidates were evaluated for a "masculine" or "feminine" position, we also asked subjects to make a series of judgments regarding the *level of skill* they would want the applicant to display in various domains before they would feel confident that the applicant either (a) had the ability to perform the skill or (b) met the minimum standard of performance on the skill (Biernat & Kobrynowicz, 1995). Nine skills were listed—including decision making, interpersonal relations, leadership, motivation, problem solving, planning, and oral communication—and subjects indicated the number of examples of each skill they would want the candidate to provide.

In keeping with the shifting standards model, subjects asked the "minimum standard" question set a lower standard for the female than the male applicant (i.e., Katherine had to produce fewer examples of her skills to meet the minimum standard than did Kenneth). At the same time, however, subjects required more examples of skill from Katherine than from Kenneth if their goal was to document ability. These two processes, setting lower standards for women, but needing more from them to make an ability attribution, can co-occur. Keeping with one of the themes of the shifting standards work, it is apparent that which pattern of effects is revealed depends, at least in part, on how one asks the questions.

Furthermore, there may be a distinction in real-world judgment between dichotomous decisions, such as hirings and promotions, and continuous judgments, such as evaluations. Dichotomous judgments are comparable to what I have described as objective ratings, in that (a) they prompt a direct comparison between targets and (b) they do not shift in meaning across social categories (e.g., being hired or not means the same thing, regardless of one's sex). On the other hand, continuous judgments of the sort that appear in evaluations are typically subjective in nature (e.g., how poorly or well an employee is performing, rated on a 1–5 scale). In general, in keeping with our research on response scale effects, objective judgments (e.g., hires) should be more likely than are subjective evaluations to reflect perceivers' mental representations, whereas subjective evaluations should be more likely to be affected by standard shifts. Of course, this is not to suggest that hires will always reveal the operation of stereotypes or that employers would be unresponsive to individuating information regarding competence—even a fairly sexist employer would most likely hire a competent woman over an incompetent man. In this case, the objective judgment would also be consistent with the perceivers' cognitive representations of the targets, though these representations would be based on accurate, diagnostic individuating information and not on stereotypes.

That subjective performance evaluations may be affected by expectancy-based standard shifts is suggested in Pettigrew and Martin's (1987) work describing the special problems faced by "solo" Blacks in work settings. These authors suggested that after being hired, solo Blacks may encounter either unreasonably low or unreasonably high expectations regarding their performance (depending, e.g., on the politics of the perceiver). In the former case, an employee may easily be able to surpass these low expectations and, therefore, might be subjectively viewed quite positively. On the other hand, employers may "act on their low expectations—in such ways as giving blacks less challenging assignments" (Pettigrew &

Martin, 1987, p. 56). This may ultimately trickle down to relatively low performance evaluations, because "objectively," the Black employee may be performing very little.

In the case of high expectations, because they are difficult to meet, even some reasonable level of objective performance may be subjectively viewed less positively than it would in the absence of such high standards. In either case, if standards based on racial or gender categories are guiding these judgments, it may be difficult to assess the validity of performance evaluations. They may be unreasonably high or unreasonably low, depending on the standards of the judge and, related to this, on the objective features of the employee's performance. It is important to recognize, of course, that judgment standards are likely to affect evaluations of all employees, not just those who belong to minority groups. In any subjective-judgment situation, evaluations are made in relation to some standard. In general, our point is that the meaning of these evaluations may be cloudy unless these standards become explicit.

The Decoding of Subjective Language

This brings us to a second "implications" question that the shifting standards model raises. Because we communicate with each other in subjective language (e.g., we are more likely to say "she's a good employee" than "she'd earn a B+ for her efforts"), it seems important to explore how listeners decode and understand evaluative judgments in everyday life. There is evidence that perceivers expect a man described as *very tall* to be taller than a woman who is similarly characterized (see Roberts & Herman, 1986), and anecdotally, it certainly seems that we are well able to take into account context and standards as we decode subjective language—remember the large cat in the small house, or consider a reference to an 80° July day in Kansas as *cool* (it *is* cool in relation to the typical Kansas summer heat). I also had the recent experience of being an external committee member on a dissertation defense for a student in a largely nonempirical field. There, I was perceived as a "statistical wizard," and I *was*, relative to the other committee members. However, this label is not readily conferred on me in my own department.

It is less clear, however, if we apply similar cognitive "corrections" when decoding other types of subjective statements or evaluations that might plausibly be affected by different stereotype-based subjective standards. Some research specifically suggests that our ability to take into account the changing subjective standards that are required for everyday speech is far from perfect. Higgins and Lurie (1983) have demonstrated a "change of standard" effect, in which subjects apparently remembered the verbal label they had attached to the criminal sentences of a fictitious "Judge Jones" (how harsh or lenient his sentences seemed to be, compared with those of other judges), but not the comparative context that led to these characterizations (see also Clark, Martin, & Henry, 1993; Higgins & Stangor, 1988). By focusing on the evaluative, subjective language, perceivers may lose sight of the original information and the standard on which it was based.

What this implies for shifting standards research is that although we make subjective judgments using shifting standards, it is the subjective language itself that may be best remembered by ourselves and by others. Thus, the application of the label *good* to both a male and a female author may ultimately lead others to accept the female as good, period. This is more likely to be true, of course, if the original subjective evaluation "she's very good" is devoid of the additional tag "for a woman."

There is one domain in which we have found evidence that perceivers do take stereotype-based standard shifts into account. Intrigued by an article on double standards of parenting that seem to operate in custodial battles (Chesler, 1991), we wondered what perceivers understand by the labels *good mother* versus *good father*. To the extent that perceivers believe that mothers do (or should do) more for their children than fathers do, they may understand the label *good parent* to imply more, or better quality, caregiving when applied to women (mothers) than to men (fathers). We simply asked subjects to listen to a vignette describing either a mother or father who was characterized as either a *good* parent or an *all right* parent of two children (see Kobrynowicz & Biernat, 1994). Subjects were then asked to make objective estimates of the frequency with which the parent engaged in a variety of child-care behaviors (e.g., how often did [parent] prepare lunch for the kids to take to school, or how many hours per week did [parent] play interactively with the children?). The *good* mother was seen to engage in significantly more behaviors (particularly those having to do with physical and emotional care) than the *good* father, as was the *all right* mother perceived to do more than the *all right* father. These data suggest that with regard to parenting, a domain in which strong gender-based expectations surely exist, perceivers understand that *good* means something different when applied to a female parent than when applied to a male parent.

We continue to pursue this line of work by focusing on factors such as the strength and accuracy of judgment-relevant stereotypes, credibility of the communicator, knowledge of the communicator's standards, and the subject's own standards as potential contributors to an individual's facility at "decoding" and interpreting others' subjective judgments. On the first point, for example, one could argue that beliefs about gender and parenting may be based on the observation of social reality: Even in two-job families, women do typically engage in more child-care activity than do men (e.g., Biernat & Wortman, 1991; Hochschild, 1989). This strong, observable association may make it likely that beliefs about parenting will function more similarly to beliefs about height than will other, less verifiable stereotypes.

CONCLUSION

This chapter has offered an overview of the shifting standards model as it relates to the issue of stereotype accuracy. Perhaps the most lucid statement this work can make is that certain types of judgments (e.g., objective judgments) are more likely to provide an accurate reflection of perceivers' mental representations of social targets than others (e.g., subjective judgments). This is not to say that objective judgments better map onto objective reality or that they are bias free. Indeed, much of our work has indicated that judgments made on objective scales are more likely than judgments made on subjective, relativistic scales to provide evidence of stereotype operation—and these stereotypes may or may not themselves be accurate. Like a number of other contributors to this volume, I recognize the difficulty of answering the accuracy question in any simple or straightforward fashion: The meaning of accuracy itself is contextual and likely to be culture specific as well (see Lee & Duenas, chapter 7, this volume). In general, however, this research raises a cautionary flag regarding experimental person perception research: Results obtained using conventional subjective scaling methods may provide a very misleading depiction of perceivers' mental representations.

Furthermore, although I have implicitly described stereotypes as relatively static beliefs, these too are subject to contextual variation. In their recent book, *Stereotyping and Social Reality*, Oakes, Haslam, and Turner (1994) wrote that "stereotypes are not the result of indiscriminate, fixed prejudices but are context-dependent statements about intergroup relations that can be influenced by a complex set of intergroup comparisons" (p. 18). Stereotypes themselves may change, or their operation may be more or less likely in certain contexts than others, and therefore the phenomenon of shifting standards may be quite variable in strength across judgment situations. Much further work is necessary to understand the various mediators and moderators of the shifting standards effect, and my hope is that this chapter points out some profitable avenues this research might take.

REFERENCES

Ashmore, R. D., & Del Boca, F. K. (1981). Conceptual approaches to stereotypes and stereotyping. In D. L. Hamilton (Ed.), *Cognitive processes in stereotyping and intergroup behavior* (pp. 1–35). Hillsdale, NJ: Erlbaum.

Bargh, J. A. (1989). Conditional automaticity: Varieties of automatic influence in social perception and cognition. In J. S. Uleman & J. A. Bargh (Eds.), *Unintended thought* (pp. 3–51). New York: Guilford Press.

Berger, J., Fisek, M. H., Norman, R. Z., & Zelditch, M., Jr. (1977). *Status characteristics and social interaction: An expectation-states approach.* New York: Elsevier.

Berger, J., Rosenholtz, S. J., & Zelditch, M., Jr. (1980). Status organizing processes. *Annual Review of Sociology, 6,* 479–508.

Berger, J., Wagner, D. G., & Zelditch, M., Jr. (1985). Introduction—Expectation states theory: Review and assessment. In J. Berger & M. Zelditch, Jr. (Eds.), *Status, rewards, and influence: How expectations organize behavior* (pp. 1–72). San Francisco: Jossey-Bass.

Biernat, M. (1993). Gender and height: Developmental patterns in knowledge and use of an accurate stereotype. *Sex Roles, 29,* 691–713.

Biernat, M., & Kobrynowicz, D. (1995). *Gender- and race-based judgment standards: Lower minimum standards and higher ability standards for devalued groups.* Manuscript under review.

Biernat, M., & Manis, M. (1994). Shifting standards and stereotype-based judgments. *Journal of Personality and Social Psychology, 66,* 5–20.

Biernat, M., Manis, M., & Nelson, T. E. (1990). [The method of triads used to ascertain gender-based beliefs about assertiveness]. Unpublished raw data, University of Michigan.

Biernat, M., Manis, M., & Nelson, T. E. (1991). Stereotypes and standards of judgment. *Journal of Personality and Social Psychology, 60,* 485–499.

Biernat, M., & Wortman, C. B. (1991). Sharing of home responsibilities between professionally employed women and their husbands. *Journal of Personality and Social Psychology, 60,* 844–860.

Chesler, P. (1991). Mothers on trial: The custodial vulnerability of women. *Feminism and Psychology, 1,* 409–425.

Clark, L. F., Martin, L. L, & Henry, S. M. (1993). Instantiation, interference, and the change of standard effect: Context functions in reconstructive memory. *Journal of Personality and Social Psychology, 64,* 336–346.

Crandall, C. S. (1994). Prejudice against fat people: Ideology and self-interest. *Journal of Personality and Social Psychology, 66,* 882–894.

Dunning, D., & Cohen, G. L. (1992). Egocentric definitions of traits and abilities in social judgment. *Journal of Personality and Social Psychology, 63,* 341–355.

Foddy, M., & Smithson, M. (1989). Fuzzy sets and double standards: Modeling the process of ability inference. In J. Berger, M. Zelditch, Jr., & B. Anderson (Eds.), *Sociological theories in progress: New formulations* (pp. 73–99). London: Sage.

Foschi, M. (1992). Gender and double standards for competence. In C. L. Ridgeway (Ed.), *Gender, interaction, and inequality* (pp. 181–207). New York: Springer-Verlag.

Goldberg, P. (1968). Are women prejudiced against women? *Transaction, 5,* 28–30.

Higgins, E. T., & Lurie, L. (1983). Context, categorization and recall: The "change of standard" effect. *Cognitive Psychology, 15,* 525–547.

Higgins, E. T., & Stangor, C. (1988). A "change of standard" perspective on the relations among context, judgment, and memory. *Journal of Personality and Social Psychology, 54,* 181–192.

Hochschild, A. (1989). *The second shift: Working parents and the revolution at home.* New York: Viking Press.

Judd, C. M., & Park, B. (1988). Outgroup homogeneity: Judgmental variability at the individual and group levels. *Journal of Personality and Social Psychology, 54,* 778–788.

Judd, C. M., & Park, B. (1993). Definition and assessment of accuracy in social stereotypes. *Psychological Review, 100,* 109–128.

Kobrynowicz, D., & Biernat, M. (1994, July). *Objective interpretation of subjective statements: Stereotypes as shifting standards.* Poster presented at the annual meeting of the American Psychological Society, Washington, DC.

Linville, P. W., & Jones, E. E. (1980). Polarized appraisals of out-group members. *Journal of Personality and Social Psychology, 38,* 689–703.

Locksley, A., Borgida, E., Brekke, N., & Hepburn, C. (1980). Sex stereotypes and social judgment. *Journal of Personality and Social Psychology, 39,* 821–831.

Locksley, A., Hepburn, C., & Ortiz, V. (1982). Social stereotypes and judgments of individuals: An instance of the base-rate fallacy. *Journal of Experimental Social Psychology, 18,* 23–42.

McCauley, C., & Stitt, C. L. (1978). An individual and quantitative measure of stereotypes. *Journal of Personality and Social Psychology, 36,* 929–940.

McCauley, C., Stitt, C. L., & Segal, M. (1980). Stereotyping: From prejudice to prediction. *Psychological Bulletin, 87,* 195–208.

McCauley, C., & Thangavelu, K. (1991). Individual differences in sex stereotyping of occupations and personality traits. *Social Psychology Quarterly, 54,* 267–279.

McConahay, J. B., Hardee, B. B., & Batts, V. (1981). Has racism declined in America? It depends on who is asking and what is asked. *Journal of Conflict Resolution, 25,* 563–579.

Nelson, T., Biernat, M., & Manis, M. (1990). Everyday base rates (sex stereotypes): Potent and resilient. *Journal of Personality and Social Psychology, 59,* 664–675.

Neuberg, S. L. (1994). Expectation–confirmation processes in stereotype-tinged social encounter: The moderating role of social goals. In M. P. Zanna & J. M Olson (Eds.), *The psychology of prejudice: The Ontario Symposium* (Vol. 7, pp. 103–130). Hillsdale, NJ: Erlbaum.

Oakes, P. J., Haslam, S. A., & Turner, J. C. (1994). *Stereotyping and social reality.* Oxford: Basil Blackwell.

Parducci, A. (1963). Range–frequency compromise in judgment. *Psychological Monographs, 77*(2, No. 565).

Parducci, A. (1965). Category judgment: A range frequency model. *Psychological Review*, 72, 407–418.

Parducci, A., & Perrett, L. F. (1971). Category rating scales: Effects of relative spacing and frequency stimulus values. *Journal of Experimental Psychology Monographs*, 89, 427–452.

Park, B., & Judd, C. M. (1990). Measures and models of perceived group variability. *Journal of Personality and Social Psychology*, 59, 173–191.

Pettigrew, T., & Martin, J. (1987). Shaping the organizational context for Black American inclusion. *Journal of Social Issues*, 43, 41–78.

Postman, L., & Miller, G. A. (1945). Anchoring of temporal judgments. *American Journal of Psychology*, 58, 43–53.

Roberts, J. V., & Herman, C. P. (1986). The psychology of height: An empirical review. In C. P. Herman, M. P. Zanna, & E. T. Higgins (Eds.), *Physical appearance, stigma, and social behavior: The Ontario Symposium* (Vol. 3, pp. 113–140). Hillsdale, NJ: Erlbaum.

Snyder, M. (1992). Motivational foundations of behavioral confirmation. In M. P. Zanna (Ed.), *Advances in experimental social psychology* (Vol. 25, pp. 67–114). San Diego, CA: Academic Press.

Spence, J. T., & Helmreich, R. (1972). The Attitudes Toward Women Scale: An objective instrument to measure attitudes toward the rights and roles of women in contemporary society. JSAS: *Catalog of Selected Documents in Psychology*, 2, 66. (Ms. No. 153)

Swim, J., Borgida, E., Maruyama, G., & Myers, D. G. (1989). Joan McKay versus John McKay: Do gender stereotypes bias evaluations? *Psychological Bulletin*, 105, 409–429.

Tajfel, H. (1969). Cognitive aspects of prejudice. *Journal of Social Issues*, 25, 79–97.

Upshaw, H. S. (1962). Own attitude as an anchor in equal-appearing intervals. *Journal of Abnormal and Social Psychology*, 64, 85–96.

Upshaw, H. S. (1969). The Personal Reference Scale: An approach to social judgment. In L. Berkowitz (Ed.), *Advances in experimental social psychology* (Vol. 4, pp. 315–371). New York: Academic Press.

Volkmann, J. (1951). Scales of judgment and their implications for social psychology. In J. H. Rohrer & M. Sherif (Eds.), *Social psychology at the crossroads* (pp. 273–294). New York: Harper.

Webster, M., Jr., & Foschi, M. (1988). Overview of status generalization. In M. Webster, Jr., & M. Foschi (Eds.), *Status generalization: New theory and research* (pp. 1–20, 477–478). Stanford, CA: Stanford University Press.

5

An Ecological View of Stereotype Accuracy

Reuben M. Baron

The problem of accuracy in stereotyping at first glance appears particularly an oxymoron type of formulation for a Gibsonian-oriented, ecological social psychologist, in the sense that stereotyping focuses on the typical case and looks to categories for meaning, whereas the ecological approach eschews the general and focuses on knowing the particular vis à vis hands-on exploration (Baron, 1988). Furthermore, my interest in the ecological approach (McArthur & Baron, 1983) was partially a reaction against the assertions of the cognitive constructivists that error predominates (cf. Nisbett & Ross, 1980). However, this paradox can be resolved once it is realized that both accuracy and stereotyping can be treated, in functional terms, as problems in how to make the best out of real-world constraints. That is, we are less cognitive misers than social realists trying to do what works in specific sociobehavioral settings.

The major thrust of this chapter is devoted to unpacking the meaning of accuracy in stereotypes from this type of ecological perspective. Because stereotypes are socially shared perceptions, the discussion of accu-

Correspondence concerning this chapter should be addressed to Reuben M. Baron, Department of Psychology, University of Connecticut, Storrs, Connecticut 06269-1020.

racy in stereotypes must go beyond individual epistemic processes. That is, stereotypes persist and are useful not only because they are helpful to individuals; they are perhaps even more useful for the functioning of groups (Dunbar, 1993; Oskamp, 1991). Thus, from an ecological perspective, the chapter presents four interrelated issues as follows: (a) the specific properties of the ecological approach relevant to accuracy, (b) the application of ecological theory to stereotypes, (c) an ecological analysis of knowledge and stereotypes, and (d) the reasons that stereotypes are ecologically accurate (or inaccurate).

SPECIFIC PROPERTIES OF THE ECOLOGICAL APPROACH RELEVANT TO ACCURACY

To put the matter most directly, the ecological approach to accuracy is important because it commits us to realism in the sense that we seek our primary constraints on the accuracy of judgments in the relations between individuals and groups that exist in the world to be discovered or detected by perceivers who are actively exploring their social environments, as opposed to assuming that all or almost all of the variance in people's judgments regarding other people originate in variations in their schemata or in the types of schemata that are primed. We now turn to a discussion of (a) how such information is to be discovered and (b) what is meant by social stimulus information within the ecological domain.

Accuracy Is for Doing

The ecological approach to accuracy, as derived from J. J. Gibson (1979), links accuracy to a few basic perspectives. First, perceiving is for doing, hence the basic criterion for accuracy has to be pragmatic in the sense of successful action. Second, because the basic functional unit for knowing in the ecological approach is the detection of *affordances*, accuracy has to be linked to (a) information that allows affordances to be detected and (b) information that allows affordances to be used to achieve goals.[1] Furthermore, the ecological approach treats information as being organized into dynamic units called *events*. There are, in turn, certain critical properties of events: During an event, certain properties of an entity will change and others will remain unchanged (structural invariants such as identity or gender remaining invariant over aging and health changes). One may also specify styles of change, such as growth or walking or interacting with friends versus strangers or with high- versus low-status others, which may or may not remain invariant over entities (*transformational invariants*). A third property of events of particular interest is that they may be induced by the external environment (e.g., weather or pathogens) or by the actor–observer's explorations of entities, including especially their interactions with other people (see below).

Given these assumptions, we begin by clarifying the meaning of *affordances*, both in general and specifically in regard to social affordances. *Affordances*, as defined by J. J. Gibson (1979), involve informational specification of what the environment offers agents "in the sense a fruit says eat me; water says drink me; thunder says fear me" (Koffka, 1935, p. 7, cited in McArthur & Baron, 1983, p. 217). J. J. Gibson maintained that these functional utilities or action possibilities may be specified extensionally in the physical properties of environmental objects, thereby providing information for perception that directly specifies the affordances available in a given entity. For example, the edibility of fruit may be specified extensionally by its color, smell, and texture. Similarly, the sexual receptivity of species in whom sexual behavior is tightly controlled hormonally may be detectable in the color, smell, posture, or gait of the female during certain phases of the estrous cycle. In such contexts, form literally follows function. In this regard, "perception in the ecological approach is

---

[1]The specific Gibsonian claim is that affordances (including social affordances) can be directly perceived, as opposed to being inferred or constructed, because they systematically constrain sources of environmental information such as the appearance or action properties of event–entity links. This claim, although central to the Gibsonian position, is not essential to our use of the affordance concept. Our position is that social affordances may be directly perceived or inferentially constructed, depending on the availability of information in the target stimulus array (e.g., the degree of ambiguity present) and the attunements of the perceiver, including needs, cultural values, and learning sets. For example, judgments of whether a given person affords help or nurturance can be rooted in direct perception, be inferred constructively, or involve some combination of epistemic modes (Baron, 1988).

not concerned with just any information. Rather it concerns the pick-up of useful information" (McArthur & Baron, 1983, p. 217).

Affordances reflect a complementary relationship between the animal and its environment (see J. J. Gibson, 1979). Specifically, affordances are animal or agent referenced in the sense that only animals with the appropriate species-specific sensorimotor sensitivities and motor competencies can detect or use particular affordances. That is, there is in any complex environment a plethora of nested affordances, only some of which are appropriate to any given animal. For example, a house may afford shelter for humans, and a hole in the wall may afford shelter for a mouse. Similarly, stairs may afford locomotion for humans, whereas a flat wall may do just as well for a spider or a fly. I have extended this idea to include cultural and personal histories and motivational states as relevant attunements for the discovery of affordances (cf. Baron, 1981; McArthur & Baron, 1983). As McArthur and Baron (1983) observed,

> the ability of Eskimos to differentiate between several varieties of snow may be related to the fact that each type of snow affords them different activities. Also, within the social realm, Gibson, Brown, and Daves (1982) demonstrated that perceptions are significantly related to sexual preference. Using a binocular rivalry paradigm, Gibson et al. found that homosexual men tended to report images of men, whereas heterosexual men reported images of women. (p. 224)

The important point here is that there is information in the environment supporting both perceptions. The variation is then a matter of attunement in the sense of what information is more likely to be resonated to.

Social affordances both share these properties and add new dimensions.

> For example, while information specifying the affordance for edibility exists in the fruit to be detected by the animal, the affordance for cooperativeness does not reside exclusively in any single object or entity. It truly only exists in the reciprocal, coordinated action of two or more individuals. That is, cooperative action involves two or more people engaged in actions that are mutually facilitative in the

sense that there is joint movement toward a common goal. Similarly, helpfulness requires a helper and a recipient, competition requires a rival, and dominance requires a subordinate. These examples are not to be viewed as metaphorical; "socialness" is taken to be a species of relational structure that exists in the world to be detected. (Baron & Boudreau, 1987, p. 1223)

Given this discussion of social and nonsocial affordances, let us see how the ecological view of accuracy falls out from assumptions regarding the nature of affordances. First, let us take a simple, nonsocial example. Specifically, if I am tired, I search an environment for an object in regard to its sitability for my particular body dimensions. Accuracy is embedded in this type of perceiving–acting cycle. The logic is exactly the same in the social realm. In the course of trying to achieve some goal, I search a behavior setting for people who afford agreeableness, given my goal of setting up a study group of people who will work well together. The accuracy then of my perception of the agreeableness is "cashed out" in terms of certain parameters of social coordination that reflect cooperation in a small-group-problem-solving context. That is, agreeableness is as agreeableness does. Similarly, in a dyadic context, the accuracy of my perception that another person is nurturant is established if when I solicit aid because of some demonstrable need, I receive a caring response in regard to the specific aid that I have requested (e.g., a book I need to solve a problem).

Accuracy Is Relational

Accuracy, when tied to social affordances and their realization, is intrinsically relational. We take this proposition to have a number of meanings, which share a higher order invariant in regard to accuracy being in the joint performance of the dance rather than in the individual dancer (Shotter, 1983). Specifically, people-referent accuracy is focused on what you attempt to do with other people and what other people attempt to do with you. The work of Newtson, Hairfield, Bloomingdale, and Cutino (1987) documents the relational–dynamic quality of specific social affordances. For example, Newtson et al. (1987) described cooperativeness in terms of the development of a common wave form for coordinated actions carried out over time. That is, there may be patterns of symmetrical or asymmetrical entrainment, in terms of the coordination of various parameters of joint social action such as pace, and pause pattern. Here, accuracy can be indexed by correlating perceived cooperativeness with an objective measure of the overlap between individual action wave forms, using a cross-spectral analysis index of coherence (Gottman, 1983). At issue is what a specific other person affords me in a kind of mutually shared social field (Asch, 1952), as opposed to a global judgment regarding whether the other person is nurturant or aggressive in general.[2]

A particularly interesting illustration of an ecological spin on the problem of the reality of relational properties is described in McArthur and Baron (1983). McArthur reported that while she traveled through Europe, several Jewish acquaintances old enough to have survived the Holocaust accurately perceived her Jewish identity from her demeanor or appearance, something Jewish acquaintances in the United States typically did not do. Although there are any number of issues that can be raised here, for the moment, this example is relevant as suggesting that even a higher order social gestalt—one's social identity—is real and perceivable, at least for certain people under certain conditions.

Basically, the proposition derived from the ecological approach described thus far is that to test for accuracy, one must transform the problem into a situation where perception-based evidence can be brought to bear, a view not too far from what we in principle seek in the judicial process. That is, at least metaphorically, we seek to move the grounds of the evidence from circumstantial and hearsay to direct datum, hence the importance given to eyewitness testimony. The ecological–perceptual approach, then, is to push toward more and more direct evidence so that the equivocality yields to information specifica-

---

[2]Here we point to a correspondence between Swann's (1984) concept of circumscribed (as opposed to global) accuracy and the present emphasis on pragmatic accuracy. The present approach differs from Swann's in that he does not allow for a stimulus-based specification of the information supporting circumscribed accuracy. Kenny's (1994) p^2 reciprocity correlation, which deals with whether the unique actions of O are reciprocated, is also relevant as a possible index of relational accuracy and is more agnostic than is the concept of Swann (1984) regarding whether the reciprocity relation is stimulus based.

tion in the sense that only that person could have produced that particular trace of behavior.

APPLYING AN ECOLOGICAL APPROACH TO ACCURACY IN STEREOTYPING

Baron (1988), in his discussion of the differences between perception and cognition, observed that there was evidence that certain events could be recognized and reacted to correctly before children's ability to label such events (Vygotsky, 1962). For example, with perceptual development, children are both increasingly able to "detect the higher order structure in events" (D. Jones, Spelke, & Alley, 1985, p. 265) and to produce events that reveal the affordances of objects.

"For example, toddlers and preschool children are especially apt to play with objects in ways that reveal their affordances. They bang on blocks on tables, squeeze clay into multiple shapes, tear and crumble paper, and so forth" (D. Jones et al., 1985, p. 265). Therefore, in regard to perception, to know whether something is breakable or holdable can be ascertained directly.

With higher order cognitive processes such as stereotyping, we run the danger of the reverse being true, in the sense that the labeling process creates the property in the absence of any hands-on interaction with the referent. Instead of "seeing is believing," *believing* is substituted for *seeing* (Hamilton, 1981; Oskamp, 1991). For example, in groupthink, the out-group may be stereotyped along dimensions that justify certain actions, but involve little, if any, in the way of perceptual grounding. In this type of context, stereotyping may yield higher order social constructions largely devoid of constraining perceptual data.

In the context of the stereotyping literature (see Ottati & Lee, chapter 2, this volume), it may be argued, however, that certain distinctions between content (stereotypes) and processes (stereotyping), as well as whether stereotypes occur at the level of individuals or are socially shared within groups, have implications for the likelihood that given stereotypes can be viewed as accurate (at least provisionally). For example, at the group level, poverty may constrain a wide range of properties, such as tendencies toward violence, poor family relations, and lack of effort. Such patterns are not arbitrary social constructions; they are objectively constrained group-trait gestalts. Furthermore, such gestalts may have sufficient stimulus grounding that they result in shared perceptions among other cultural groups, which can be said to be accurate in the basic ecological sense of being, based on shared information as opposed to shared bias (McArthur & Baron, 1983).

EXPECTANCIES, ATTUNEMENTS, AND STEREOTYPES

Insight into issues at the level of process can be achieved if we compare the concepts of expectancies and attunements. Specifically, although both expectancies and attunements make for selectivity in information processing, they do so in very different ways. To use Piaget's terminology, expectancies foster assimilation of discrepant input to the existing frame; the operative idea is that expectancies look toward confirmation as opposed to fidelity to the world.

On the other hand, attunements are like a tuning fork or a channel selector: They resonate to or accommodate to what is out there. That is, attunements help us get in touch with relevant aspects of the world. For example, consider what it means to have an "educated eye" idea regarding modern art. To begin with, it involves getting rid of conventional expectancies regarding what good art is all about and learning to look at subtle variations in combinations of color and shape to pick up certain visual rhythms. Note that this requires extensive contact with modern art and artists. Moreover, just as in the social domain, contact is a necessary, but not sufficient, condition (Amir, 1969). Contact has to be under favorable conditions—as in Aronson's jigsaw (Aronson & Bridgeman, 1979), with its cooperative framing of the contact. In the art example, a comparable analogy might be sharing one's viewing with a more experienced lover of modern art, who points out what to look for.[3] In both the art-viewing and the integration situation, the goal is to appropriately differentiate the target— or in the Gibsonian metaphor, we seek to create perceptual learning in regard to an increasingly educated distribution of attention. When this occurs, the major source of variation is in the "object of judgment" as opposed to the "judgment of the object" (Asch, 1952, p. 424).

On the basis of this analysis, we now have a useful way of differentiating ways that stereotyping functions at the process level. First, stereotypes may be related to expectations. We have certain expectations and beliefs about certain social groups. If we stereotype professors as intelligent, we expect them to behave intelligently when we meet them. On the other hand, stereotypes may resemble Gibsonian attunement. That is to say, a perceiver's schemata may affect the stimulus information to which the perceiver is attuned. For example, social groups are complex stimuli. Stereotypes in the context may lead us to focus on one set of properties rather than another. This distinction in terms of whether stereotypes function as expectancies or attunements is particularly important in regard to the detection of negative as opposed to positive properties. It may be assumed that the more adaptively relevant the property, the more important it is, particularly at the group level, for stereotypes to function as attunements.

AN ECOLOGICAL PERSPECTIVE ON THE VALENCE OF STEREOTYPES

The ecological perspective allows one a principled way of differentiating between the inclusion of negative and positive properties in stereotypes, using the constraint of adaptive information. Specifically, while it is em-

---

[3] In the cognitive realm, Vygotsky's (1978) zone of proximal development (ZPD) makes an analogous point in regard to the value of a more competent other in raising the performance level of a novice. In the present example, joint problem solving may function as a "social tool" in the sense that partners are able to attain affordances for solving a problem that are unattainable at the individual level (Baron & Misovich, 1992).

pirically true that most social stereotypes contain both positive and negative attributes, the ecological approach predicts a predominance of negative attributes, because knowing negative attributes has greater adaptive
payoff. A good evolutionary argument for this focus is provided by Fox
(1992), who argued that stereotypes are necessary for human survival. In
this regard, it is particularly important to focus on negative properties. For
example, negative stereotypes help us react to emergency situations. Knowing gangsters are dangerous, we tend to run away when facing a group of
gangsters with guns. As Fox (1992) pointed out, the essence of stereotyping is that "it is fast and gives us a basis for immediate action in uncertain circumstances" (p. 140). Fox's emphasis on immediacy is in keeping
with the perceptual-attunement view of schemata accuracy.

Furthermore, although this same derivation would be possible for any
approach that is grounded in an evolutionary perspective (Caporeal &
Brewer, 1991; Fox, 1992), there is one aspect of such a derivation that is
more obligatory from a Gibsonian-perceptual perspective. Specifically, the
more adaptively relevant a property, such as distinguishing predator versus prey or benevolence versus malevolence, or ingroup versus outgroup,
the more one would expect social stimulus information would be available to specify the property (McArthur & Baron, 1983). For example, if it
can be claimed that it is more adaptively relevant to detect mental illness
than whether people have a good sense of humor, mental illness is more
likely than a sense of humor to be clearly specified in terms of structural
and transformational invariants that are readily detectable—such as appearance, gait, and reactions to distance-reducing gestures, such as personal space invasion. Moreover, as Baron and Misovich (1993) pointed
out, the more adaptively significant the property, the more likely it will
have cross-modal specification; that is, negative attributes are more likely
than positive properties to be specified in terms of converging sights,
smells, and sounds, a derivation relatively specific to J. J. Gibson's (1979)
brand of functionalism.

In addition, to stimulus specification, the previous analysis also
strongly fits the ecological postulate that "perceiving is for doing." That is,
it is particularly important that attunements to negative properties focus

on affordances for overcoming or escaping from the dangerous entity. In this regard, it is possible that negative stereotypes will be more affordancelike in content.

ECOLOGICAL ANALYSES OF THE ENVIRONMENTAL CONSTRAINTS ON KNOWLEDGE AND STEREOTYPES

To firmly establish the relevance of the ecological approach to stereotype accuracy, it is necessary to specify in greater depth how the environment may objectively constrain stereotypes and stereotyping. Strange as it may seem, I proposed in Baron (1991) that the best source for wedging in a realism constraint could be found in Heider (1990), in regard to two related propositions. First, Heider (1990) commented that "it makes a difference whether the source of the cognitive unit is in the restraints of the cognitive apparatus, or whether the source is the environment, and the cognitive apparatus only imitates the environment" (p. 51). Furthermore, "our cognitive apparatus divides the world into units and interstices between units, into the important modal entities or events and the less important, derived shadow entities. There must be something corresponding to all that outside in reality, the structure of the world must be such that by means of these divisions and distinctions we can describe the world better" (Heider, 1990, p. xvii). Given this type of ecological realism, one crucial test of the accuracy of stereotypes is then whether they allow us to describe other people or groups better.

At issue here is a view that fits Heider's (1990) brand of realism in the sense that divisions of the world made by the cognitive apparatus, including social stereotypes, can under certain conditions imitate the environment. Accuracy here has two foci: (a) the extent to which the sources of our cognitive units are in the world and (b) the "straight" perceptual view, which ignores the issue of how well the cognitive apparatus is attuned to the structure of the world and directly concentrates on unmediated knowing based on the stimulus specification of affordances. I propose that both perspectives are ecological in the sense that they share a commitment to realism as the final arbiter of accuracy.

TWO VERSIONS OF ACCURACY IN STEREOTYPING

Given the above analysis, I would propose, two approaches to accuracy in stereotyping are suggested by the ecological approach: a mediated versus a nonmediated case.

The Mediated Case and Schematic Knowledge

Here what is at issue is well framed by Heider (1990) in terms of whether a division of the world mediated by a given social stereotype helps us know the world better in the sense of our keying into the actual organization of the target entity or environment. For example, if a particular group has a hierarchical structure, such as a dominance hierarchy, does having a social stereotype aid or hinder us in placing ourselves correctly into this dominance hierarchy? If I was a young boy transferring to a new middle school, this certainly would qualify as useful information to me. Here, potentially relevant stereotypes pertain to perceiving correctly the dimensions on which the dominance hierarchy rests—for example, athletic skills, strength, social skills, and academic ability. A similar problem may exist at the adult level as a person sizes up the "singles scene" in a new city—is status based on occupation, athletic prowess, worldly sophistication, ability to race cars, or dancing skills?

In regard to the boy, he may, because of a particular social stereotype based on urban–rural differences (he may be moving from a large city to a small town), focus on the wrong dimension, for example, focus on strength or athletic prowess, when in this small town, which houses a university, the dominance hierarchy is based on academic standing and social skills. Here, we have a relatively pragmatic criterion to use in determining the accuracy of the stereotype. That is, had he invoked a "university town" as opposed to a "rural town" stereotype, he would have done much better in the pragmatic sense of detecting the appropriate social affordances for bossing versus being bossed.

If one is willing to assume that experts have better schemata in the previously discussed sense than novices, the work of Wright and Mischel (1987; cf. Wright, 1988) becomes relevant. Specifically, experienced observers rated campers as high in aggression when they frequently reacted to frustration with aggression, whereas novices followed an out-of-role attributional schema and weighted children highest in aggression if they reacted to praise with aggression. That is, a child who displayed aggression in frustrating, but not nonfrustrating, situations was seen as a good example of an aggressive child by expert observers. Children who react to nonfrustrating situations, such as, being praised, with aggression are in this context not highly aggressive, but emotionally disturbed. These distinctions are missed by novices. In effect, schemata have the ability to help perceivers navigate through a plethora of affordances, with the payoff being more effective interaction strategies.

This type of analysis of how stereotypes can be accurate is constrained in terms of both the antecedents and consequences of stereotypes in a manner that can be related to Neisser (1976) and Shepard's (1984) attempts to give recognition to ecological constraints on schema. Specifically, the present emphasis on having a "better" schema corresponds in Neisser's (1976) frame to the schema correctly or incorrectly directing people where to look. This treatment of the functioning of a schema is ecological in the sense that a person's schema functions in an accommodation as opposed to an expectancy-confirmation (assimilation) mode. That is, Neisser (1976) treats schemata as devices for improving perceptual learning. For example, in areas such as chess, it has often been demonstrated that chess masters look more at the board than do novices (cited in Neisser, 1976). Moreover, the memories of the layout of the chessboard are superior for experts in relation to the memory of novices only when the board involves an actual game; arbitrary, random displays are not better remembered (Neisser, 1976). I take the latter finding to indicate that stimulus-level constraint occurs only when the world is organized—not when ambiguity prevails. This approach also resembles Shepard's (1984) proposals, regarding how motor schemata such as the scripts for playing golf can be constrained by the actual movements in playing golf. Specifically, accuracy arises when schemata, rather than being arbitrary, are grounded or constrained by the actual properties of the activity in regard to functionally significant correspondences. Shepard's approach argues that it is necessary for schemata to be isomorphic with the structure of the world if they are to facilitate mastering the world. I propose that the nearest analogue to Shepard's proposal in the social stereotyping realm is Aronson's (Aronson & Bridgeman, 1979) jigsaw paradigm, because in this situation, (a) racial contact is organized and not random and (b) it is organized around a joint-problem-solving activity that could very well create perceptual learning because the activity directs attention to positive social affordances. (See page 440 for an elaboration of this interpretation.)

Unmediated Accuracy and Affordances

Here, I essentially seek to find an ecological grounding for Devine's (1989) finding that what differentiates nonprejudiced from prejudiced reactions to Blacks is the ability to inhibit or suppress one's stereotypic beliefs. The argument is that by suspending one's stereotypes, one treats each individual in terms of a specific-relational set of affordances that are both stimulus and relationship constrained. Specifically, I base my reactions on directly checking out the affordances offered by the boys in this new middle school, interaction by interaction. That is, just as a child may evaluate the breakability of an entity by banging it against a table, I seek to find social activities that are diagnostic for getting to know other individual children—the equivalent of a series of social litmus tests (see Baron & Misovich, 1993). Such tests would be designed by active perceivers to ascertain whether the other boys were hostile, friendly, outgoing, and so on, vis à vis their social overtures.

E. E. Jones (1993) summarized this approach as follows: "Over time perceivers can implement what amount to experimental designs in coping with the response variations of others—particularly those responses that have personalistic significance for perceivers" (p. 660). The essence of this approach is to make perceivers active in the world in regard to creating interactive arrangements that afford "opportunities for diagnostic revelations" (E. E. Jones, 1993, p. 660). In effect, just as children who want to learn about breakability bang objects against a hard, as opposed to a soft, surface, so accuracy in the social realm may rest on selecting the correct interaction surfaces. What is being assumed is that if given social properties exist, then if certain actions are taken, certain events will normally result. For example, if a paper cup affords crushing when an adult grasps the cup and squeezes, it should crush (Kirsh, 1992). Similarly, a person who is said to be high in dominance should, when offered the opportunity to control a situation, take advantage of it, whereas a submissive person will not. That is, it is assumed that if people are motivated to ascend a dominance hierarchy, they will seek to boss others rather than be bossed by them (Sadalla, Kenrick, & Vershure, 1987).

Indirect support for this line of reasoning can be found in Kendrick, McCreath, Govern, King, and Bordin's (1990) exploration of how different behavior settings recruit occupants with appropriately different personality variations (e.g., people high in dominance for athletic settings and people high in sociability for church settings). Assuming that certain roles are better fitted by people with certain characteristics than others, accuracy here is tested by fit. Moreover, in optimally or overstaffed settings, people who do not fit are expelled (Barker, 1968).

In the spirit of "perceiving is for doing," these last observations involve testing the accuracy of a social judgment by observing people's social performance in diagnostic situations. In this regard, perhaps one can put an ecological spin on the classic contact hypothesis (Amir, 1969), given the provision that contact per se is necessary, but not sufficient; in the above terms, contact per se may not be diagnostic enough for one to suspend their social stereotypes. However, Aronson's jigsaw (Aronson & Bridgeman, 1979) may be, because its cooperative framing of social contact creates mutual informational dependence (the event activity test) in regard to successful problem solving. For example, O must be competent if he or she knows something I do not know and supplies the relevant information when I need it. In this example, the accuracy of the competence perception becomes a social affordance because it emerges in the context of a joint problem-solving system (see footnote 3).

In summary, one can achieve accuracy in knowing the properties of other people by creating better schemata, including social stereotypes, with *expert versus novice* being a type of paradigmatic case. Alternately, one can bypass stereotypes and attempt to know the other people directly by creating situational tests that are diagnostic for the properties you seek to know in the spirit of King Solomon, who created a test (threatening to cut the baby in two) to establish which of two claimants to a baby was the real mother (Baron & Misovich, 1993).

WHY ARE STEREOTYPES ACCURATE (AND INACCURATE)?

Group Size

Different social stereotypes, in the example I gave earlier of a transfer student, were seen to differentially affect accuracy of social perception. Here, the better stereotypes were better because they provided a more effective social information sampling plan for a particular setting, in the sense of being more sensitive to the actual properties of the social organization of dominance. Alternately, in a small school, for example, social knowing could be carried out in an unmediated way with useful information being obtained through diagnostic, personalized encounters. However, the more personalized perceptual approach becomes less feasible as group size exceeds a certain level (Dunbar, 1993). Indeed, Dunbar proposed that there is a critical reciprocal relationship between treating other people in terms of types or categories and group size; beyond a certain group size, it is not possible to secure firsthand social knowledge about other people. When groups exceed a certain size (e.g., 50–150), language develops as a mechanism that allows other people who cannot be directly interacted with to be treated as types or categories:

> The ability to categorize individuals into types clearly makes it possible to create much larger groups than is possible by direct interaction. One need only learn how to behave toward a general type of

individual rather than having to learn the nature of each individual relation. (Dunbar, 1993, p. 693)

Moreover, categorical types of "social bookkeeping" (Dugatkin & Wilson, 1993, p. 701) facilitate the hierarchical organization of groups. Thus, in an interesting twist on conventional thinking, it appears that social stereotyping, which is usually seen as a way of reducing cognitive complexity, actually increases social complexity!

Effects of Role

When a group becomes large enough so that there is a regular division of roles, there may even be a conflict between the accuracy of individualized, directly achieved personal knowledge and the successful functioning of the organization in regard to the adequacy of role performance. Steiner (1955) pointed out that personalized accuracy outcomes may be dysfunctional at the organizational level. For example, if one correctly perceives one's supervisor as having various negative traits (e.g., being arrogant or disagreeable), this perception may get in the way of a good supervisor–subordinate role relationship and, hence, be detrimental to organizational functioning. Here "ignorance is bliss" so long as the supervisor's negative traits do not impair his or her ability to carry out his or her organizational role. For example, insensitivity to subordinates may make for effective leadership in certain organizational contexts (Fiedler, 1967). In such a context, treating this supervisor as a category may result in pragmatic accuracy at the organizational level.

Accuracy and Invariant Properties

There is another way to think about the potential accuracy of categorical knowing, including social stereotypes. Think, in this regard, about the concept of events as a source of information about people's invariant properties. Specifically, an ecological criterion for invariance is that the property remains correctly recognizable over various types of changes or transformations. As noted earlier, personal identity, gender, and race normally remain invariant over changes in age, health, social power, marital status, and so on. A similar case could be made for certain personality-type attributes, such as type A versus type B or introversion versus extraversion or certain mood disorders, such as depression. Indeed, a part of their defining characteristic is that there is invariance over change, whereas other attributes may show strong Personality × Situation interactions (e.g., agreeableness, assertiveness, and conscientiousness).

Pseudo Versus Real Invariants in Stereotypes

If we scale this idea up to the social group level, the issue is whether the group property remains invariant across different behavior settings, historical epochs, geographical constraints, and so on. As I point out below, a good deal of the content of social stereotypes does not hold up well against this type of criterion. That is, we need to distinguish between pseudo and real invariants, with *pseudo* invariants representing a kind of culturally induced meta-self-fulfilling prophecy by creating constraints in the sense of varying opportunities for acting. For example, Jews in Eastern Europe were restricted to certain occupations in certain countries, forced to live in ghettos, and so on, thereby constraining the existence of certain traits, such as being clannish, miserly, cunning, or studious, which constitute aspects of the classic stereotype of Jews. Similarly, today in this country, Blacks are channeled into certain athletic activities, such as basketball, or certain criminal activities constrained by a slum culture, which, in turn, realistically generate aspects of the stereotype of Black Americans as having athletic and criminal traits (Niemann & Secord, 1994). Furthermore, certain physical properties of the target group may realistically constrain the content of stereotypes. For example, the stereotype that Asian American high school students do well academically in the United States can have an objective basis. Specifically, Chinese American students are, on average, neither as athletically skilled as Black Americans nor as politically or culturally sophisticated as White Americans (Sue & Okazaki, 1990). Because they cannot do well athletically or politically, to survive in this society, they may orient their time and effort for better school performance (Ottati & Lee, chapter 2, this volume).

How then do we determine the accuracy of the stereotypes of Jews,

Black Americans, and Chinese Americans? To deal with the problem, one must change frames and test for invariance. Does the trait change dynamically with different cultural constraints, either cross-sectionally or historically? For example, in biblical times and now in regard to the state of Israel, Jews were (are) perceived as bold and aggressive, whereas for 200 years in Eastern Europe they were seen as meek. More generally, the issue is the invariance of the trait over setting and historical circumstances. Are certain traits more stable than others? What traits of Black Americans remain the same or change when there is a move from the ghetto to suburbia?

Accuracy in this context would be a convergence between the stereotyped trait description and what remained invariant. For example, certain temperamental differences might remain invariant across changes in setting, or certain differences in body type (e.g., height and muscularity) might not change even when social class changes occur. Other beliefs have changed as the racial group has changed. For instance, the belief that the Chinese are superstitious (Katz & Braly, 1933), although perhaps historically true in the 1930s, has changed as the Chinese have changed (Ottati & Lee, chapter 2, this volume). Such differences might, in turn, coincide with Campbell's (1967) treatment of the "kernel of truth hypothesis" (Oskamp, 1991, p. 29) as being at least partially based on traits on which a group differs most in fact from another group. That is, such traits are the ones most likely to enter into the stereotypes (Oskamp, 1991). For example, if in fact Jews in the United States are more emotionally expressive than White, Anglo-Saxon Protestants, expressiveness differences are highly likely to be included in ethnic stereotypes (as illustrated by the dining scenes in Woody Allen's *Annie Hall*).

To Campbell's treatment of the problem, I would add that such properties are likely to have strong stimulus specification, given their high adaptive relevance. Moreover, stimulus specification in this view includes the role of dynamic factors. That is, a dynamic criterion for accuracy is that the stereotype changes when historical conditions change the property, as in the Chinese example cited above. Specifically, whereas height remains invariant over social change, superstitiousness does not.

SPECIFICITY CONSTRAINTS ON SOCIAL STEREOTYPING: AMERICAN VERSUS MEXICAN PUNCTUALITY

Perhaps the most dramatic way to understand certain potential disadvantages of social stereotyping is to focus on a current social stereotype that appears to be accurate. During a recent conference on the problem of accuracy in stereotyping (Lee & Duenas, chapter 7, this volume), an often-cited example was the belief that Mexican businesspeople are less concerned with punctuality than are their American counterparts. Because this characterization came from a Mexican professor employed in a business school, we would appear to have the best-case scenario for evaluating this property as an example of accuracy in stereotyping. However, even here one has to be wary. One problem with stereotyping is not the inaccuracy of the characterization per se, but its overgeneralization. That is, is the proposition that typical Mexican businesspeople are late, or is the proposition that most of the Mexican businesspeople I have interacted with are late, or is the proposition even broader—are all Mexicans (not just businesspeople) habitually unconcerned with punctuality, or even more extremely, are all Mexicans lazy?

Because the above is surely not a uniquely ecological formulation of the disadvantages of social stereotyping, what would be relatively unique? First, we ask, where is the source of the characterization—is it in the cognitive apparatus as existing only top-down, or is it in the environment so that the affordance structure of the referent drives the labeling. In terms of the earlier examples, punctuality is more likely a product of the perception of affordance information than laziness, which goes considerably beyond the information given, in that it implies an intention to avoid work, a property more difficult to give a stimulus-specification description. In ecological terms, the next issue is whether even for punctuality there is an informational specification possible so that we can demonstrate that punctuality is in the object of judgment as opposed to being in the judgment of the object. For example, what would be self-rated or subjected to consensual agreement, a shared bias or shared information specifying a social affordance? In this context, it is quite possible that punctuality is not a meaningful or relevant dimension for Mexican businesspeople doing business with other Mexican businesspeople. Here, the error in stereotyping lies in the very application of this category. In this case, punctuality is not an invariant property (e.g., affordance) of doing business, but a culturally stereotyped category. For example, whereas fairness in exchange or the detection of cheating may capture invariant properties of doing business, punctuality may not. That is, it appears that all societies are attuned to information specifying cheating, whereas it is unlikely that all societies are attuned to punctuality (Tooby & Cosmides, 1992). Indeed, it has been proposed that the detection of cheating is a constraint on the nature of the operation of the cognitive apparatus (Cosmides, 1989).

Thus, in evaluating social stereotyping, one possible source of inaccuracy is that the attribute largely exists in the eyes (more precisely, the categories) of the beholder. Furthermore, from an ecological perspective, the perceptual apparatus is attuned only to useful information—punctuality specification may not constitute cross-culturally significant, useful information, whereas cheating does. Therefore, to apply such a judgment in a society where punctuality is not relevant quite likely means that it will be difficult, if not impossible, to find a consensus based on a shared informational attunement. At least indirect support for the cultural specificity of certain traits comes from Wright and Mischel's (1987) finding that in a camp for disturbed children, higher accuracy was obtained for judgments of aggressiveness (a more universal property) than conscientiousness. Another related possibility, of course, is that aggressiveness is constrained bottom-up, whereas conscientiousness is at least partially created top-down by the labeling process. Operationally, this means, for example, that Mexican self-ratings may not yield good correlations with outsider (e.g., U.S. businesspeople's) ratings and that an outsider consensus of American observers will have a strong component of shared cultural bias.

Another possibility is suggested by the affordance constraint that opportunities or functional utilities must be viewed relationally. To wit: Punctuality may be relationally constrained so that it exists only at the level of an interaction between American and Mexican businesspeople; it is not a property of Mexican–Mexican business exchanges. That is, it exists only in the specific synergy or coordination of certain types of people. Devoid of such a context, punctuality derives its meaning top-down, largely free of any correspondence to social environmental constraints. It becomes, in effect, a classic example of "believing as seeing" (Oskamp, 1991).

CONCLUSION

Social Versus Cognitive Complexity

Dunbar's (1993) coevolution model—which includes circular relations among group size, language development, and treating other people as types—is hypothesized to provide a perspective on both the evolution and current functioning of social stereotypes in a way that supports the ecological perspective. Recall that in my introductory remarks, I proposed that we need to go beyond the individual level and consider how "social facts" are involved in the stereotyping process and that we are less "cognitive misers" than "social realists" trying to do what works.

First, this approach is ecological because in the conventional approaches to stereotyping, social facts do not function as constraints on either the origins or accuracy of stereotypes. Moreover, within the mainstream constructive view, the utility of stereotyping is typically seen in terms of using the cognitive apparatus to achieve categories that allow us to avoid confronting social complexity. In contradistinction, Dunbar's (1993) approach allows us to create a social realism based on two social facts: (a) Increases in group size are complexly related to type or categorical thinking, including social stereotyping. Specifically, once a group exceeds a certain size, personal contact knowing becomes increasingly difficult; furthermore, categorical thinking allows groups to grow larger without becoming chaotic or fissioning. (b) Treating people as types, as opposed to individuals, facilitates the development of role-typehierarchical organizations.

These social facts provide support for a new view of the relationship between social and cognitive complexity—categorical thinking at the within-group level may be essential to group complexification. Here, accuracy is a matter of the ability of the categories the group comes up with to get the right people into the right roles. Kenrick et al.'s (1990) research regarding the tendency of different behavior settings to recruit people with different personality types speaks to this type of process. For example, people high in assertiveness may indeed do better in athletic than church settings. Steiner's (1955) distinction between accuracy in person perception at the individual or dyadic level versus the organizational level speaks to this precise problem, given that treating other people as types may facilitate the development of group stratification.

In summary, groups and behavior settings allow a different frame for accuracy that, while failing to respect diversity at the individual or dyadic level, may be considered accurate if they allow people to be fitted into roles that facilitate the adaptive functioning of the group. Returning to our transfer student example, accuracy at the individual level is whether this student correctly places himself where he belongs in the sense he knows who to, and who not to, act differentially toward. Now we are looking at the other side of the coin: the selection of people into slots in a role hierarchy in terms of whether they fit group socialization criteria for membership (Moreland & Levine, 1982). Group-level accuracy here is pragmatic in the sense of whether the people they select (a) accept the overtures and (b) rise in the group to successfully fill role gaps as they occur over time.

Viewed thus, the ecological-realist emphasis on "social facts" and social stereotyping do not constitute an oxymoron relationship. Indeed, given the present view that cognitive and social complexity are mutually constraining, they may be seen as having coevolved in the service of adaptive functioning at the group level.

REFERENCES

Amir, Y. (1969). Contact hypothesis in ethnic relations. *Psychological Bulletin, 71,* 319–342.

Aronson, E., & Bridgeman, D. N. (1979). Jigsaw groups and the desegregated classroom: In pursuit of common goals. *Personality and Social Psychology Bulletin, 5,* 438–446.

Asch, S. (1952). *Social psychology.* New York: Prentice Hall.

Barker, R. G. (1968). *Ecological psychology.* Stanford, CA: Stanford University Press.

Baron, R. M. (1981). Social knowing from an ecological perspective: A consideration of the relative domains of power for cognitive and perceptual modes of knowing. In J. H. Harvey (Ed.), *Cognition, social behavior, and the environment* (pp. 61–89). Hillsdale, NJ: Erlbaum.

Baron, R. M. (1988). An ecological framework for establishing a dual-mode theory of social knowing. In D. Bar-Tal & A. Kruglanski (Eds.), *The social psychology of knowledge* (pp. 48–82). Cambridge, England: Cambridge University Press.

Baron, R. M. (1991). A meditation on levels of structure. *Contemporary Psychology, 36,* 566–567.

Baron, R. M., & Boudreau, L. (1987). An ecological perspective on integrating personality and social psychology. *Journal of Personality and Social Psychology, 53,* 1222–1228.

Baron, R. M., & Misovich, S. J. (1992). The social constitution of personal change: An ecological interpretation. In Y. Klar, J. D. Fisher, J. M. Chinsky, & A. Nadler (Eds.), *Self-change: Social psychological and clinical perspectives* (pp. 179–195). New York: Springer-Verlag.

Baron, R. M., & Misovich, S. J. (1993). An integration of Gibsonian and Vygotskian perspectives on changing attitudes in group contexts. *British Journal of Social Psychology, 32,* 53–70.

Campbell, D. T. (1967). Stereotypes and the perception of group differences. *American Psychologist, 22,* 817–829.

Caporeal, L. R., & Brewer, M. B. (1991). Reviving evolutionary psychology: Biology meets society. *Journal of Social Issues, 47,* 187–195.

Cosmides, L. (1989). The logic of social exchange: Has natural selection shaped how humans reason? Studies with the wagon selection task. *Cognition, 31,* 187–276.

Devine, P. G. (1989). Stereotypes and prejudice: Their automatic and controlled components. *Journal of Personality and Social Psychology, 56,* 5–18.

Dugatkin, L. A., & Wilson, D. S. (1993). Language and levels of selection. *Behavioral and Brain Sciences, 16,* 4.

Dunbar, R. I. M. (1993). Coevolution of neocortical size, group size and language in humans. *Behavioral and Brain Sciences, 16,* 681–735.

Fiedler, F. E. (1967). *A theory of leadership effectiveness.* New York: McGraw-Hill.

Fox, R. (1992). Prejudice and the unfinished mind: A new look at an old failing. *Psychological Inquiry, 3,* 137–152.

Gibson, J. J. (1979). *The ecological approach to visual perception.* Boston: Houghton Mifflin.

Gibson, M., Brown, E. C., & Daves, W. F. (1982). Sexual orientation as measured by perceptual dominance in binocular rivalry. *Personality and Social Psychology Bulletin, 8,* 494–500.

Gottman, J. M. (1983). *Time series analysis: A comprehensive introduction for social scientists.* Cambridge, England: Cambridge University Press.

Hamilton, D. L. (1981). Illusory correlation as the basis for stereotyping. In D. L. Hamilton (Ed.), *Cognitive processes in stereotyping and intergroup behavior* (pp. 115–144). Hillsdale, NJ: Erlbaum.

Heft, H. (1993). A methodological note on overestimates of reaching distance: Distinguishing between perceptual and analytical judgments. *Ecological Psychology, 5,* 255–271.

Heider, F., & Benish-Weiner, M. (Ed.). (1990). *Fritz Heider: The notebooks: Vol. 6. Units and coinciding units.* New York: Springer-Verlag.

Janis, I. L. (1982). *Groupthink* (2nd ed.). Boston: Houghton-Mifflin.

Jones, D., Spelke, E., & Ally, T. (1985). Workgroup on perceptual development. In W. H. Warren & R. E. Shaw (Eds.), *Persistence and change* (pp. 259–268).

Jones, E. E. (1993). Afterword: An avuncular view. *Personality and Social Psychology Bulletin, 19,* 657–660.

Katz, D., & Braly, K. (1933). Racial stereotypes of one hundred college students. *Journal of Abnormal and Social Psychology, 28,* 280–290.

Kenny, D. A. (1994). *Interpersonal perception: A social relations analysis.* New York: Guilford Press.

Kenrick, D. T., McCreath, H. E., Govern, J., King, R., & Bordin, J. (1990). Person–environment intersections: Everyday settings and common trait dimensions. *Journal of Personality and Social Psychology, 58,* 685–698.

Kirsh, D. (1992). *Preparation: How to overcome the limitations of perceptual control.* Unpublished manuscript, University of California at San Diego.

McArthur, L. Z., & Baron, R. M. (1983). Toward an ecological theory of social perception. *Psychological Review, 90,* 215–238.

Millikan, R. (1984). *Language, thought and other biological categories.* Cambridge, MA: MIT Press.

Moreland, R. L., & Levine, J. M. (1982). Socialization in small groups: Temporal changes in individual–group relations. In L. Berkowitz (Ed.), *Advances in experimental social psychology* (Vol. 15, pp. 137–192). New York: Academic Press.

Neisser, U. (1976). *Cognition and reality.* San Francisco: Freeman.

Newtson, D., Hairfield, J., Bloomingdale, J., & Cutino, S. (1987). The structure of action and interaction. *Social Cognition, 5,* 191–237.

Niemann, Y. F., & Secord, P. F. (1994). *The social ecology of stereotyping.* Unpublished manuscript, University of Houston, Psychology Department, Houston, TX.

Nisbett, R. E., & Ross, L. (1980). *Human inference: Strategies and shortcomings in social judgment.* Englewood Cliffs, NJ: Prentice Hall.

Oskamp, S. (1991). *Attitudes and opinions* (2nd ed.). Englewood Cliffs: NJ: Prentice Hall.

Sadalla, E. K., Kenrick, D. T., & Vershure, B. (1987). Dominance and heterosexual attraction. *Journal of Personality and Social Psychology, 52,* 730–738.

Shepard, R. (1984). Ecological constraints on internal representations: Resonant kinematics of perceiving, imagining, thinking and dreaming. *Psychological Review, 91,* 417–447.

Shotter, J. (1983). "Duality of structure" and "intentionality" in an ecological psychology. *Journal for the Theory of Social Behavior, 13,* 19–44.

Steiner, I. (1955). Interpersonal behavior as influenced by accuracy of social perception. *Psychological Review, 62,* 268–274.

Stephan, W. (1991). Intergroup relations and prejudice. In R. M. Baron & W. G. Graziano (Eds.), *Social psychology.* New York: Holt, Rinehart & Winston.

Sue, S., & Okazaki, S. (1990). Asian American educational achievements: A phenomenon in search of an explanation. *American Psychologist, 43,* 913–920.

Swann, W. B. (1984). Quest for accuracy in person perception: A matter of pragmatics. *Psychological Review, 91,* 457–477.

Tooby, J., & Cosmides, L. (1992). The psychological foundations culture. In J. H. Barkow, L. Cosmides, & J. Tooby (Eds.), *The adapted mind* (pp. 19–36). London: Oxford University Press.

Vygotsky, L. (1962). *Thought and language* (E. Hanfmann & G. Vakar, Trans.). Cambridge, MA: Harvard University Press.

Vygotsky, L. S. (1978). *Mind in society: The development of higher psychological processes* (M. Cole, V. John-Steiner, S. Scribner, & E. Soubernen, Eds. and Trans.). Cambridge, MA: Harvard University Press.

Wright, J. (1988). An alternative paradigm for studying the accuracy of person perception: Simulated personalities. In D. M. Buss & N. Cantor (Eds.), *Personality psychology: Recent trends and emerging directions* (pp. 61–81). New York: Springer-Verlag.

Wright, J. C., & Mischel, W. (1987). A conditional approach to dispositional constructs: The local predictability of social behavior. *Journal of Social Psychology, 53,* 1159–1177.

6

Stereotypes, Base Rates, and the Fundamental Attribution Mistake: A Content-Based Approach to Judgmental Accuracy

David C. Funder

W e realize that something is a snake and immediately respond to it on the basis of what we believe to be true about snakes in general. We realize somebody is a librarian, or an extravert, and respond to that person on the basis of what we believe to be true about librarians or extraverts. Every new object, and every new person, that we encounter is almost immediately categorized in the light of the similarity we perceive between it, or him or her, and other objects or persons we have encountered in the past. Is this kind of categorization and subsequent response on the basis of preexisting knowledge a good thing to do?

The social psychological literature contains two firm and unequivocal answers to this question: no and yes. That is, in a fairly amazing twist of scientific progress, over the past half-century, social psychology has managed to develop *two* independent research literatures—both active, in-

The research described in this chapter was supported by National Institute of Mental Health (NIMH) Grant R01-MH42427 to me. I am grateful for the helpful comments of Lee Jussim, Yueh-Ting Lee, Clark McCauley, and Tom Malloy.

Correspondence concerning this chapter should be addressed to David C. Funder, Department of Psychology, University of California, Riverside, California 92521.

fluential, and even famous—that reach diametrically opposite conclusions on this matter. The contradiction does not seem to be noted very often; an informal survey of several social psychology textbooks indicates that the two literatures are generally safely ensconced away from each other, in separate chapters. These two literatures comprise research on stereotypes and research on base rates, respectively.[1]

STEREOTYPES

The literature that says no, we should not categorize those we meet and treat them according to our knowledge of their categories is, of course, the classic stereotyping literature that is the topic of so much of this book (e.g., Allport, 1954; Bar-Tal, Graumann, Kruglanski, & Stroebe, 1989; Ehrlich, 1973; Hamilton, 1981; Katz & Braly, 1933; LaPiere, 1936). The term *stereotype* is usually attributed in this context to the commentator Walter Lippman (1922). He used the term to describe the fixed and harmful images that various European nationalities stubbornly held of each other and which, he believed, helped incline them to go to war. The more general definition, the one that has gained common currency both in everyday speech and in the psychological literature, is that a *stereotype* is a preexisting representation of a type of person. The connotation, almost uniformly, is that this representation has an overly powerful effect on human judgment (see Ottati & Lee, chapter 2, this volume).

Since at least 1970, the nearly constant message of the stereotypes literature has been that as soon as we know what category a person belongs to—an ethnic minority, an occupation, or a place of residence—we "rush to judgment" and conclude that the individual possesses all or most of the prototypic traits that we tend to associate with his or her category. Whatever the poor individual is *actually* like, by contrast, and in particular whatever he or she actually does in our presence, will tend to be ignored. Indeed, social psychology's belief in this principle is so strong that when

---

[1]Research on stereotypes is usually discussed in a chapter entitled "Prejudice" or "Social Problems," whereas research on base-rate underutilization is usually found in a chapter entitled "Person Perception" or "Social Cognition."

Locksley (Locksley, Borgida, Brekke, & Hepburn, 1980; Locksley, Hepburn, & Ortiz, 1982) and, more recently, Jussim (1993) tried to argue that people do not *always* ignore individuating information in favor of group stereotypes, their arguments were viewed as controversial (e.g., Rasinski, Crocker, & Hastie, 1985).

So the message is that we use stereotypes too much. Whenever we can, we should ignore them. Wouldn't the world be a wonderful place if only we could judge every person, and indeed every instance, on the basis of individual merits and not be misled by all that baggage of usually incorrect information about the attributes of his or her or its category?

BASE RATES

The literature that says yes, we should categorize those we meet and treat them according to our knowledge of their categories comprises the somewhat more recent, but nearly as popular, research on base-rate utilization. The message of this literature is that we do not use our categorical knowledge, here called *base rates* instead of *stereotypes*, nearly as much as we should. Indeed, our failure to use base rates sufficiently has been dubbed the "base-rate fallacy" (e.g., Bar-Hillel, 1980; Kahneman & Tversky, 1973).

The message of the base-rate literature is that we often possess pre-existing, probabilistic representations of what people (or things) are generally like. But we do not use that information enough. As soon as we are confronted with an individual instance of a category, such as an actual person, we are overwhelmed by the salience of this stimulus, and our more general knowledge goes out the window. We base our judgment entirely on what we see directly; more "pallid" information, such as categorical data, is ignored. Indeed, social psychology's belief in this conclusion is so strong that when some commentators, such as Koehler (1993, 1994, in press), state that we sometimes can use base rates appropriately, their statements are also treated as highly controversial.

The conventional view, rather, is that we are generally trapped by our cognitive limitations, such as the protagonist of Nisbett, Borgida, Crandall, and Reed's (1976) classic "Volvo" story (see also Ross, 1977). This story is not an experiment, nor is it even apparently a true anecdote. It is a hypothetical case, used to illustrate how salient, individualized information overwhelms base rates. To abbreviate, the story is that you have just read up on Volvos in *Consumer Reports* or some other reliable source and found out that there were, say, 10,000 satisfied Volvo owners and only 1,000 dissatisfied owners. You are considering buying one yourself when your neighbor tells you a vivid story of his brother-in-law's Volvo, which broke down on the freeway, caught on fire, and had to be sold for scrap. What you should rationally do, say Nisbett et al., is update your statistics to be 10,000 happy owners and 1,001 unhappy owners. Instead, though, the individual case is so overwhelming that you suddenly have deep doubts about something about which you really have little more information than you did before.

The conclusion, then, is that we do not use base rates enough. But wouldn't the world be wonderful if we could only learn to make judgments like true Bayesian statisticians and give more weight to what we know to be true about the world in general (e.g., group and probabilistic data) rather than allowing ourselves to be so distracted by the salient aspects of particular cases?

WHAT IS GOING ON HERE?

So, on the one hand, we have a literature that tells us that we apply our categorical knowledge to our evaluation of individual cases too much. On the other hand, we have a literature that says we apply such knowledge to our judgments not nearly enough. How is such a contradiction possible? I can offer three answers.

The first and most general answer is that this is just yet another example of a sort of all-too-common scientific myopia. It stems from a failure of individual investigators to appreciate, or often even to know about, any literature beyond the narrow segment in which they are directly working. As a result, literatures can develop along contradictory tracks for years before it occurs to anybody that they need to be reconciled or integrated in some way. This is a fairly routine happening; such myopia is found throughout science—certainly not just psychology—and, in this light, there is nothing unprecedented, or even very remarkable, about the contradiction that motivates this chapter.

A second, more specific answer is that these two contradictory literatures both developed under the influence of a common and more basic assumption, which has permeated social psychology for decades: People are usually wrong. Social psychology is an extraordinarily cynical field, it sometimes seems, and is particularly prone to the bias of seeing any general human judgmental tendency as likely to be misguided (Funder, 1987, 1992; Lopes, 1991). In the present case, we can see one similarity between the belief that people use categorical information way too much and the belief that people use categorical information not nearly enough: In both cases, people are portrayed as judgmentally hapless, making errors that are frequent, basic, and consequential. The small problem, however, is that what we really seem to have here is a case of "damned if you do and damned if you don't."

THE FUNDAMENTAL EVALUATION MISTAKE

I would like to propose a third reason for the existence of this contradiction, which I think is the most basic and most important. Both of these literatures exhibit a failure to appreciate the fundamental difference between *cognitive process* and *social content* and the fact that considerations of cognitive process, by themselves, are irrelevant to accuracy. Accuracy is a matter of social content.

This pair of failures can be distilled into what could be named the *fundamental evaluation mistake*. This mistake appears in the stereotypes literature, in the base-rate literature, and in many other research areas that purport to examine judgmental error. The fundamental evaluation mistake is to evaluate a judgment in terms of the cognitive process by which it was made rather than in terms of empirical evidence gathered from the social world that shows it to be right or wrong.[2]

---

[2]This mistake is a special case of what philosophers call the *genetic fallacy*, which is to decide the truth value of an argument on the basis of its origin rather than its logic or evidence. (I am grateful to Albert Pepitone for his remedial instruction on this matter.) Another special case is the *ad hominem* fallacy, in which an argument is deemed false because of who makes it rather than on logical or empirical grounds.

Stereotype researchers assume that any judgment based on a stereotype is wrong, and base-rate researchers assume that any judgment based on a base rate is right. But these assumptions speak to the cognitive process by which the judgment was made, not to its external validity. As I have argued elsewhere, the cognitive process of judgment is just one part of the larger interpersonal process that leads from real properties of people to accurate or inaccurate judgments of those properties. The study of cognitive process is insufficient by itself to address accuracy issues because it omits any consideration of what might be true about the target of judgment and how that truth might be revealed and observed in social interaction (Funder, in press).

Historically and up to the present day, stereotype researchers have studied the effects on judgment of preexisting, categorical knowledge structures—stereotypes—that do happen to be wrong, or at least highly exaggerated. In many cases, the stereotypes to be studied, such as racial and gender stereotypes, were selected precisely because they were believed not only to be wrong, but to be the source of significant social problems. The original motivation for much research on stereotypes, as well as for Lippman's coining of the very term *stereotype*, was to address problems of racism and other kinds of prejudice that have harmful effects.

As a result of this orientation, the definition of *stereotype*—sometimes explicitly, more often just implicitly—shifted from a preexisting, categorical knowledge structure to a preexisting, categorical knowledge structure that is wrong. In that light, it becomes unsurprising that research results have shown how the use of stereotypes can unfairly bias judgments and cause other problems, and it has been a small step for the researchers to conclude—again, sometimes explicitly, but usually just implicitly—that all use of such preexisting, categorical knowledge is bad. It *was* bad, in all of the examples they studied.

Researchers on the use of base rates began with a very different orientation, starting with putatively normative models of decision making based loosely on Bayesian statistical theory. Triggered largely by the early work of Kahneman and Tversky (e.g., 1973), researchers set up artificial judgment situations in which stimuli were designed to correspond to one or more of the terms in a mathematized model of how judgments *should* be made. These models sometimes were expected utility formulas drawn from economics and business.

An essential term in the Bayesian decision-making formula is *prior probability*, the chances of an outcome being true in the absence of—"prior to"—any information about the particular case to be analyzed.[3] A very simple way (in fact, in many cases, an oversimplified way) to obtain such a prior probability is to find out or to estimate the base rate. The base rate is the percentage of true cases over the total number of similar cases in the past. The main (and often overlooked) conceptual complication in determining the base rate is trying to figure out exactly what is meant by "similar" cases (Bar-Hillel, 1990; Koehler, in press). The main empirical complication, once the category of relevant cases is (somehow) defined, is obtaining accurate data on frequencies of prior outcomes.

In experiments, this number can be, and often is, simply presented to subjects. Kahneman and Tversky's (1973) famous "lawyer–engineer" problem, for example, begins with the bald statement that an individual comes from a population of 30 engineers and 70 lawyers. The subject is then given more information about this individual, such as that he has no interest in politics and enjoys mathematical puzzles, that is obviously designed to sound engineerlike and very unlawyerlike. But if the subject's subsequent estimate of the probability that the individual is a lawyer falls much below 70%, the subject is deemed to have committed the base-rate fallacy.

The preexisting categorical information that base-rate researchers provide to their subjects is always above reproach. It is sometimes attributed to an unimpeachable source, such as *Consumer Reports*, but more often the information is simply provided to the subject by the experimenter as part of the stimulus protocol. When that is the case, of course, the information might as well come from God. The subject is not supposed, in-

---

[3]For example, the prior probability of there being a monster in Loch Ness is low; therefore, we might require more than one eyewitness that a monster was there before we believed. The prior probability that Loch Ness is wet and cold is higher, however, so for that claim, one witness would probably be deemed entirely sufficient.

deed is not allowed, to question the source or truth of this information. Any failure on the subject's part to accept and to use this information, full strength, no matter how it is presented, will be dubbed a fallacy and an error.

The base-rate researchers' practice of providing their subjects preexisting, categorical information that happens to be correct seems to have led them to assume that any use of such information is good and to interpret the underuse of such information as a serious judgmental error. From the beginning, the definition of a base rate—sometimes explicitly, more often just implicitly—has been that it is a preexisting, categorical knowledge structure that happens to be right. The persistent lament that emanates from the base-rate literature is about how tragic it is that such categorical, probabilistic information about group properties is not always used, that people pay too much attention to unreliable individuating information instead.

Of course, the opposing, central conclusions of the two literatures are both wrong, because both embody the fundamental evaluation mistake. Knowing whether a judge used a preexisting knowledge structure tells us nothing about his or her accuracy unless we determine, first, whether the knowledge contained in these structures is right or wrong. That is precisely the issue that occupies most of the other chapters in this book. For present purposes, it is sufficient to note that the use of stereotypes or base rates neither promotes nor harms accuracy, in itself. Rather, their use promotes accuracy when the stereotypes or base rates are themselves accurate and harms accuracy when they are inaccurate. But research that only examines *whether* these knowledge structures affect judgment—which is to say, 99.9% of the research in both literatures—does not begin to address this issue one way or the other.

This is precisely the reason that the research represented in this volume is so important and even overdue. What is needed, concerning stereotypes as well as other areas of research on social judgment, is more attention to the interpersonal content of judgment rather than just its cognitive process. In the present case, this translates to a shift from just asking "do stereotypes/base rates affect judgment?" to also asking "are stereotypes/base rates accurate?" What we desperately need to know is, Which preexisting, categorical structures of probabilistic knowledge—call them *stereotypes*, call them *base rates*—are right and which are wrong, when, and to what extent?

ACCURACY RESEARCH

Research aimed at these questions, such as contained in this volume, provides an important step toward addressing the even more basic question: Which of the judgments we make of each other (and even of ourselves) are right, which are wrong, and when? Research aimed at this question stems from the *accuracy paradigm* (Funder, in press; Funder & West, 1993).

The essence of the accuracy paradigm is to look at what a judgment says, not just at how it was made, and then to seek empirical evidence as to whether what this judgment says is true, really is true. Of course, the answer will always be a matter of degree. No judgment is 100% correct all of the time. But the purpose of the accuracy paradigm is to learn more about the circumstances under which judgments are more likely to be more accurate. This purpose requires a focus on content.

THE ACCURACY PROJECT

In my laboratory, which we call the Riverside Accuracy Project, we focus on the accuracy of judgments of personality. We are interested in the judgments that people make of the degree to which they or others are *critical*, *dependable*, or *talkative*. Trait terms like these describe patterns of behavior and simultaneously refer to the psychological properties of the person being described that produce these behavioral patterns (Funder, 1991, in press).

How can we evaluate whether judgments of such personality traits are accurate or not? Such evaluation requires that our research look not just at the judge and his or her cognitive processes, but at the person who is the target of judgment. We need to find out what that person is like and to what degree a given judgment accurately characterizes him or her.

Determining the answer to this question is no simple matter. By what criteria can anybody say what somebody's personality is really like? The usual criterion for personality judgment, over the years, has been inter-judge agreement (Funder & Colvin, in press). The more that different judges of a personality—including the person in question him or herself—agree with each other, the more likely they are to be assumed to be accurate. It does seem to be logical that two judgments that disagree cannot both be accurate; in that sense, agreement is relevant to accuracy. But it also must be acknowledged that agreement, far from guarantees accuracy; two judgments can be in perfect agreement, yet both be perfectly wrong. The other category of possible criteria for accuracy is that of direct behavioral observation. The industrial/organizational (I/O) literature for years has used various measures of work output and job performance as criteria for evaluating the accuracy of employers' judgments of their employees (e.g., Borman, White, Pulakos, & Oppler, 1991). But this work, while extremely valuable, is a bit more narrowly focused than research on personality judgment. Sophisticated researchers in the I/O domain have concluded that even constructs like *competence* or *performance* must be operationalized through multiple measures to be assessed with any validity (Pulakos, Borman, & Hough, 1988). Personality constructs are even broader, and the need for multiple indicators concomitantly is even more urgent (Funder, 1991).

The bottom line, therefore, is that the evaluation of personality judgment requires that as many and as diverse criteria as possible be used and that we constantly do all we can to come up with more. Unfortunately, many personality researchers for years have been content to use only self-reports and, occasionally, peer judgments as their measures of traits. But others, notably the project by J. H. Block and Block (e.g., 1980), have taken on the difficult business of trying constantly to formulate new and different ways to assess personality, without neglecting the tried and (maybe) true. Other researchers more recently have begun to include behavioral as well as judgmental criteria for the evaluation of accuracy (e.g., Funder & Sneed, 1993; Gormly, 1984; Levesque & Kenny, 1993).

Such a multifaceted approach is used in our research. Our project in

Riverside includes self-judgments of personality by about 160 undergraduates (80 of each sex), using an instrument that we use often, the (modified) California Q-sort (Bem & Funder, 1978; Block, 1978). This is a very broadly ranging assessment instrument that consists of 100 phrases, such as "is critical and skeptical; not easily impressed," each printed on a separate card. The task of a judge using this instrument is to sort these cards into a forced, peaked, 9–step distribution ranging from *not at all (or negative) characteristic* (1) to *high characteristic* (9) of the person being described. We also obtained self-judgments using several more conventional personality questionnaires.

Similar data, Q-sort and questionnaire ratings, about our subjects were obtained as well from two college acquaintances, two hometown acquaintances, and both parents (when available). As you can imagine, the result already is an extremely large data set that affords multiple analytical possibilities that we are already beginning to exploit (e.g., Funder, Kolar, & Blackman, in press). But that is just the beginning. As shown in Figure 1, we also videotaped each subject's behavior in seven laboratory situations. Each was about 5 min long and included interactions with a friend and with a stranger under unstructured, cooperative, and competitive circumstances, as well as a discussion in a larger group. These interactions are currently in the process of being coded with a 64–item behavioral Q-sort, as well as with other instruments (e.g., Sneed, 1994).

And there is more. Each of our subjects (who survived to that point) completed a diary form every evening for 8 days, where he or she noted the salient events of the day and how he or she felt about them. Finally, each subject wore a pager for 8 days and was beeped four times each day. The subject wrote down what he or she was doing when beeped, who else was present, and how he or she felt about it (Spain, 1994; cf. Csikszentmihalyi & Larson, 1992).

Our research is organized around four general variables that seem to affect accuracy: (a) the possibility that some individuals are better at judging personality than are others; (b) the possibility that some individuals are easier to judge than are others (Colvin, 1993); (c) the possibility that some traits are easier to judge accurately than are others (Funder & Colvin,

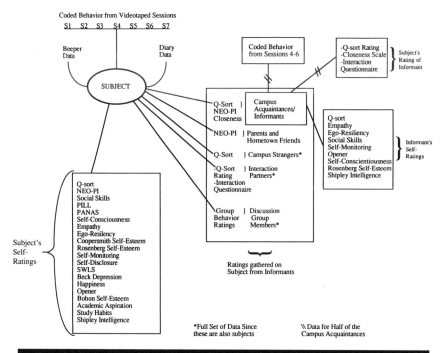

Coded Behavior from Videotaped Sessions
S1 S2 S3 S4 S5 S6 S7

Beeper Data

Diary Data

Coded Behavior from Sessions 4-6

-Q-sort Rating
-Closeness Scale
-Interaction Questionnaire } Subject's Rating of Informant

SUBJECT

Q-Sort }
NEO-PI
Closeness

Campus Acquaintances/ Informants

NEO-PI } Parents and Hometown Friends

Q-Sort } Campus Strangers*

Q-Sort } Interaction
Rating   Partners*
-Interaction
Questionnaire

Q-sort
Empathy
Ego-Resiliency
Social Skills
Self-Monitoring
Opener
Self-Conscientiousness
Rosenberg Self-Esteem
Shipley Intelligence } Informant's Self-Ratings

Q-sort
NEO-PI
Social Skills
PILL
PANAS
Self-Consciousness
Empathy
Ego-Resiliency
Coopersmith Self-Esteem
Rosenberg Self-Esteem
Self-Monitoring
Self-Disclosure
SWLS
Beck Depression
Happiness
Opener
Bohon Self-Esteem
Academic Aspiration
Study Habits
Shipley Intelligence

Subject's Self-Ratings

Group } Discussion
Behavior   Group
Ratings   Members*

Ratings gathered on Subject from Informants

*Full Set of Data Since these are also subjects

\\ Data for Half of the Campus Acquaintances

Figure 1

A schematic representation of the data gathered by the Riverside Accuracy Project. The aim of this project is to evaluate the accuracy of personality judgment through as many and as diverse criteria as possible, including self- and other-judgments, but also including behavior in seven videotaped settings and reports of daily activities gathered through diary and beeper (pager) reports. S1–S7 = Experimental Sessions 1–7, PILL = Pennebaker Inventory of Limbid Languidness, PANAS = Positive Affect Negative Affect Scale, SWLS = Satisfaction With Life Scale.

1988; Funder & Dobroth, 1987); and (d) the possibility that some kinds and amounts of information are more likely to yield accurate judgments than are others (e.g., Colvin & Funder, 1991; Funder & Colvin, 1988).

For present purposes, the central issue is not the results we have obtained, but the method we use. This method is to try to use all of the various criteria we have available for evaluating judgmental accuracy, in the service of better understanding the variables, such as the four just summarized, that seem to make accuracy more and less likely. It is a difficult method. Individual studies almost always use just one or two of the available criteria, and the construction of something like coded behavior into a criterion for evaluating a personality judgment can be an extremely difficult and time-consuming task in itself. One of my graduate students has completed a dissertation on how to convert behavioral observations into criteria for at least some personality traits (Sneed, 1994), and another has worked on converting the information in the diary and beeper data into similarly useful criteria (Spain, 1994). Both projects are major undertakings, yet are relatively small parts of the effort that ultimately will be required.

This is what comes of being a philosophical realist, or "neo-Allportian" (Funder, 1991), about personality traits. I believe that they are not mere social constructions; I think something out there really exists. But that belief behooves one to act accordingly. It entails research that not only focuses on how "impressions" of personality are "socially constructed" or how certain kinds of stimuli can lead to certain kinds of judgments, but also addresses, as well as it can, what the attributes of the persons judged might actually be. In different but complementary ways, that is the kind of research that is presented throughout this volume.

CONCLUSION

The contradiction between the classic sterotype and base-rate literatures can be resolved by noting that both focus too exclusively on the cognitive processes rather than the interpersonal content of judgment. The use of stereotypes and base rates is neither good nor bad for judgmental accuracy; that depends on whether the content of the stereotypes and base rates is itself accurate or inaccurate. Research to examine the accuracy of stereotypes must use multifaceted criteria to assess the actual properties of the individuals being described. One example of the use of such multifaceted criteria, the Riverside Accuracy Project, has been described. The Accuracy Project concerns the accuracy of judgments of the personalities of individuals, rather than group stereotypes. Nonetheless, it, along with the research described by the other chapters in this volume, illustrates the kind of spadework that will be necessary as we try to match our individual judgments and group stereotypes to what may or may not be the underlying reality.

REFERENCES

Allport, G. W. (1954). *The nature of prejudice.* Springfield, MA: Addison-Wesley.

Bar-Hillel, M. (1980). The base-rate fallacy in probability judgments. *Acta Psychologica, 44,* 211–233.

Bar-Hillel, M. (1990). Back to base rates. In R. M. Hogarth (Ed.), *Insights in decision making: A tribute to Hillel J. Einhorn* (pp. 200–216). Chicago: University of Chicago Press.

Bar-Tal, D., Graumann, C. F., Kruglanski, A. W., & Stroebe, W. (1989). *Stereotyping and prejudice: Changing conceptions.* New York: Springer-Verlag.

Bem, D. J., & Funder, D. C. (1978). Predicting more of the people more of the time: Assessing the personality of situations. *Psychological Review, 85,* 485–501.

Block, J. (1978). *The Q-sort method in personality assessment and psychiatric research.* Palo Alto, CA: Consulting Psychologists Press.

Block, J. H., & Block, J. (1980). The role of ego-control and ego-resiliency in the organization of behavior. In W. A. Collins (Ed.), *Minnesota symposium on child psychology* (Vol. 13). Hillsdale, NJ: Erlbaum.

Borman, W. C., White, L. A., Pulakos, E. D., & Oppler, S. H. (1991). Models of supervisory job performance ratings. *Journal of Applied Psychology, 76,* 863–872.

Colvin, C. R. (1993). Judgable people: Personality, behavior and competing explanations. *Journal of Personality and Social Psychology, 64,* 861–873.

Colvin, C. R., & Funder, D. C. (1991). Predicting personality and behavior: A boundary on the acquaintanceship effect. *Journal of Personality and Social Psychology, 60,* 884–894.

Csikszentmihalyi, M., & Larson, R. (1992). Validity and reliability of the Experience Sampling Method. In M. W. deVries (Ed.), *The experience of psychopathology: Investigating mental disorders in their natural settings* (pp. 43–57). Cambridge, England: Cambridge University Press.

Ehrlich, H. J. (1973). *The social psychology of prejudice.* New York: Wiley.

Funder, D. C. (1987). Errors and mistakes: Evaluating the accuracy of social judgment. *Psychological Bulletin, 101,* 75–90.

Funder, D. C. (1991). Global traits: A neo-Allportian approach to personality. *Psychological Science, 2,* 31–39.

Funder, D. C. (1992). Everything you know is wrong. *Contemporary Psychology, 37,* 319–320.

Funder, D. C. (in press). On the accuracy of personality judgment: A realistic approach. *Psychological Review.*

Funder, D. C., & Colvin, C. R. (1988). Friends and strangers: Acquaintanceship, agreement, and the accuracy of personality judgment. *Journal of Personality and Social Psychology, 55,* 149–158.

Funder, D. C., & Colvin, C. R. (in press). Congruence of self and others' judgments of personality. In R. Hogan, J. Johnson, & S. Briggs (Eds.), *Handbook of personality psychology.* Orlando, FL: Academic Press.

Funder, D. C., & Dobroth, K. M. (1987). Differences between traits: Properties associated with interjudge agreement. *Journal of Personality and Social Psychology, 52,* 409–418.

Funder, D. C., Kolar, D., & Blackman, M. (in press). On the basis of agreement among judges of personality: Interpersonal relations, similarity, and acquaintanceship. *Journal of Personality and Social Psychology.*

Funder, D. C., & Sneed, C. D. (1993). Behavioral manifestations of personality: An ecological approach to judgmental accuracy. *Journal of Personality and Social Psychology, 64,* 479–490.

Funder, D. C., & West, S. G. (1993). Consensus, self–other agreement, and accuracy in personality judgment: An introduction. *Journal of Personality, 61,* 457–467.

Gormly, J. (1984). Correspondence between personality trait ratings and behavioral events. *Journal of Personality, 52,* 220–232.

Hamilton, D. L. (Ed.). (1981). *Cognitive processes in stereotyping and intergroup behavior.* Hillsdale, NJ: Erlbaum.

Jussim, L. (1993). Accuracy in interpersonal expectations: A reflection–construction analysis of current and classic research. *Journal of Personality, 61,* 638–668.

Kahneman, D., & Tversky, A. (1973). On the psychology of prediction. *Psychological Review, 80,* 237–251.

Katz, D., & Braly, K. (1933). Racial stereotyping in one hundred college students. *Journal of Abnormal and Social Psychology, 28,* 280–290.

Koehler, J. J. (1993). The base rate fallacy myth. *Psycoloquy* [On-line serial], *4*(49). Available FTP: Hostname: princeton.edu Directory: pub/harnad/Psycoloquy/1993.volume.4 File: psycoloquy.93.4.49.base-rate.1.koehler

Koehler, J. J. (1994). Base rates and the "illusion illusion." *Psycoloquy* [On-line serial], *5*(9). Available FTP: Hostname: princeton.edu Directory: pub/harnad/Psycoloquy/1994.volume.5 File: psycoloquy.94.5.9.base-rate.9.koehler

Koehler, J. J. (in press). The base rate fallacy myth. *Behavioral and Brain Sciences.*

LaPiere, R. T. (1936). Type-rationalizations of group antiplay. *Social Forces, 15,* 232–237.

Levesque, M. J., & Kenny, D. A. (1993). Accuracy of behavioral predictions at zero acquaintance: A social relations analysis. *Journal of Personality and Social Psychology, 65,* 1178–1187.

Lippman, W. (1922). *Public opinion.* New York: Harcourt, Brace.

Locksley, A., Borgida, E., Brekke, N., & Hepburn, C. (1980). Sex stereotypes and social judgment. *Journal of Personality and Social Psychology, 39,* 821–831.

Locksley, A., Hepburn, C., & Ortiz, V. (1982). Social stereotypes and judgments of individuals: An instance of the base-rate fallacy. *Journal of Experimental Social Psychology, 18,* 23–42.

Lopes, L. L. (1991). The rhetoric of irrationality. *Theory and Psychology, 1,* 65–82.

Nisbett, R. E., Borgida, E., Crandall, R., & Reed, H. (1976). Popular induction: Information is not always informative. In J. Carroll & J. Payne (Eds.), *Cognitive and social behavior.* Potomac, MD: Erlbaum.

Nisbett, R., & Ross, L. (1977). *Human inference: Strategies and shortcomings of social judgment.* Englewood Cliffs, NJ: Prentice Hall.

Pulakos, E. D., Borman, W. C., & Hough, L. M. (1988). Test validation for scientific understanding: Two demonstrations of an approach to studying predictor–criterion linkages. *Personnel Psychology, 41,* 703–716.

Ross, L. (1977). The intuitive psychologist and his shortcomings. In L. Berkowitz (Ed.), *Advances in experimental social psychology* (Vol. 10, pp. 174–214). New York: Academic Press.

Sneed, C. D. (1994). *Situational influences on the perception and expression of behavior.* Unpublished doctoral dissertation, University of California, Riverside.

Spain, J. S. (1994). *Personality and daily life experiences: Evaluating the accuracy of personality judgments.* Unpublished doctoral dissertation, University of California, Riverside.

Stereotype Accuracy in Multicultural Business

Yueh-Ting Lee and Guillermo Duenas

There is no such thing as human nature independent of culture.

(Geertz, 1973, p. 49)

Given that psychology is so immersed in culture, it must be organized around those meaning-making and meaning-using processes that connect man to culture. This does not commit us to more subjectivity in psychology; it is just the reverse. By virtue of participation in culture, meaning is rendered public and shared. Our culturally adapted way of life depends upon shared meanings and shared concepts and depends as well upon shared modes of discourse for negotiating differences in meaning and interpretation.

(J. Bruner, 1990, pp. 12–13)

Special thanks are extended to Albert Pepitone for his insightful comments on various drafts of this chapter and to Linda Albright and Victor Ottati for their helpful and constructive comments on our final version of this chapter. We are also grateful to the following people: the participants at the Bryn Mawr conference for their helpful comments, Clark McCauley and Lee Jussim for their editorial suggestions, and Lucia Sullivan and Shelley Baum-Brunner for proofreading this chapter for us. However, any shortcoming or weakness in the chapter is our own.

Correspondence can be addressed either to Yueh-Ting Lee, Department of Psychology, Westfield State College, Westfield, Massachusetts 01086 (Y_LEE@FOMA.WSC.MASS.EDU) or to Guillermo Duenas, School of Business Administration, Philadelphia College of Textiles and Science, School House Lane and Henry Avenue, Philadelphia, Pennsylvania 19144 (DUENASG@HARDY.TEXSCI.EDU).

WHAT IS WRONG WITH PSYCHOLOGY AND MANAGEMENT?

Although American psychology, especially American mainstream so-cial psychology, has historically and currently neglected the role of culture in its theories and research (Campbell, 1975; Gielen, 1994; Ich-heiser, 1949, 1970; Lee, 1994b; Pepitone, 1989), an increasing number of social scientists have come to realize the influence of culture on social be-havior and social development. If there were a market in academic ideas, instead of simply a market in academic personnel, it is a fairly safe bet that stock in the concept of culture would be on the rise (Rosen, 1991). Today, for example, culture and diversity are important issues in national and in-ternational organizations and management (see Hall & Hall, 1990; Hatch, 1993; Hofstede, 1991; Schein, 1985). Much money has been spent on di-versity management workshops and on total quality management train-ing (Carey, 1994; Cox, 1993). Although many organizations began to introduce diversity or cultural awareness training programs to meet the challenge of the future workforce (e.g., more minority employees, more female employees, and more international or foreign workers/ businesspersons), the outcomes of these workshops and training activities are seldom assessed (Carey, 1994; Chu & McCauley, 1995) or are even un-expectedly negative (Jackson et al., 1992). In this chapter, we propose that considering stereotype accuracy could help corporations and organiza-tions improve their management of national and international business and collaboration with various cultural groups. To understand stereotype accuracy, we suggest examining the ways stereotyping impacts worker re-lations.

THE BASIS OF CONFLICT: DIFFERENTIAL MEANINGS OF CULTURAL STEREOTYPES

White workers, when asked to list as quickly as possible a few words or expressions about Blacks, Chinese, Japanese, and Mexicans, tend to asso-ciate Blacks with sports, rap music, and dance; Chinese with food; Japanese with cars (Lee, Pellicci, & Hogan, 1994); and Mexicans with *mañana* (tomorrow). Similarly, Mexicans tend to describe Americans as machines or robots. These stereotypes may negatively influence the relations among people from various cultures.

In both domestic and international business or management, it is often argued that destructive conflicts can arise from the negative stereotypes that one cultural group holds against another (e.g., Borisoff & Victor, 1989). Examples include tension in the workplace, loss of productivity, and low morale. However, are these conflicts always due to the negative stereotypes toward outgroups? Perhaps not.

Attributes perceived as negative by one cultural group may not be perceived as negative by another. For example, in an experiment, Lee and Ottati (1995) found that independent of American negative stereotypes toward Chinese people, Chinese subjects were proud of the fact that Americans perceived the Chinese as inhibited, at least as long as the Chinese perceived the description as accurate. On the other hand, when Americans perceived the Chinese as dishonest, Chinese subjects felt offended, mainly because Chinese subjects did not think dishonest accurately described Chinese people.

It seems, then, that accuracy may be as important as, if not more than, the valence of stereotypes in determining intergroup conflict or harmony. Obviously, the meanings that stereotypes hold for individuals are important when we deal with discussing stereotype accuracy, especially in regard to understanding intercultural behavior and management (see also Osgood, 1979). As noted in the introductory chapter (Jussim, McCauley, & Lee, this volume), stereotypes need to be viewed multidimensionally—for example, for accuracy (i.e., accurate vs. inaccurate) and valence (i.e., positive vs. negative). Similarly, research on attitude measures (also see Ajzen, 1988; Ajzen & Fishbein, 1980; Fishbein & Ajzen, 1975) has suggested that beliefs about the attitude object can be measured separately from the evaluation of these beliefs.

It should be made clear, however, that accuracy and valence (e.g., the positivity and negativity of stereotypes) are complicated and interrelated issues. On the one hand, the accuracy and valence of stereotypes can be independent of each other. On the other hand, they are interrelated when both cultures agree on the difference in behavior, but label or interpret it evaluatively. In other words, people of various cultures may use different traits to accurately describe the same perceived difference in behavior. For example, the inhibited behavior can be objectively perceived, but culturally interpreted. Although Americans negatively stereotype the Chinese as inhibited, the Chinese who are exposed to Confucian culture do not perceive it this way. To them, it is a virtue to have an inhibited personality (see Lee, 1993). For Confucians, it means self-control and a decent desire not to impose on others. For Americans, it is a lack of motivation, a lack of genuineness, or a neurotic repression.[1]

In the same manner, rural people in the Third World (e.g., in China) may bathe less often than do urban Americans. If traveling to China, urban Americans may call the rural Chinese dirty; visiting the United States, rural Chinese perhaps call the urban Americans "shower addicts." Mexicans may call Americans "machines," whereas Americans call Mexicans lazy or "*mañana* people." From a cross-cultural perspective, E. M. Bruner (1956) examined stereotypic perceptions between Hidatsa Indians and local ranchers of European extraction (i.e., the "Yankees") in the Dakotas (also see D. T. Campbell, 1967; LeVine & Campbell, 1972). Bruner found that the Hidatsa Indians regarded their own behavior as generous and unselfish and regarded the Yankees as stingy and selfish. Simultaneously, the Yankees considered their own behavior as thrifty and provident, but considered the Hidatsa Indians to be profligate and improvident. Both groups accurately perceived these cultural differences, but used different labels to describe them.

Thus, the meanings that stereotypes hold for individuals are related not only to valence, but also to accuracy. One of the basic arguments in this chapter is that stereotype accuracy (or inaccuracy) depends on the meaning of stereotypes. Simply put, how do we interpret stereotypes? What do they (e.g., stereotypic beliefs and behaviors) mean to us and to other people? We attempt to answer these questions from a cultural perspective,

---

[1]The argument that Chinese inhibitedness is more related to genetics than to culture is no different from the debate on nature and nurture. Our view is that social stereotypes are culturally or socially determined and shared.

emphasizing the meanings that various stereotypes hold with various cultural groups in national and international business or in cross-cultural management.

STEREOTYPE ACCURACY AND MEANING IN MANAGING CULTURAL DIFFERENCES

Cultural Stereotype Accuracy–Meaning (CSAM) Model

In this chapter, we propose a different approach to stereotype accuracy (and inaccuracy): the cultural stereotype accuracy–meaning (CSAM) model. Though a detailed discussion of this theoretical perspective may go beyond the scope of our chapter, the CSAM model should be delineated here as much as possible. Basically, the CSAM model holds that the degree of stereotype accuracy (or inaccuracy) depends on how the meanings of cultural stereotypes are understood by stereotyping and stereotyped cultures. The meanings of cultural stereotypes may play a pivotal role in cultural interaction (e.g., cross-cultural perception, communication, and international business and/or management).

What is the rationale of the CSAM model? First, from the perspective of interpersonal perception, Kenny's (1994) research on the weighted average model has dealt with similar meaning systems (i.e., r^2: the extent to which a behavior "is given the same meaning by two perceivers," p. 64). If the degree to which two individuals accurately perceive an act or behavior depends on how these two perceivers interpret that act or behavior, then it may be true that the accuracy of two cultural groups' perceptions may be correlated with the extent to which the two cultures interpret the same behavior or act. For example, in the eyes of urban Americans, it is dirty that the rural Chinese bathe only once a month in winter. On the other hand, it is "shower-addicted" that urban Americans bathe every day.

Second, stereotype accuracy is not absolute, but relative. That is to say, the shared beliefs (or standards) within a social or cultural group may determine how we judge ourselves and others. Theoretically or empirically, Ashmore and Longo (chapter 3, this volume) and Biernat (chapter 4, this volume) have touched on how different standards (e.g., "shifting standards," or "in whose heads are stereotypes?") are related to stereotype accuracy and inaccuracy.

Third, perception (including stereotype) accuracy may be dynamic and circumscribed because of time and space change (see Baron, chapter 5, this volume; McArthur & Baron, 1983). A stereotype of the Chinese as superstitious may have been accurate in the 1930s, but not true today because of time change (Lee, 1995; Lee & Ottati, 1995). In the meanwhile, a stereotype of Mexicans as *mañana* people may be true in the United States, where most Americans impose their own values and beliefs on Mexicans. On the other hand, it may not be true in Mexico, where Mexicans share their own cultural values and beliefs with their compatriots.

Finally, as has been discussed previously, cross-cultural and anthropological evidence suggests that the essence of understanding stereotype accuracy may lie in understanding the *meanings* that people from different cultures attach to perceptions, behaviors, rules, events, and so on. This requires achieving a certain degree of mutual cultural understanding.

Considering the application of the CSAM model, we believe it useful in such a way that the ultimate goal of understanding stereotype accuracy will lead to more effective management of cross-cultural differences (including cross-cultural interaction, diversity workshops, and cross-cultural training programs). For example, many diversity workshops and cross-cultural training programs in national or multinational organizations are obstructed by the stereotypes that members of different cultural groups have of each other. Though the difficulty in achieving successful cross-cultural communication and collaboration stems many times from the inaccuracy of the cultural stereotypes (Hall & Hall, 1990), discovering accuracy in cultural stereotypes is an equally important means of achieving cross-cultural understanding and effective international management.

Two Assumptions Regarding Cultural Stereotype Accuracy

Traditionally, researchers in cross-cultural communication and management hold that to facilitate cross-cultural communication, people from different cultures should "avoid stereotyping" (e.g., Borisoff & Victor, 1989;

Coyne & O'Neil, 1992). But is stereotyping really avoidable? Not really. We cannot avoid stereotyping because it is the very basic mechanism people use to cope with the complexity implied by the encounter with a culture alien to their own (Ottati & Lee, chapter 2, this volume). Instead, the meanings of cultural stereotypes must be made explicit and analyzed by the participants. By assessing their accuracy and inaccuracy, participants gain understanding of the other's culture and of their own.

To be more specific, we generalize two theoretical assumptions in this chapter, based on the CSAM model. First, stereotype accuracy lies in the reflection of cultural difference and identity.[2] That is, stereotypic perceptions may accurately capture objective cultural difference and evaluatively correspond to cultural identity. Cultural evaluations (or identities) would be of no avail if people did not first grasp the meanings of those cultural values and beliefs (e.g., cultural stereotypic beliefs). If Culture A is objectively different from Culture B, people's perceptions (including stereotypes) may accurately capture the differences between these two cultures (i.e., correspondence between perceived difference in behavior and objective cultural difference in behavior). If one culture accepts those cultural differences (reflected or captured by cultural stereotypes), this culture may tend to identify itself with stereotypes (i.e., cultural identity), regardless of whether they are positive or negative in the eye of another culture.

The second assumption is that stereotype accuracy (or inaccuracy) depends on the cultural standards that people tend to use. The standards can be understood only through a series of stereotype exposure analyses, that is, analyzing cultural stereotypes step by step. To say it in another way, what you mean may be different from what we mean. For example, Culture Y thinks its perceptions of Culture X are accurate, whereas Culture X thinks Culture Y's stereotypes are inaccurate. The different meanings that stereotypes hold to cultural groups can be discovered through a systematic stereotype assessment.

---

[2]Though the concept of stereotype accuracy as a reflection may not be most desirable, it has often been used in other empirical research (see Jussim, 1991; Triandis & Vassiliou, 1967). Put another way, *stereotype accuracy* may be defined as the correspondence between perceived cultural difference and objective cultural difference.

In the following, we analyze two cross-cultural cases in detail so as to test the two assumptions above. It may be true that our case studies are not methodologically held in high regard by some rigorous behavioral scientists, but these cases at least help us to understand cultural stereotype accuracy and inaccuracy and the CSAM model. These two cases are related to cross-cultural management or international business. The first case pertains to stereotypes between Asians and Americans. The second case is about stereotypic perceptions between Mexicans and Americans.

CASE STUDY 1

How do Eastern people usually see Westerners when they meet to do business? They may have some stereotypes of each other. Apropos of the supervisor–subordinate relationship, Americans are perceived as easygoing, equal, and informal in their workplace (Brislin, 1993). The Japanese or Chinese are usually perceived as rigorous, hierarchical, and unequal (Lee, 1993, 1995; Pye, 1992). Are these stereotypes accurate? Let us examine the following case, summarized from Brislin (1993).

Interactions Between Asians and Americans in the Workplace

This cross-cultural case involves Peter Reed (an American employee in Japan) and Hiumi Watanabe (a Japanese boss).

> The relationship between Peter and Mr. Watanabe started out well because Mr. Watanabe recognized Peter's abilities and the quality of his work. After 3 months, however, tensions began to arise because Mr. Watanabe believed that the boss had a right to direct the behavior of his employees. He was accustomed to his workers saying the equivalent of "yes, sir!" when he made a suggestion. Peter certainly knew that Mr. Watanabe was the boss, but Peter did not see the distinction between himself and his boss to the extent that his Japanese coworkers did. Thus, Peter undoubtedly felt more free to express his disagreement with his boss than did his Japanese coworkers. He believed that superiors and subordinates could even become

good friends (e.g., having lunch together, calling each other by first names, and playing sports together during free time). As time went on, the relationship between Peter and Mr. Watanabe deteriorated. Peter was not happy with his boss, nor was Mr. Watanabe pleased with Peter's performance. Eventually, Peter was asked to consider changing companies.

Case Analysis: Empirical Evidence and Cultural Identity

To a large extent, this cross-cultural conflict may be related to the fact that Peter did not accurately understand the cultural meanings of Japanese supervisor–subordinate relations; nor did Mr. Watanabe accurately know the cultural meanings of American supervisor–subordinate relations. There was very low correspondence between either Peter's or Mr. Watanabe's perceived work relations and the objective work relations. This case suggests one objective cultural difference between Westerners and Easterners in the workplace.

The East–West cultural differences in Case Study 1 are supported by two empirical studies of cross-cultural management. One is Hofstede's (1991) IBM study of power distance. The other is Bond's international survey of Confucian work dynamism (Chinese Culture Connection, 1987). For instance, in the 1960s and 1970s, Hofstede (1991) did a series of international studies for IBM that contained 53 cultures. Four dimensions were obtained: (a) power distance (i.e., the extent to which the less powerful members of organizations and institutions accept and expect that power is unequally distributed), (b) individualism and collectivism (i.e., the degree to which individuals are integrated to groups), (c) masculinity and femininity (i.e., the distribution of roles between sexes), and (d) uncertainty avoidance (i.e., the use of rules and laws to avoid uncertainty in the future; Hofstede, 1991; Hofstede & Bond, 1988). As can be seen in Table 1, it was found that Hong Kong, Taiwan, and Japan were higher on the power distance than was the United States (also see Bond, Wan, Leong, Giacalone, 1985; Hofstede, 1980; Triandis, Brislin, & Hui, 1988).

In the late 1970s and early 1980s, Bond and other psychologists (Chinese Culture Connection, 1987) performed another international study by

Table 1

Scores on Power Distance in IBM Research and on Confucian Work Dynamism in Chinese Value Survey.

Selected countries	Power distance	Confucian work dynamism
Australia	36	31
Brazil	69	65
Germany	35	31
Great Britain	35	25
Hong Kong	68	96
India	77	61
Japan	54	80
South Korea	60	75
The Netherlands	38	44
Singapore	74	48
Sweden	31	33
Taiwan	58	87
United States	40	29

NOTE: Higher numbers mean greater power distance and Confucian work dynamism. *Power distance* means the extent to which the less powerful members of organizations and institutions accept and expect that power is unequally distributed. *Confucian work dynamism* means ordering relationships and observing this order, thrift, and persistence. Data are from "The Confucius Connection: From Cultural Roots to Economic Growth," by G. Hofstede & M. Bond, 1988, *Organizational Dynamics*, 16, pp. 12–13.

administering a Chinese Value Survey to subjects from 22 cultures. Four factors were obtained: Integration (e.g., harmony with groups); Human-Heartedness (e.g., kindness), Confucian Work Dynamism (e.g., ordering relationships and observing this order, thrift, and persistence), and Moral Discipline (e.g., moderation, having few desires). It was found that Brazil and many Asian cultures (e.g., China, Japan, South Korea, and Singapore) were very high on Confucian dynamism; the Netherlands, Sweden, and West Germany took a middle position; and the United States, Britain, New Zealand, and Canada were very low (Hofstede & Bond, 1988). Obviously, ordering relationships and observing this order are part of Confucian culture. In this sense, stereotypes do reflect and correspond to the objective cultural differences.

The stereotypes of Americans as easygoing and equal and the stereotypes of Japanese as rigorous, unequal, and hierarchical perhaps suggest not only differences between, but also identities within, Japanese and American culture. What is the meaning of American and Japanese cultural identity in the case above?

To answer this question, we first refer to social identity theory (cf. self-categorization theory in Oakes, Haslam, & Turner, 1994, p. 94). According to Tajfel and Turner (Tajfel, 1981; Tajfel & Turner, 1986), social identity theory holds that group members attempt to see their group differentiated from other groups and are motivated to preserve and achieve positive group distinctiveness, which in turn serves to protect, enhance, preserve, or achieve a positive social identity for the members of the group. Positive social identity can be achieved in many cases through appropriate intergroup social comparison. Thus, in the same vein, cultural identity could be interpreted as the positive beliefs and values that people in a culture hold and of which they are proud. Intergroup contact may increase both the awareness of one's group membership and loyalty to his or her cultural values (e.g., Asian respect vs. American equality). As Lee (1994a) suggested, the mainland Chinese may not realize their Chinese identity until they come to the United States for the first time. Similarly, Americans may not feel their national or cultural identity until they visit a foreign country or culture. Furthermore, in intercultural contact, the values and beliefs of one culture may be differentiated from those of another culture so as to protect cultural identity. For example, American subordinates may feel very proud to be equal and informal with their supervisors in Japan. In the eyes of many Americans, equality is meant to be a part of American cultural heritage. Like Peter, many Americans tend to identify themselves with their own culturally different values and stereotypic beliefs (i.e., cultural identity) in a foreign culture.

On the other hand, Japanese and Chinese workers may feel proud to be hierarchical and obedient to authority. Like China, Japan holds Confucian beliefs. Confucius said, "Let the prince be a prince, the minister a minister, the father a father, and the son a son" (Shi, 1988, p. 65). In Confucian culture, the stability of society is based on hierarchical and unequal relationships. The *wu lun*, or five relationships, are ruler–subject, father–son, older brother–younger brother, husband–wife, and older friend–younger friend (Hofstede & Bond, 1988; Lee, 1993). The junior (e.g., subordinate/son/student) ought to respect and be obedient to the senior (e.g., supervisor/father/professor), who should, in return, protect and be concerned with the former. In the eyes of many Asians, unequal relationships are understood as (or meant to be) part of their cultural identity. Many Asians may identify themselves with their own culturally different values and stereotypic beliefs (i.e., cultural identity) when interacting with Americans.

Perhaps the earlier analyses suggest that cross-cultural training programs or diversity workshops should consider the meanings of stereotypes. For example, both Asian and American workers can be encouraged to discuss mutual stereotypes openly from a cultural accuracy–meaning perspective. Specifically, they can be taught (a) how people from different cultures (e.g., "we" and "they") understand "our" and "their" own stereotypic beliefs and (b) how those stereotypic beliefs are appreciated and valued (i.e., liked or disliked) by "us" and "them."

CASE STUDY 2

The two cultures of Case Study 1, Japan and the United States, are far from each other geographically, and there may be more differences between a Western culture and an Eastern culture than between two Western cultures. But Case Study 2 deals with two cultural groups— Mexicans and Americans—who are not far from each other in North America. They meet for the purpose of doing business together. The case is a composite of situations that Guillermo Duenas has found over the years in his consulting and training experience. We use it to illustrate the degree of stereotype accuracy (or inaccuracy) through the following analysis.

Managing Cultural Differences Between Mexicans and Americans

The situation entailed a series of meetings between representatives of an American company and those of a Mexican company, who were exploring the possibility of forming a joint venture to manufacture and distribute the products of the American company in Mexico. The meetings took place in Mexico City.

Right from the outset, the Americans wanted to start the meetings before 9:00 a.m. The Mexicans, on the other hand, proposed to meet after 9:00 a.m. After a couple of 1-week visits to Mexico, the Americans perceived the meetings as going nowhere. Although the Americans had tried to focus the meetings on the items listed in a previously agreed on agenda, this had been an impossible task because the Mexicans, in the eyes of the Americans, seemed to want to talk about anything except the business issues at hand. Besides this, the Americans had tried to have the Mexicans accomplish certain tasks by certain dates, and although the Mexicans agreed to the deadlines, they seldom finished the work by the agreed on time. On the other hand, the Mexicans were frustrated because they felt that in the meetings, the Americans insisted on reaching conclusions before everyone had gained a good understanding of the issues involved. Besides, they thought that the Americans had an obsession with having tasks finished by agreed on dates even if all the information needed was not yet available or the thoroughness in the analysis of all relevant data had not yet been achieved. Once in one of the meetings, one of the American representatives made an open statement that the meeting was leading nowhere and that he believed the possibility of reaching a mutually beneficial agreement did not exist. He added that he did not understand how any kind of business could be done in a country like Mexico where no one gave a damn about time and accomplishing things within given deadlines and according to set agendas. He continued to say that he came to Mexico only to confirm what he had already heard about Mexicans, namely, that they were the *mañana* people: Why do something today if you can do it tomorrow? One of the Mexican representatives responded to the comments of the American visitor. He said that he could not understand why Americans insisted on treating people like machines. In his view, Americans planned everything in a mechanical way and expected people to behave according to rigid schedules and inflexible goals. He concluded by saying that the visitor's behavior in that meeting had confirmed his opinion of Americans being like robots. At this point, both parties decided to end the meeting and reevaluate the possibilities of the two groups doing business together.

Case Analysis: Stereotype Accuracy and Inaccuracy Assessment and Stereotype Exposure Analysis[3]

The stereotypes that cultures have of each other help them make sense of a situation that otherwise would be totally absurd. The stereotypes in the case cited obstructed cross-cultural communication and understanding. The question that we address is: How can participants in a cross-cultural situation assess the accuracy of their stereotypes and use this knowledge to increase the effectiveness with which they manage their cultural differences? Figure 1 may help us to understand this question. The following stereotype accuracy/inaccuracy assessment process assumes that a facilitator trained in cross-cultural communication and conflict management will help both groups gain an understanding of each other's culture and negotiate new rules of interaction that may lead the groups to manage more effectively their cultural differences. The process consists of the following 10 steps.

Step 1

Clearly state the stereotype that the stereotyping group has of the other in the specific situation in which the groups are interacting and in relation to the communication problem they are having. The facilitator may have to do this with each group separately.

---

[3]Cultural stereotype exposure analysis in Case Study 2 is different from the contact hypothesis (see Allport, 1954; Amir, 1969; Brewer & Miller, 1988; Brislin, 1993; Miller & Brewer, 1984). First, the former emphasizes the meaning of beliefs, perceptions, and behaviors, whereas the latter does not. Second, stereotype exposure analysis emphasizes the specific (mental) understanding of the meanings of stereotypes step by step, whereas the contact hypothesis emphasizes general (physical) interaction among groups.

Figure 1

American stereotype of Mexicans: Mexicans are the "mañana people."

Example

The Americans stated, "Mexicans are the mañana people." They made this statement in the specific context of the meeting they were having with the Mexicans to discuss a possible joint venture. The specific communication problem they faced was a stalemate situation in which people did not listen to each other anymore. This was the problem that triggered the use of the stereotype to vent the anger and frustration felt.

Step 2

Ask the stereotyping group to make explicit the meaning they attach to the stereotype they have of the other group.

Example

The Americans would be asked, "Could you explain what you mean by 'Mexicans are the mañana people'?" They would explain, "Oh, well ... Mexicans do not have a sense of urgency. Mexicans have no concept of planning. Mexicans go around in circles without ever getting to the bottom line."

Step 3

Of the prior explanations, select those for which observable behaviors, according to the stereotyping group, could be recorded in the specific situation at hand.

Example

In the meeting, the Mexicans did not hand in a report on time; the Mexicans did not follow the agenda.

Step 4

Identify the more general cultural issues to which these behaviors are related.

Example

Concept of time: the Mexicans did not hand in the report on time.

Concept of planning: the Mexicans did not follow the agenda.

Step 5

Ask the stereotyping culture to explain what these concepts mean in their culture.

Example

Concept of time: "In my culture, we take time seriously." "Setting deadlines means to do what was said would be done within the agreed on time frame."

Step 6

Validate the stereotyping group's understanding of their own culture—or self-perception—by comparing it with widely accepted cultural research of their culture.

Example

Self-perception: "In my culture, we take time seriously." "In my culture, setting deadlines means to do what was said would be done within the agreed on time frame."

Cultural research: Americans are a time-monochronic culture. They follow plans religiously (Hall & Hall, 1990). Americans are a low-context culture (Hall & Hall, 1990).

Step 7

Ask the stereotyped group what these concepts mean in their culture.

Example

Concept of time: "In my culture, unexpected things may come up that may require changing your priorities. This requires a flexible sense of time." "In my culture, it is understood that if we say we will do something within a certain time frame, we mean we will do our best to meet that deadline."

Step 8

Validate the stereotyped group's understanding of their own culture, or self-perception, against widely accepted cultural research.

Example

Self-perception: "In my culture, unexpected things may come up that may require changing your priorities. This requires a flexible sense of time."

Cultural research: Mexicans' concept of time is polychronic. They do several things at the same time (Hall & Hall, 1990; see Table 2).

Self-perception: "In my culture, it is understood that if we say we will do something within a certain time frame, we mean we will do our best to meet that deadline."

Cultural research: Mexicans are a high-context-communication culture (Hall & Hall, 1990; see also Table 3).

Step 9

Make a cross-cultural comparison of the validated explanations of the two groups of their own culture regarding the specific cultural issues being discussed and, by doing this, check the accuracy of the stereotype.

The intention here is that people from the stereotyped culture will see things about their culture that they did not see before. On the other hand, people from the stereotyping culture ought to be able to identify their inaccurate (and accurate) understandings of the other culture, as well as their judgments that are based on lack of information about the other culture's reasons for their behavior.

Table 2	

Comparison of Monochronic and Polychronic People

Monochronic people	Polychronic people
Do one thing at a time	Do many things at once
Concentrate on the job	Are highly distractible and subject to interruptions
Take time commitments (e.g., deadlines and schedules) seriously	Consider a time commitment an objective to be achieved, if possible
Are low context and need information	Are high context and already have information
Are committed to the job	Are committed to people and human relationships
Adhere religiously to plans	Change plans often and easily
Are concerned about not disturbing others; follow rules of privacy and consideration	Are more concerned with those who are closely related (family, friends, and close business associates) than with privacy
Emphasize promptness	Base promptness on the relationship
Are accustomed to short-term relationships	Have a strong tendency to build lifetime relationships

NOTE: Data are from *Understanding Cultural Differences* (p. 15), by E. Hall & M. Hall, 1990, Yarmouth, ME: Intercultural Press.

The result of the comparison would lead to realizations of the following sort.

Mexicans: We realize now that you (the Americans) treat time and deadlines in a different way than we do and that you always mean what you say. For instance, if you say, "This should be ready by Friday," then you mean Friday. So you are right in thinking that we do not have a sense of urgency. Consequently, in your eyes, we deserve to be called the mañana people. Our behavior must drive you crazy. Furthermore, if we were to

Table 3

Comparison of Low- and High-Context-Communication Cultures

High-context-communication cultures	Low-context-communication cultures
Include Japanese, Arabs, and Mexicans	Include North Americans and some Europeans
Well-developed social networks	Segregated relationships
Information is already in the person. People do not need detailed or specific information	Information is in the explicit code. People need detailed or specific information
Human relations are more important than facts	Facts are more important than human relations
Shared information; everyone stays informed	Information is controlled by a few top decision makers

NOTE: Data are from *Understanding Cultural Differences* (pp. 6–9), by E. Hall & M. Hall, 1990, Yarmouth, ME: Intercultural Press.

work together in a joint venture, we would have to come to an agreement on whose concept of time we would use, yours or ours, or if together we should come up with a new way of thinking of deadlines.

Americans: We realize that you have a different concept of time and that when we called you "laid-back," it was because we thought your definition of deadlines was the same as ours. We also see now that in a country like yours, where priorities may change in unexpected ways, our insistence on keeping a tight schedule, no matter what, is perceived by you as acting like robots. If we were to adopt your view of time and take into account your context, we would understand that you also take deadlines seriously. Consequently, the stereotype of you as the mañana people would not apply.

At this point in the comparison, both groups would have agreed on the following: (a) Measured against the standards used by the Americans to make judgments in their own culture, their stereotype of Mexicans is accurate. (b) Measured against the standards used by the Mexicans to make judgments in their own culture, the stereotype is inaccurate. (c) If in future meetings, both groups were to adopt the other's view, the stereotype would be either accurate or inaccurate *for all*. (d) If the two groups were to define a new concept of punctuality, then the accuracy of the stereotype would be assessed against the newly agreed on concept of punctuality.

Step 10

On the basis of the newly gained understanding of both groups' cultures, the two groups must negotiate rules of interaction with which both groups can live. This requires achieving a certain degree of "cultural harmonization." Only then will the two groups be able to manage their cultural differences effectively. This cross-cultural negotiation is done with the facilitator attending to the differences in negotiating styles and practices typical of each culture.

However, as far as cross-cultural training programs and diversity workshops are concerned, two issues should be made clear here. First, in a cross-cultural situation in which communication has broken down because of mutual misunderstandings derived from unchecked stereotypes, to each stereotype held by one group, there is a corresponding counterstereotype held by the other. For example, in the case that has been analyzed here, to the stereotype "Mexicans are the mañana people," there is the counterstereotype "Americans are like machines," which can also be systematically analyzed or assessed through the 10 steps above.

Second, although we go through these steps, it means neither that we can resolve all intergroup conflicts nor that we can definitely achieve cultural harmony. In other words, there may still be problems between groups or cultures. Intercultural negotiation rules (e.g., stereotype exposure analysis), though sometimes necessary, may not be sufficient.

DISCUSSION

CSAM Model: Comparisons Between the Cases

Obviously, Case 1 was different from Case 2 in the following ways. First, Case 1 pertained to the cultural difference between Easterners and Westerners, whereas Case 2 involved the difference between two North American cultures: Mexico and the United States. Second, Case 1 was quantitatively supported and discussed, whereas Case 2 was qualitatively and systematically analyzed. Third, in Case 1, stereotype accuracy was understood as the reflection of cultural difference and identity (equality vs. respect or rigorous vs. easygoing in the workplace), whereas in Case 2, stereotype accuracy lay in the systematic stereotype exposure analysis or the using of different cultural standards (e.g., mañana vs. machinelike in terms of a sense of time).

However, these cases are interrelated. First, stereotype accuracy can be understood as the correspondence between perceived difference in each culture's behavior and the objective difference in each culture's behavior. Second, stereotype accuracy depends on how people of stereotyping and stereotyped cultures interpret stereotypes. The meanings of stereotypes play an important role in human behavior and beliefs. The ultimate goal of this understanding is more effective management of cross-cultural differences. We call this approach to stereotype accuracy the *cultural stereotype accuracy–meaning model.*

Specifically, in the analysis of Case 1, the stereotypes of Americans and Asians are probabilistically accurate because they reflect certain objective differences between cultures (i.e., reflection of intercultural differences). In keeping with the research by McCauley and his colleagues (McCauley, Stitt, & Segal, 1980), some stereotypes can function as predictions rather than prejudice. Furthermore, if one culture accepts (i.e., understands the meaning of) those stereotypes and even feels proud of them, people in this culture may tend to identify themselves with those stereotypes (i.e., cultural identity). In other words, the meanings of stereotypic perceptions or observations may accurately capture cultural differences and cultural identity. This is consistent with our first assumption that stereotype accuracy lies in the reflection of cultural difference and identity.

Apropos of the analysis of Case 2, the stereotype exposure analysis suggests that in a cross-cultural situation, it is critical to show how stereotype accuracy and inaccuracy are a result of the way in which the stereotyping and stereotyped groups understand *their own* cultural values, beliefs, assumptions, and so on. That is, the degree of accuracy (or inaccuracy) depends on how stereotyping and stereotyped cultural groups use their criteria to understand the meanings behind those stereotypic beliefs and behaviors. This understanding may be gained through stereotype assessment or stereotype exposure analysis. For instance, Mexicans are situation or context oriented, whereas Americans are task oriented. Whether Mexicans are mañana people or Americans are machinelike depends on who sees it and how it is interpreted. Therefore, in keeping with our second assumption, stereotype accuracy is contingent on the cultural standards we tend to use.

One may raise the following question, Does Case 1 seem to be a different evaluation, whereas Case 2 seems to be different meaning? Not really. Though we agree that a difference in meaning is not necessarily a difference in valence, as we discussed in the beginning, evaluations (of one's cultural values and stereotypic beliefs) or identities (with those values or stereotypes) in Case 1 would be of no avail if people do not first grasp the *meanings* of those cultural values and stereotypic beliefs. In other words, both cases emphasize the meaning or understanding of cultural stereotypes and cultural differences.

Take Case 1, for example. These stereotypes of American culture or Japanese culture correspond to the cultural reality, in our opinion (as a third party), but both Peter and Mr. Watanabe may understand only the meaning of his own respective cultural values and stereotypes (e.g., equality vs. respect/hierarchy), view these values and stereotypes as positive, and finally tend to identify himself with them. A person (e.g., Peter) from Culture A (e.g., United States) may not understand the meaning of the values and stereotypes related to Culture B (e.g., Japan) to the extent that another person (e.g., Mr. Watanabe) from Culture B does. Similarly, in Case 2, we (i.e., authors or facilitators), as a third party, think stereotypes of Mexicans or Americans are accurate and inaccurate but depend also on who the stereotyping and stereotyped groups are and how they are interpreted. Mañana may be an accurate stereotype for Americans, but an inaccurate stereotype for Mexicans. In terms of valence, this stereotype may be negative. American businessmen sometimes say "Mexicans are mañana people," so as to express their frustration and anger, whereas Mexicans may refuse to accept it or refuse to identify themselves with it. Instead, they call Americans "machines." In brief, with the emphasis on how stereotypes are understood, both cases have revealed unpleasant conflict and frustration between cultures, and the CSAM model may help people of different cultures to cope with unpleasant conflict and frustration and to manage their cultural differences more effectively.

Applications of Stereotype Research to Cross-Cultural Training and Management

Although there are many approaches to diversity workshops and cross-cultural training programs (see Chu & McCauley, 1995), our current CSAM model suggests that the meanings of stereotypes (or the way to understand stereotypes) play a very important role in stereotype accuracy (and inaccuracy) in our cross-cultural management.

Succinctly put, these two cases, though different, are both consistent with the CSAM model in that they offer us the idea that cultural stereotype accuracy or inaccuracy depends on the cultural meanings that stereotypes hold to people, that is, how they understand or interpret cultural stereotypes. This cultural understanding is not easily achieved if researchers in psychology and management are not culture oriented. It would be naive to underestimate the difficulty of achieving true cross-cultural understanding, which Duenas (1994) called "intercultural understanding." As he observed:

> "Intercultural understanding" is not only about "understanding another culture"—as is usually defined in the literature of cross-cultural management. Rather, it is about trying to understand the world using another culture's meanings and theories, and developing the emotional empathy that goes with this experience. Furthermore, it is also about understanding the world in completely new ways. (p. 210)

Only through this kind of intercultural understanding can the various cultural groups invent new rules of interaction that may lead to a better management of cultural differences.

To be more explicit and relevant, if big money in national or international corporations or business is not enough to resolve stereotype problems, then it seems likely that there is enough accuracy in stereotypes to make accuracy worth studying. At least the way to approach stereotypes in cross-cultural programs should be assessed and reconsidered.

In the United States, although many diversity workshops are organized to eliminate stereotypes at colleges or in companies each year, participants still have the same stereotypes after their workshops. If people continue to use certain stereotypes, that may mean some stereotypes are accurate. We, psychologists and other social scientists, may consider stereotype accuracy and inaccuracy simultaneously. In other words, the traditional way to approach stereotypes in the diversity workshops or in cross-cultural training programs should be reconsidered.

CONCLUSION

Two main conclusions can be reached from this analysis. First, some stereotypes are accurate when they objectively reflect cultural differences, as can be seen in Case 1. Stereotypes may suggest cultural differences and identity. At this point, discovering the meanings of cultural stereotypes may help us to understand and appreciate cultural differences and identity.

Second, the degree of stereotype accuracy (or inaccuracy), as can be seen in Case 2, depends on what cultural standards people use, who the stereotyping groups are, and who the stereotyped groups are. A cultural stereotype may be accurate when the standards of behavior of the stereotyping culture are used and, at the same time, inaccurate when the standards of the culture being stereotyped are used. The stereotype exposure analysis (or the assessment of stereotype accuracy) proposed in Case 2 helps us to see the meaning of the "mañana people" or "machines."

There are a number of implications in this research. First, in keeping with cultural relativism, understanding stereotype accuracy does not suggest that one culture's ways or views are better than another's. The purposes of our CSAM model are (a) to increase cultural understanding and appreciation (e.g., cultural relativism, diversity, and identity) and (b) to achieve cultural harmony (Triandis, 1994) in communication and inter-action between social groups and nations.

Second, studying the accuracy of cultural stereotypes is not a way of *preventing conflict* between the interacting groups. We believe that the CSAM model we propose here is a useful mechanism to *manage conflict* more effectively and may help us to better grasp the positive and negative connotations of cultural stereotypes and expressions.

Third, realization of stereotype accuracy and inaccuracy in one's per-ception of another culture does not necessarily ensure improved collabo-ration between the groups. There may be other factors involved (e.g., per-sonality or politics). However, we believe that the understanding and assessment of the meanings of cultural stereotypes are the first steps. From there, cultural groups may come to understand the accuracy and inaccu-racy of their perceptions and then negotiate rules of interaction, which they may have to invent, to achieve cultural harmony. Therefore, when we believe that cultural stereotypes have a kernel of truth or accuracy and try to understand the meanings behind them, we will be more sensitive to them and be able to participate in national and international business or cross-cultural collaboration more effectively.

Finally, let us end this chapter with the following questions. If people inevitably use cultural stereotypes, why do psychologists, management re-searchers, and other social scientists or cross-cultural trainers insist on changing their stereotypes rather than changing our research approach by considering stereotype accuracy and inaccuracy simultaneously? Although national and international corporations, agencies, and institutions have invested a tremendous amount of money and time to resolving cultural or gender stereotype problems (e.g., diversity workshops and cross-cultural training programs), why has this approach not worked? Is it pos-sible that there is enough accuracy in stereotypes to make the accuracy and inaccuracy worth studying simultaneously?

REFERENCES

Ajzen, I. (1988). *Attitudes, personality, and behavior.* Stratford, England: Open Uni-versity Press.

Ajzen, I., & Fishbein, M. (1980). *Understanding attitudes and predicting social behavior.* Englewood Cliffs, NJ: Prentice Hall.

Allport, G. (1954). *The nature of prejudice.* Reading, MA: Addison-Wesley.

Amir, Y. (1969). Contact hypothesis in ethnic relations. *Psychological Bulletin, 71,* 319–343.

Bond, M., Wan, K., Leung, K., & Giacalone, R. (1985). How are responses to verbal insults related to cultural collectivism and power distance? *Journal of Cross-Cultural Psychology, 16,* 111–127.

Borisoff, D., & Victor, D. (1989). *Conflict management.* Englewood Cliffs, NJ: Prentice Hall.

Brewer, M., & Miller, N. (1988). Contact and cooperation: When do they work? In P. A. Katz & D. Taylor (Eds.), *Toward the elimination of racism: Profiles in controversy.* New York: Plenum.

Brislin, R. (1993). *Understanding culture's influence on behavior.* Forth Worth, TX: Harcourt Brace Jovanovich.

Bruner, E. M. (1956). Primary group experience and the process of acculturation. *American Anthropologist, 58,* 605–623.

Bruner, J. (1990). *Acts of meaning.* Cambridge, MA: Harvard University Press.

Campbell, D. T. (1964). Distinguishing differences of perception from failures of communication in cross-cultural studies. In F. S. Northrop & H. H. Livingston (Eds.), *Cross-cultural understanding: Epistemology in anthropology.* New York: Harper & Row.

Campbell, D. T. (1967). Stereotypes and the perception of group differences. *American Psychologist, 22,* 817–829.

Campbell, D.T. (1975). On the conflicts between biological and social evolution and between psychology and moral tradition. *American Psychologist, 30,* 1103–1126.

Carey, J. (1994). Multinational enterprises. In L. L. Adler & U. P. Gielen (Eds.),*Cross-cultural topics in psychology* (pp. 155–163). Westport, CT: Praeger.

Chinese Culture Connection. (1987). Chinese values and the search for culture-free dimensions of culture. *Journal of Cross-Cultural Psychology, 18,* 143–164.

Chu, J. Y., & McCauley, C. (1995). *Cross-cultural training.* Manuscript in preparation, Department of Psychology, Bryn Mawr College, Pennsylvania.

Cox, T. (1993). *Cultural diversity in organizations: Theory research and practice.* San Francisco: Berrett-Koetiler.

Coyne, R., & O'Neil, J. (1992). *Organization consultation: A casebook.* Newbury Park, CA: Sage.

Duenas, G. (1994). Toward a theory of intercultural learning. *Teoria Sociologica, 2* (3), 193–215.

Fishbein, M., & Ajzen, I. (1975). *Belief and attitude, intention and behavior: An introduction to theory and research.* Reading, MA: Addison-Wesley.

Geertz, C. (1973). *The interpretation of cultures.* New York: Basic Books.

Gielen, U. P. (1994). American mainstream psychology and its relationship to international and cross-cultural psychology. In A. L. Communian & U. P. Gielen (Eds.), *Advancing psychology and its applications: International perspectives.* Milan, Italy: FrancoAngeli.

Hall, E. T. (1976). *Beyond culture.* New York: Anchor Press/Doubleday.

Hall, E., & Hall, M. (1990). *Understanding cultural differences.* Yarmouth, ME: Intercultural Press.

Hatch, M. J. (1993). The dynamics of organizational culture. *Academy of Management Review, 18,* 657–693.

Hofstede, G. (1980). *Culture's consequences: International differences in work-related values.* Newbury Park, CA: Sage.

Hofstede, G. (1991). *Cultures and organizations: Software of the mind.* New York: McGraw-Hill.

Hofstede, G., & Bond, M. (1988). The Confucius connection: From cultural roots to economic growth. *Organizational Dynamics, 16,* 4–21.

Ichheiser, G. (1949). Sociopsychological and cultural factors in race relations. *American Journal of Sociology, 54,* 395–401.

Ichheiser, G. (1970). *Appearances and realities: Misunderstanding in human relations.* San Francisco: Jossey-Bass.

Jackson, S., & associates. (1992). *Diversity in the workplace: Human resources initiatives.* New York: Guilford Press.

Jussim, L. (1991). Social perception and social reality: A reflection and construction model. *Psychological Review, 98,* 54–73.

Kenny, D. (1994). *Interpersonal perception: A social relations analysis.* New York: Guilford Press.

Lee, Y. T. (1993). Perceived homogeneity and familial loyalty between Chinese and Americans. *Current Psychology, 12,* 260–267.

Lee, Y. T. (1994a). Stereotypes, ingroup homogeneity and social identity theory in intergroup contact and comparison. *Teoria Sociologica, 3,* 162–175.

Lee, Y. T. (1994b). Why does American psychology have cultural limitations? *American Psychologist, 49,* 524.

Lee, Y. T. (1995). A comparison of politics and personality in China and in the U. S.: Testing a "kernel of truth" hypothesis. *Journal of Contemporary China. 9,* 56-68.

Lee, Y. T., & Ottati, V. (1993). Determinants of ingroup and outgroup perceptions of heterogeneity: An investigation of Sino–American stereotypes. *Journal of Cross-Cultural Psychology, 24,* 298–318.

Lee, Y. T., & Ottati, V. (1995). Perceived ingroup membership salience and stereotype threat homogeneity as a function of group. *Personality and Social Psychology Bulletin, 21,* 610–619.

Lee, Y. T., Pellicci, J., & Hogan, D. (1994, April). *Outgroup negativity and positivity vs. optimal ingroup favoritism: Stereotypes in our daily life.* Paper presented at the 65th Annual Conference of the Eastern Psychological Association, Providence, RI.

LeVine, R. A., & Campbell, D. T. (1972). *Ethnocentrism.* New York: Wiley.

McArthur, L. Z., & Baron, R. M. (1983). Toward an ecological theory of social perception. *Psychological Review, 90,* 215–238.

McCauley, C., Stitt, C. L., & Segal, M. (1980). Stereotyping: From prejudice to prediction. *Psychological Bulletin, 87,* 195–208.

Miller, N., & Brewer, M. (Eds.). (1984). *Groups in contact: The psychology of desegregation.* Orlando, FL: Academic Press.

Oakes, P. J., Haslam, S. A., & Turner, J. C. (1994). *Stereotyping and social reality.* Cambridge, MA: Basil Blackwell.

Osgood, C. E. (1979). *Focus on meaning.* New York: Mouton.

Pepitone, A. (1989). Toward a cultural psychology. *Psychology and Developing Society, 1,* 5–19.

Pye, L. W. (1992). *Chinese negotiation style: Commercial approaches and cultural principles.* New York: Quorum Books.

Rosen, L. (1991). The integrity of cultures. *American Behavioral Scientist, 34,* 594–617.

Schein, E. H. (1985). *Organizational culture and leadership.* San Francisco: Jossey-Bass.

Shi, J. (1988). *Selected readings from famous Chinese philosophy.* Beijing: People's University Press (in Chinese and English).

Tajfel, H. (1981). *Human groups and social categories.* Cambridge, England: Cambridge University Press.

Tajfel, H., & Turner, J. C. (1986). The social identity theory of intergroup behavior.

In S. Worchel & W. G. Austin (Eds.), *Psychology of intergroup relations* (pp. 7–24). Chicago: Nelson-Hall.

Triandis, H. (1994). *Culture and social behavior.* New York: McGraw-Hill.

Triandis, H., Brislin, R., & Hui, H. (1988). Cross-cultural training across the individualism–collective divide. *International Journal of Intercultural Relations, 12,* 269–289.

Triandis, H., & Vassiliou, V. (1967). Frequency of contact and stereotyping. *Journal of Personality and Social Psychology, 7,* 316–328.

PART THREE

Empirical Studies of Accuracy and Inaccuracy in Stereotypes

8

Motivations and the Perceiver's Group Membership: Consequences for Stereotype Accuracy

Carey S. Ryan

S ocial stereotypes have long been assumed to be inaccurate. This assumption underlies nearly all of the most influential theories of stereotyping and prejudice (Ryan, Park, & Judd, in press), including, for example, scapegoating (Dollard, Doob, Miller, Mowrer, & Sears, 1939), realistic group conflict theory (Sherif & Sherif, 1953), and social cognition theories of social categorization (Hamilton & Trolier, 1986). Despite the ubiquity of this assumption, however, there have been few empirical investigations of stereotype accuracy. Furthermore, the work that has been done has focused primarily on whether particular cultural stereotypes are accurate or inaccurate (e.g., Abate & Berrien, 1967; McCauley & Stitt, 1978; Swim, 1994) or on the complex methodological issues involved in the assessment of stereotype accuracy (e.g., Judd & Park, 1993; McCauley & Stitt, 1978). There has been little research concerning the psychological factors

Preparation of this chapter was partially supported by National Institute of Mental Health (NIMH) Grant R03-MH53509–01. I acknowledge with gratitude the extensive advice of Charles Judd and Bernadette Park and the helpful comments of Richard Moreland and John Levine.

Correspondence concerning this chapter should be addressed to Carey S. Ryan, Department of Psychology, University of Pittsburgh, Pittsburgh, Pennsylvania 15260. Electronic mail may be sent to cryan@vms.cis.pitt.edu.

that may lead some people to be more (or less) accurate than others. (See Judd & Park, 1993, and Ryan et al., in press, for critiques of previous accuracy research.) The purpose of this chapter is to consider the role of one social psychological factor that may affect stereotype accuracy, namely, the perceiver's group membership.

Although the perceiver's group membership has important implications for perceptions of social groups (Linville, Fischer, & Salovey, 1989; Park & Rothbart, 1982), its effects on stereotype accuracy have received little attention. Indeed, previous research appears to be limited to two studies, one examining stereotype accuracy for business and engineering majors (Judd, Ryan, & Park, 1991) and one examining stereotype accuracy for Democrats and Republicans (Judd & Park, 1993). These studies revealed consistent ingroup–outgroup differences in stereotype accuracy. Specifically, stereotypes of outgroups were characterized by greater exaggeration and overgeneralization than were stereotypes of ingroups. Furthermore, subjects demonstrated greater sensitivity to actual between-attributes differences in the characteristics of ingroups as compared with outgroups. Finally, Judd and Park (1993) found that ingroup–outgroup differences in stereotype accuracy were greater for subjects who were more strongly affiliated with their ingroup.

In this chapter, I extend this work to demonstrate that the effects of the perceiver's group membership on stereotype accuracy depend both on the characteristics of the group to which the perceiver belongs and on the particular form of stereotype accuracy that is examined. I begin by providing an overview of four forms of stereotype accuracy and provide a rationale for expecting that qualitatively distinct perceiver-group memberships may lead to different types of inaccuracy. I then present two empirical studies of stereotype accuracy. The first one examines ethnic minority and majority groups that have a history of conflict, strong group loyalties, and a clear disparity in social status, namely, Black Americans and White Americans. The second study examines a type of group membership that has rarely been considered in the stereotyping literature: membership in an interested third party (Billig, 1976).

The accuracy criteria used in both studies are derived from subjects' self-ratings. Because these self-ratings are provided by random samples of group members, they can be considered unbiased estimates of the actual self-ratings of group members. In essence, then, in this chapter, I am defining accuracy as the extent to which subjects' perceptions of a group correspond to the aggregated self-perceptions of the members of that group. (See Judd & Park, 1993; Judd et al., 1991; Ryan et al., in press, for more detailed discussions of the pros and cons of various accuracy criteria.)

HOW MIGHT QUALITATIVELY DISTINCT PERCEIVER-GROUP MEMBERSHIPS AFFECT DIFFERENT FORMS OF STEREOTYPE ACCURACY?

In recent research, stereotypes have been conceptualized as including two primary components: the perceived stereotypicality of a group (i.e., the perceived extremity of the central tendency) and the perceived dispersion, or diversity, of group members (Park & Judd, 1990). For example, two persons may agree that women are generally quite nurturant, but they may perceive very different degrees of dispersion among women. One person may perceive women as being highly diverse, whereas the other may perceive women as being tightly clustered around the group's central tendency. This distinction is important because of its implications for subsequent group-relevant judgments. That is, the perception of variability among group members reflects a degree of uncertainty in the group stereotype. People who perceive greater diversity among group members are, therefore, less likely to use the stereotype to judge individual group members because they perceive it as less likely to apply (Ryan, Judd, & Park, 1993). Furthermore, stereotypic accuracy is not necessarily related to dispersion accuracy (Judd & Park, 1993; Ryan et al., in press); it is, therefore, important to assess the accuracy of both stereotype components.

Assessing the accuracy of social perceptions, however, is highly complex, both conceptually and methodologically. A number of researchers have written about the difficulties involved in accuracy assessment, partially in response to Cronbach's (1955) critical analysis of the use of discrepancy scores as an indicator of accuracy. These discussions are available both in the person-perception literature (e.g., Funder, 1987) and in the stereotyping literature (e.g., Judd & Park, 1993; Ryan et al., in press). I, therefore, review only those methodological issues that are necessary to the discussion that follows. Interested readers should refer to these other papers for more detailed discussions of the methodological problems involved in accuracy assessment.

Of particular interest to the present discussion are the two kinds of measures that have been used to assess stereotype accuracy: discrepancy scores and within-subject sensitivity correlations. Most often, researchers examining stereotype accuracy have used discrepancy scores to assess the extent to which subjects over- or underestimate the actual characteristics of a group. For each subject, a discrepancy score is computed to assess the difference between the subject's perception of the group's stereotypicality and an accuracy criterion that is intended to reflect the actual stereotypicality of the group. Stereotypes would be considered exaggerations to the extent that perceptions of the group's central tendency overestimate the actual central tendency of the group on stereotypic dimensions and underestimate the actual central tendency of the group on counterstereotypic dimensions (Judd & Park, 1993). That is, in the case of exaggeration, the group is perceived to conform to the stereotype to a larger extent than it actually does. Similarly, a discrepancy score can be computed to assess the extent to which subjects under- or overestimate the actual dispersion of group members. To the extent that the actual dispersion of group members is underestimated, stereotypes would be characterized as overgeneralizations about the group (Judd & Park, 1993). Note, however, that discrepancy scores must be limited to the assessment of relative differences in accuracy; they cannot be used to assess accuracy in an absolute sense (Cronbach, 1955; Judd & Park, 1993; Ryan et al., in press). This is because of various response language confounds, or biases, that may result from the type of judgment task or from systematic differences among subjects in their use of response scales. For example, previous research indicates that the standard deviation measure of perceived group dispersion yields systematically higher judgments than does the range measure (Judd et al., 1991).

Within-subject sensitivity correlations provide a conceptually and methodologically distinct measure of stereotype accuracy. This measure involves computing, for each subject across attributes, the correlation between a subject's judgments of the group and the group's actual standing on each dimension. Correlations can be computed to assess the extent to which subjects' perceptions of the group's central tendency are sensitive to the group's actual central tendency from one attribute dimension to another. Similarly, they can be computed to assess the extent to which subjects' perceptions of a group's dispersion correspond to the actual dispersion of group members from one attribute dimension to another. Higher correlations reflect greater accuracy, that is, greater sensitivity to variations between attributes in the group's actual characteristics. Within-subject correlations are not vulnerable to the sorts of confounds that occur for discrepancy scores and, therefore, provide an appealing assessment alternative.

As I indicated above, these measures are also conceptually distinct, so that one might expect the effects of the perceiver's group membership on accuracy to depend not only on the type of group membership but also on the kind of accuracy that is examined. Groups may differ in the extent to which each of two general types of motivations is likely to operate: the desire to know and have a relatively accurate conception of social reality, to predict and control one's environment (e.g., Fiske, 1993), and the desire for a positive social identity (e.g., Tajfel & Turner, 1986). For example, one might expect individuals who belong to less powerful groups to be more strongly motivated to attain an accurate conception of more powerful outgroups. Furthermore, certain group memberships are likely to be more central to one's social identity, thereby increasing the motivation to attain a positive social identity with respect to that group. To the extent that group memberships differ in the relative importance of these motivations, then, there may be different effects on discrepancy measures of stereotype accuracy than on sensitivity-correlation measures.

Consider the effects of the perceiver's group membership on stereotype accuracy from a social identity perspective. According to social identity theory, individuals are motivated to maintain a positive social identity, and this is based primarily on self-categorization into meaningful social groups and comparisons with other group members (Tajfel & Turner, 1986; Turner, Hogg, Oakes, Reicher, & Wetherell, 1987). Individuals accentuate between-groups differences and within-group similarities to strengthen their social identity. The implications of this for discrepancy measures of stereotype accuracy seem clear. The accentuation of between-groups differences should lead to stereotype exaggeration (i.e., overestimation of the prevalence of stereotypic attributes and underestimation of the prevalence of counterstereotypic attributes), and the accentuation of within-group similarities should lead to overgeneralization (i.e., underestimation of the dispersion of group members), both of which are assessed by discrepancy scores (Judd & Park, 1993; Ryan et al., in press). Discrepancy measures of accuracy, then, should be strongly influenced by the desire to maintain a strong group identity. On the other hand, social identity theory does not make predictions about sensitivity-correlation measures of stereotype accuracy, which reflect the ability to discern a group's standing on one attribute dimension versus another; for example, the ability to discern whether Black Americans are more academically intelligent than they are athletic. Thus, there is no compelling reason, either conceptually or methodologically, why social identity motivations should influence sensitivity correlations.

Now consider the effects of the motivation to have an accurate conception of social reality on stereotype accuracy. The effects of this motivation seem clear for sensitivity-correlation measures. It seems reasonable that a strong motivation to have an accurate understanding of a group should be reflected in higher sensitivity correlations. A strong motivation to attain an accurate knowledge of, for example, Black Americans should enable one to discern whether the group is more academically intelligent than athletic. However, one might expect an accuracy motivation to have less influence on discrepancy measures. Discrepancy measures assess a systematic tendency to under- or overestimate a group's characteristics. Although the lack of motivation to attain an accurate conception of a group should indeed result in higher discrepancies (i.e., greater inaccuracy), such an effect will be apparent only if the individual displays a systematic tendency in one direction or another; for example, toward the underestimation of dispersion or the overestimation of stereotypicality. Otherwise, positive and negative discrepancies will offset each other, resulting in lower discrepancies whether the individual is highly or weakly motivated to attain an accurate conception of the group.

Of course, the motivations to strengthen social identity and to obtain an accurate conception of a group may often go hand in hand, resulting in similar effects on different measures of stereotype accuracy. Consider, for example, the case of membership in an occupational group that involves the motivation for a positive and relatively strong identification with the group as well as the need for a relatively accurate conception of that group, especially as compared with some other occupational outgroup. One might expect to find that the members of such groups have stereotypes of their own group that are much more accurate than their stereotypes of the outgroup, regardless of the type of accuracy examined. That is, such group members are likely to demonstrate less stereotype exaggeration and overgeneralization in their stereotypes of their own group, as well as greater sensitivity to between-attributes differences in its actual characteristics. In other instances, however, motivations associated with group membership may conflict with one another, perhaps resulting in greater accuracy on one type of accuracy measure and less accuracy on another. In this chapter, I consider two such cases: ethnic minority (i.e., Black American) versus majority (i.e., White American) group membership and membership in a relatively neutral third party that has an interest in attaining an accurate conception of two other target groups (Billig, 1976), that is, Independents versus Democrats and Republicans in the United States.

To summarize, there are four forms of accuracy that are of concern in the present chapter: the extent to which the group's actual stereotypicality (i.e., the actual extremity of the central tendency) is under- or overestimated, the extent to which the group's actual dispersion is under- or overestimated, sensitivity to differences in the actual central tendency of the group from one attribute to another, and sensitivity to differences in the actual dispersion of the group from one attribute to another. Furthermore, certain motivations that are likely to be associated with group membership may result in some types of groups being more accurate on one measure, but less accurate on another. In general, I am concerned with the motives to maintain a positive social identity, which is likely to lead one to accentuate between-groups differences and within-group similarities, thereby affecting discrepancy measures, and the need for a relatively accurate understanding of a group as a whole, which may be most evident in higher sensitivity correlations.

ETHNIC MINORITY VERSUS MAJORITY GROUP DIFFERENCES IN STEREOTYPE ACCURACY

Social psychologists have long been interested in the social perceptions and behavior of minority versus majority group members, because of the implications for understanding social problems involving stereotyping, prejudice, and social change. Belonging to a social group that constitutes the minority of some larger group is believed to provide different sorts of psychological experiences than those experienced by members of the majority. For example, minority group members may encounter opposition to their beliefs and behaviors much more frequently than do members of a majority. Minority group members may therefore be especially vulnerable to social alienation and exclusion. Moreover, minority group members may be forced to adopt the majority group's behaviors and attitudes or to learn certain styles of interaction, in an effort to influence indirectly the views of majority group members. It seems reasonable, then, that there may be rather different motivations affecting the kinds of group-relevant judgments that ethnic minority versus majority group members make. Social psychologists have provided compelling evidence that this may indeed be the case.

Consider, for example, the work on minority versus majority group differences in the perceived variability of social groups. Although this research has defined minorities and majorities almost exclusively in terms of the number of group members, it has obvious implications for members of ethnic groups. Researchers working from social identity theory

(Tajfel & Turner, 1986), and, more recently, from self-categorization theory (Turner et al., 1987), have argued that there are threats to positive social identity associated with minority status, for example, social alienation and exclusion. These sorts of threats should lead to greater category accentuation on the part of minority group members, as they attempt to strengthen their group identity in response to the threat. Thus, some researchers have demonstrated that members of a minority group perceive their own group to be less variable than a majority outgroup (Simon, 1992; Simon & Brown, 1987). Other research also suggests that group membership may be more psychologically meaningful to minority group members than to majority group members. For example, Ellemers (1993) showed that members of groups that have lower status and relatively impermeable boundaries tend to be more highly identified with their group. Other researchers argued that membership in a majority group is less central to one's social identity than membership in a minority group (Abrams, 1994; Brewer, 1993; Mullen, 1991).

This research suggests, then, that minority group members will demonstrate greater inaccuracy when accuracy is assessed using discrepancy scores. That is, minority group subjects should demonstrate greater exaggeration and overgeneralization in their stereotypes of their ingroup and outgroup as compared with majority group subjects who feel less threatened and for whom group membership may be less psychologically meaningful. To understand the effects that minority versus majority group membership might have on sensitivity correlations, let us now consider research concerning the effects of status differences on interpersonal perceptions.

Fiske (1993) argued that people are more attentive to those who are more powerful, in an effort to predict and perhaps influence their outcomes. Black Americans may find themselves in a less powerful position in relation to White Americans, particularly in a predominantly White environment. Black Americans may, therefore, be more highly motivated to attain an accurate conception of White Americans, which, as I indicated earlier, should lead to higher sensitivity correlations. More specifically, I would expect minority group members to demonstrate as much sensitivity to actual differences in the prevalence of attributes for the outgroup as they do for their own group. Conversely, because understanding the minority group is much less important to members of the majority, majority group members would be expected to demonstrate greater sensitivity to actual differences in the prevalence of attributes for their own group as compared with their perceptions of the minority outgroup. In other words, majority group members ought to be much more accurate in their judgments of their own group than in their judgments of the outgroup, when sensitivity correlations are examined. And minority group members should exhibit little, if any, difference in the accuracy of their perceptions of their own group versus the outgroup.

In an effort to test these hypotheses, I asked random samples of Black American and White American college students at the University of Colorado at Boulder to provide judgments of stereotypicality and dispersion for both their ingroup and outgroup. Stereotypicality was assessed by asking subjects to estimate the percentage of group members that they believed would have certain traits or that would agree with various attitude statements. These traits and attitude statements were either stereotypic or counterstereotypic of the group and either positive or negative in valence. The specific attributes are given in Table 1. Dispersion was assessed by having subjects indicate where they believed the two most extreme (i.e., highest and lowest) members of a group would fall along each of these same attribute dimensions. Subjects made identical judgments for their ingroup and outgroup, and target-group order was counterbalanced across subjects.

After judging both target groups, subjects responded to 13 items assessing their familiarity with members of the outgroup. For example, subjects used 7–point scales to indicate the extent to which their friends in high school were members of the outgroup and the extent to which their current friends were outgroup members. Finally, subjects rated themselves on each of the same attribute dimensions listed in Table 1; these self-ratings were used to compute the actual stereotypicality and dispersion of the group. Because random samples of students participated, with a 94% participation rate, subjects' self-ratings provided unbiased estimates of the

	Table 1	

Attribute Dimensions as a Function of Stereotypicality and Valence

Stereotypic	Counterstereotypic
	Positive
Athletic	Academically intelligent
Dance well	Participates in campus social activities
Strong emotional bonds	High SAT math scores
to family	At least one parent has a college degree
"I believe taking Ethnic Studies	Parents' combined annual income
courses is an important part	is greater than $50,000
of a college education."	
	Negative
Sexually aggressive	Self-centered
Likely to drop out of college	"I have usually been given whatever material
Financial support from	things I needed or wanted without having to
athletic scholarships	work for them."
Grew up in a household in	Spends money frivolously
which the father was absent.	"I considered skiing opportunities an
	important factor in deciding to attend CU."

NOTE: Stereotypic attributes are stereotypic of Black Americans and counterstereotypic of White Americans; counterstereotypic attributes are counterstereotypic of Black Americans and stereotypic of White Americans. CU = Colorado University.

actual self-perceptions of the members of these groups. Thus, as I indicated earlier, accuracy was defined as the extent to which subjects' judgments of the group reflected the aggregated self-perceptions of the members of that group.

I first examined discrepancies between subjects' perceptions of the stereotypicality of the group and the group's actual stereotypicality derived from members' self-ratings. These discrepancies were analyzed as a function of subject group, target group, and attribute stereotypicality, with repeated measures on the last two factors. The results are displayed in Figure 1. Stereotype exaggeration refers to the overestimation of stereotypic

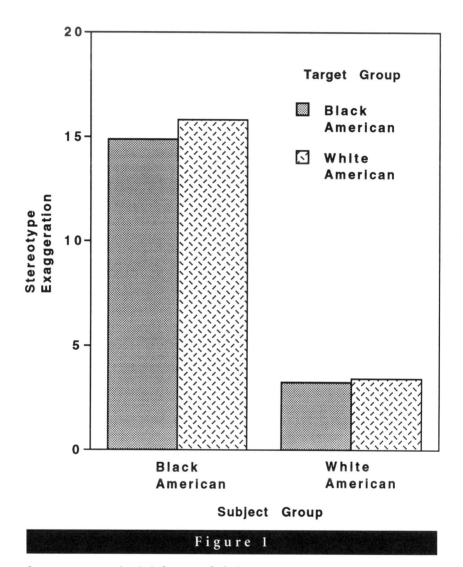

Figure 1

Stereotype exaggeration in judgments of ethnic groups.

versus counterstereotypic attributes. As the figure indicates, overall, subjects perceived both groups to be more stereotypic than the group members perceived themselves to be, $F(1, 89) = 113.85$, $p < .001$. In addition, this difference depended on subject group, so that Black American subjects overestimated the stereotypicality of both groups to a larger extent

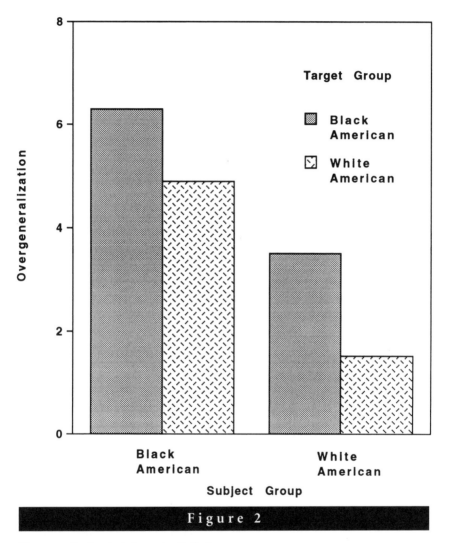

Figure 2

Overgeneralization in judgments of ethnic groups.

than did White American subjects, $F(1, 89) = 45.60$, $p < .001$. Interestingly, this difference did not depend on target group. That is, Black American subjects exhibited greater stereotypic inaccuracy than did White American subjects, and this was as true for the Black American target group as for the White American target group.

I similarly examined discrepancies between subjects' perceptions of the dispersion of the groups and the actual dispersion (i.e., range) of group members' self-ratings. These results are displayed in Figure 2. *Overgeneralization* refers to the tendency to underestimate the actual dispersion of the group. Note that while subjects exhibited a general tendency to overgeneralize, this may simply be a function of the particular task subjects were asked to complete. Previous work indicates that subjects tend to underestimate the range of distributions (Judd et al., 1991). My primary interest was in the effects of subject group and target group. As Figure 2 indicates, Black American subjects underestimated dispersion more than did White American subjects, $F(1, 89) = 21.70$, $p < .001$. In addition, all subjects underestimated the dispersion of the Black American target group more than they did the White American target group, $F(1, 89) = 65.05$, $p < .001$.

In summary, the results of the discrepancy analyses are in keeping with predictions from social identity theory. On the whole, Black American subjects showed greater stereotype exaggeration and overgeneralization in their perceptions of both their ingroup and their outgroup, as compared with White American subjects.

A different pattern of results emerged, however, when within-subject sensitivity correlations were examined. Recall that these correlations indicate the extent to which subjects are sensitive to between-attributes differences in the stereotypicality (or dispersion) of the group members' self-perceptions, with higher correlations reflecting greater sensitivity. The mean sensitivity correlations for perceived stereotypicality indicate that overall, Black American subjects were more sensitive to such differences than were White American subjects (Ms = .413 and .358, respectively), $F(1, 91) = 5.68$, $p < .02$. In other words, Black American subjects were more accurate. Furthermore, Black American subjects displayed a much smaller difference than did White American subjects in their sensitivity to actual differences in the prevalence of attributes for their own group, as compared with the outgroup, $F(1, 91) = 3.92$, $p = .05$. Indeed, Black Americans were actually somewhat more accurate in their judgments of the outgroup ($M = .479$) than in their judgments of the ingroup ($M =$

.347), and White Americans were much more accurate in their judgments of the ingroup ($M = .483$) than the outgroup ($M = .232$). Finally, overall, subjects demonstrated greater accuracy in their judgments of the White American target group than in their judgments of the Black American target group ($Ms = .481$ and $.289$, respectively), $F(1, 91) = 73.02$, $p < .001$.

Now let us turn to sensitivity correlations for perceived dispersion. These correlations assess the correspondence between subjects' perceptions of group dispersion and the actual dispersion of self-reported judgments from one attribute dimension to another. Overall, White American subjects were more accurate than Black American subjects ($Ms = .123$ and $.014$, respectively), $F(1, 89) = 4.88$, $p < .05$; and judgments of the White American target group were more accurate than judgments of the Black American target group ($Ms = .134$ and $.003$, respectively), $F(1, 89) = 9.02$, $p < .01$. But there was also a reliable Subject Group × Target Group interaction, $F(1, 89) = 3.87$, $p = .05$, so that Black American subjects were slightly more accurate (or less inaccurate) in their judgments of the outgroup ($M = .034$) as compared with judgments of the ingroup ($M = -.007$); White American subjects, on the other hand, were much more accurate in their judgments of the ingroup ($M = .234$) than in their judgments of the outgroup ($M = .012$). Results from within-subject sensitivity-correlation measures of accuracy, then, demonstrate a much smaller target-group difference on the part of Black American subjects. Furthermore, Black American subjects were more accurate in the first analysis. And, although White American subjects were more accurate overall in the second analysis, this was due to the particularly high accuracy with which they judged their own group. Finally, all subjects were more accurate in their judgments of the White American target group.

One might wonder what influence familiarity with the outgroup might have on stereotype accuracy, particularly for these two groups. Black American college students on a predominantly White American college campus are undoubtedly more familiar with the outgroup than are White American college students. Furthermore, greater familiarity with the outgroup might explain the lack of a target-group difference in the sensitivity correlations of Black Americans. Note, however, that differences in familiarity with the outgroup cannot account for the greater accuracy of White Americans when discrepancy scores were analyzed. Furthermore, I examined the extent to which familiarity with the outgroup correlated with the within-subject sensitivity correlations. Recall that subjects responded to a series of items assessing their familiarity with members of the outgroup. A principal components analysis of these items yielded one factor, accounting for 47% of the variance. (The eigenvalue for this factor was 6.09, with the next largest eigenvalue equal to 1.49.) These items were, therefore, combined into a single Outgroup Familiarity factor score, which was then correlated with each of the two within-subject sensitivity correlations for each subject group separately. Although these analyses revealed a tendency for greater familiarity with the outgroup to be related to more accurate perceptions of the outgroup, none of the correlations were reliable. Perhaps somewhat surprisingly, then, familiarity with the outgroup did not influence the extent to which subjects' perceptions of the groups accurately reflected the group members' aggregated self-reports. Next, let us consider the effects of a different sort of perceiver-group membership, that is, membership in an interested third party, on discrepancy and within-subject sensitivity-correlation measures of stereotypic accuracy.

THE PERCEIVER AS AN INTERESTED THIRD PARTY

Understanding the effects of membership in an interested third party seems important to our understanding of stereotypes, conflict resolution, and intergroup relations. It is a role that perceivers often play—sometimes formally, as in the case of jurists or mediators in contract disputes, and sometimes informally, as in the case of bystanders who observe an important event. It seems reasonable to expect differences in stereotype accuracy as a function of perceivers' membership in an interested third party as compared with their membership, for example, in an ingroup or outgroup. Let us consider one particular case—that of Independents' perceptions of Democrats and Republicans in the United States.

Independents have a qualitatively different sort of relationship to the

Democratic and Republican parties than do the members of these groups themselves. First, as the label suggests, *Independents* are unlikely to have a social identity based on membership in either target group. At the same time, they do not truly seem to be outgroup members. Rather, Independents appear to be part of a much looser and more informal group. They are often wooed by both target groups during election campaigns. And they generally do not compete with either of the target groups in any significant way. They would not, therefore, seem particularly motivated to distinguish themselves from either of the target groups in the same way that ingroups and outgroups, or minorities and majorities, might. In addition, given that Democrats and Republicans are clearly the dominant forces in U.S. politics, Independents have a clear interest in attaining a relatively accurate conception of the two target groups' positions on political issues.

What predictions could we make about the accuracy of Independents' perceptions of Democrats and Republicans? First, we would expect Independents' perceptions of the two target groups to be about equally accurate, regardless of the type of accuracy that is examined. That is, we would not expect to find the sort of target-group difference in accuracy that would be expected from perceivers who are members of one of the two target groups being judged. And, because they are likely to be interested in, and familiar with, the two parties, Independents should generally be at least as accurate as the group members themselves. Furthermore, because Independents ought to be least affected by the sorts of motivations that lead to stereotype exaggeration and overgeneralization, their stereotypes should be more accurate than those of outgroup members as shown in discrepancy scores. Finally, members of an interested third party are presumably motivated to obtain a relatively accurate understanding of the groups, although this may be less true for them than for ingroup members, for whom such information may prove more useful in daily social interactions. Independents should therefore be relatively sensitive to between-attributes differences in the actual characteristics of both target groups (i.e., have relatively high sensitivity correlations), although possibly less so than ingroup members. Recall, however, that in a previous study of stereotype accuracy for Democrats and Republicans, Judd and Park (1993) found that ingroup stereotypes were more accurate than outgroup stereotypes, whether the accuracy measures were discrepancy scores or within-subject sensitivity correlations. Moreover, this was particularly true for individuals who were more strongly affiliated with their ingroup. Thus, on the basis of Judd and Park's findings, we would expect Independents to be less accurate than ingroup members, with respect to both discrepancy scores and sensitivity correlations, because Independents' affiliation with Democrats and Republicans is clearly weaker.

To test these predictions, I analyzed data from the 1976 National Election Study, conducted by the Survey Research Center at the University of Michigan. I computed the same two measures of stereotype accuracy examined by Judd and Park (1993) in their previous analyses of these same data. Specifically, I computed discrepancies between respondents' perceptions of each target group and the mean of the target-group members' self-reports on each of the 10 national policy issues listed in Table 2, as well as within-subject correlations reflecting the extent to which respondents' perceptions of each target group's positions were sensitive to actual differences in the group members' self-reported positions from one policy issue to another. Unlike Judd and Park (1993), however, I computed these measures not only for Democratic and Republican respondents, but also for those respondents who indicated that they were either Independent or "other."

Group members' self-ratings again constituted the accuracy criterion. And, again, because self-ratings were provided by random samples of group members, these self-ratings provide unbiased estimates of the group members' actual self-ratings. Note, however, that in these data, perceived group stereotypicality and the accuracy criterion are based on attitudes only; they did not include any personality traits. It seems reasonable that individuals would be better able to identify their true attitudes toward national social policy issues, as opposed to their true personality traits. Self-reports in this case, then, may provide a better accuracy measure and minimize social desirability problems that are often associated with self-reports (Judd & Park, 1993; Ryan et al., in press).

Table 2

Policy Issues Used in Assessment of Stereotype Accuracy for Political Parties

Policy issue	Endpoints on attitude scale
Government- guaranteed job	1 = *Government should see to job and good standard of living* 7 = *Government should let each person get ahead on his or her own*
Rights of accused	1 = *Protect rights of accused* 7 = *Stop crime regardless of rights of accused*
School busing	1 = *Bus to achieve integration* 7 = *Keep children in neighborhood schools*
Aid to minorities	1 = *Government should help minority groups* 7 = *Minority groups should help themselves*
Government role in health insurance	1 = *Government insurance plan* 7 = *Private insurance plans*
Liberalism– Conservatism	1 = *Extremely liberal* 7 = *Extremely conservative*
Government response to urban unrest	1 = *Solve problems of poverty and unemployment* 7 = *Use all available force*
Legalization of marijuana	1 = *Make use of marijuana legal* 7 = *Set penalties higher than they are now*
Tax-rate changes	1 = *Increase the tax rate for high incomes* 7 = *Have the same tax rate for everyone*
Women's rights	1 = *Women and men should have an equal role* 7 = *Women's place is in the home*

NOTE: From "Definition and Assessment of Accuracy in Social Stereotypes," by C. M. Judd and B. Park, 1993, *Psychological Review, 100*, p. 125. Adapted with permission of the author.

Discrepancy scores were computed by subtracting the criterion from perceived values for the Republican target group and by subtracting perceived values from the criterion for the Democratic target group. Higher values therefore indicate the extent to which respondents overestimated the stereotypicality of the target group, that is, how conservative Republicans are and how liberal Democrats are. Overall, the mean discrepancies indicated that subjects overestimated how liberal Democrats are and underestimated how conservative Republicans are. However, this may reflect a tendency to overestimate liberalness in general. Alternatively, it may reflect a tendency to give low responses because the liberal response was always the low end of the response scale. In any case, this sort of elevated-response bias is confounded with absolute levels of stereotype accuracy, which prevents conclusions concerning absolute levels of stereotype exaggeration (Judd & Park, 1993).

Discrepancies were analyzed as a function of subject group and target group, with repeated measures on the last factor. The analysis revealed a main effect for subject group, indicating that Independents were more accurate ($M = .14$) in their judgments of the two parties' positions than were the Democratic and Republican subjects combined ($M = .26$), $F(1, 1893) = 14.59$, $p < .001$. Overall, then, Independents were much less likely to overestimate the stereotypicality of the two groups. Unexpectedly, the target-group difference for Independents was virtually the same as for Democratic and Republican subjects $F(1, 1893) < 1$. However, the mean discrepancies for Democratic and Republican subjects judging the Democratic and Republican target groups were .89 and $-.37$, respectively; for Independents, these means were .79 and $-.52$. Note, then, that the target-group difference for Independents may simply reflect the response bias toward the overestimation of liberalness (or toward the use of the low end of the response scale). That is, the difference between the absolute values of the two target groups for Independents ($M = .27$) is much smaller than that for Democratic and Republican subjects combined ($M = .52$).

Perhaps more interesting are the direct comparisons between overall stereotypicality estimates for Independents versus ingroup members and outgroup members. In keeping with the notion that inaccuracy in discrepancy scores may result from a motivation to distinguish one's group from an outgroup, the data indicated that Independents were much more accurate than outgroup members ($Ms = .13$ and .42, respectively), $F(1, 1893) = 49.15$, $p < .001$. In other words, Independents were much less prone to stereotype exaggeration than were outgroup members. In addition, Independents were just as accurate as ingroup members ($Ms = .13$ and $.09$, respectively, $p > .10$). This seems somewhat surprising, given Judd and Park's (1993) finding that ingroup members who are more strongly affiliated with their group tend to demonstrate greater accuracy for the ingroup. That is, Independents who were not affiliated with the target group at all were just as accurate as ingroup members, at least on this measure of stereotype exaggeration.

I also examined within-subject sensitivity correlations, which I have argued may reveal a different pattern of effects, depending on the motivations that are associated with the particular group membership. This analysis revealed little difference in Independents' sensitivity to between-attributes differences in Democrats' versus Republicans' positions on the 10 policy issues ($Ms = .23$ and $.19$, respectively). Furthermore, although only marginally reliable, the target-group difference for Independents was smaller than that for Democrats and Republicans combined ($Ms = .04$ and $.11$, respectively), $F(1, 539) = 2.78$, $p < .10$. In contrast to the discrepancy scores, however, Independents were no more accurate (and no less accurate, $M = .21$) than were Democratic and Republican subjects combined ($M = .23$), $F(1, 539) < 1$. Moreover, Independents were not reliably more accurate than outgroup members ($Ms = .21$ and $.18$, respectively, $p > .10$); however, they were reliably less accurate than ingroup members ($Ms = .21$ and $.28$, respectively), $F(1, 539) = 5.05$, $p < .05$.

In summary, examining stereotype accuracy for a group in the role of an interested third party has yielded a pattern of effects that cannot be entirely predicted by previous research on ingroup–outgroup differences in stereotype accuracy. The lack of a target-group difference in the accuracy of Independents, the lack of stereotype exaggeration for Independents as compared with outgroup members, and the higher sensitivity to between-attributes differences for ingroup members versus Independents are all in keeping with previous work. However, Independents, who by definition were unaffiliated with the target groups, were just as accurate as ingroup members on the discrepancy measure of accuracy.

CONCLUSION

The primary purpose of this chapter was to demonstrate the need to examine more fully the influence of group membership on the accuracy with
which social groups are perceived. Perceivers may belong to many kinds
of social groups; the type of motivations associated with various group
memberships seems likely to affect one's perceptions, resulting in different levels of accuracy on different kinds of accuracy measures. Two types
of group membership differences were examined: ingroup versus outgroup
versus interested third party differences, and ethnic minority versus majority group differences. Four types of stereotype accuracy were examined:
two discrepancy measures, assessing stereotype exaggeration and overgeneralization, and two types of within-subject correlations, assessing sensitivity to between-attributes differences in the group's actual stereotypicality and the actual dispersion of group members. Note that the accuracy
criteria used in this research were derived from group members' self-
ratings. Thus, stereotype accuracy has been defined here as the extent to
which subjects' perceptions of a group correspond to the aggregated self-
perceptions of the members of that group.

Recent research examining ingroup–outgroup differences in stereotype accuracy for business and engineering majors (Judd et al., 1991) and
Democrats and Republicans (Judd & Park, 1993) has indicated that ingroup members have more accurate stereotypes than outgroup members
on both discrepancy and within-subject correlation measures of accuracy.
I have argued that these results may be due to the motivations associated
with these kinds of group memberships. That is, these group members
may be more motivated to attain both a positive social identity and a relatively more accurate conception of their ingroup than of their outgroup,
thus affecting discrepancy measures and within-subject correlations in a
similar manner. More specifically, because discrepancies assess stereotype
exaggeration and overgeneralization (Judd & Park, 1993), these types of
stereotype accuracy should be strongly influenced by the motivation to attain a positive social identity. On the other hand, within-subject sensitivity correlations may be more strongly influenced by the need to attain a

relatively accurate conception of social reality. In the studies just mentioned, these motivations may work together resulting in more accurate stereotypes of ingroups than outgroups on both discrepancy and correlation measures of accuracy.

Several findings provide at least partial support for this interpretation. First, I examined stereotype accuracy for groups that would be expected to have qualitatively different sorts of relationships to the groups being judged. Thus, the study of Black American and White American college students' stereotypes indicated that White Americans were more accurate on discrepancy measures. In other words, Black Americans demonstrated greater stereotype exaggeration and overgeneralization. These findings make sense from a social identity perspective, in which membership in an ethnic minority group is seen as more central to social identity, because of greater exposure to social threats and the relative inability of members to move across group boundaries. Ethnic minority group members, in an effort to attain a positive social identity, would be expected to accentuate group differences, resulting in greater inaccuracy on discrepancy measures. The examination of within-subject sensitivity correlations, however, yielded a different picture. On these measures, Black American subjects demonstrated somewhat greater accuracy and virtually no target-group difference. That is, they were equally accurate in their judgments of the Black American and White American target groups. White American subjects, on the other hand, showed much greater accuracy in perceptions of their own group than in their perceptions of the outgroup. Furthermore, all subjects were significantly more accurate in their judgments of the White American target group. These findings are in keeping with the notion that members of an ethnic minority group may be more motivated to attain a veridical picture of a majority outgroup than vice versa. Ethnic minority group members, who must interact daily in a predominantly majority context, would be expected to be more highly motivated to understand the characteristics of the majority group than vice versa.

In a second study, members of an interested third party (i.e., Independents vs. Democrats and Republicans), who should be less subject to social identity motivations, demonstrated greater stereotype accuracy than did the members of the target groups when discrepancy measures of accuracy were examined. Furthermore, members of an interested third party were more accurate than outgroup members but just as accurate as ingroup members. These findings do not clearly follow from previous research on ingroup–outgroup differences in stereotype accuracy. That is, given that Independents, by definition, are weakly affiliated with both Democrats and Republicans, they would be expected to demonstrate less stereotype accuracy than would the members of those groups.

This research underscores the importance of assessing stereotype accuracy in the context of qualitatively different sorts of group memberships, as well as the need to use conceptually distinct measures to assess stereotype accuracy. Of course, in future research, significant dimensions of, and motivations associated with, group membership should be identified and empirically assessed. Their consequences for perceptions of social groups and the accuracy of those perceptions can then be examined in a more precise and systematic fashion. Another interesting possibility for future research is to examine the relationship between perceivers' membership status in groups they have chosen to join and various types of stereotype accuracy. Perceivers' relationships to groups seem likely to change as they undergo socialization by the group to fulfill certain roles. The psychological process of becoming a group member may indeed begin well before formal entry into the group, continuing as the individual becomes a full-fledged group member and, ultimately, perhaps leaving the group (Levine & Moreland, 1994). Individuals' perceptions of both their own group and relevant outgroups are likely to change throughout this process (Brown & Wootton-Millward, 1993), resulting in differences in levels of stereotype accuracy among group members.

Finally, I wish to argue that it is time for social scientists to turn their attention to more process-oriented issues concerning the possible causes and consequences of differences in levels of stereotype accuracy rather than simply examining particular cultural stereotypes with the hope of being able to pronounce them to be inaccurate (or accurate). Thus, attention should be given to different types of group memberships, their social psychological characteristics, their effects on perceptions of groups, the relative accuracy of those perceptions, and, ultimately, the consequences of these perceptions for group-relevant judgments.

REFERENCES

Abate, M., & Berrien, F. K. (1967). Validation of stereotypes—Japanese versus American students. *Journal of Personality and Social Psychology, 7,* 435–438.

Abrams, D. (1994). Political distinctiveness: An identity optimising approach. *European Journal of Social Psychology, 24,* 357–365.

Billig, M. (1976). *Social psychology and intergroup relations.* London: Academic Press.

Brewer, M. B. (1993). The role of distinctiveness in social identity and group behaviour. In M. A. Hogg & D. Abrams (Eds.), *Group motivation: Social psychological perspectives* (pp. 1–16). New York: Harvester Wheatsheaf.

Brown, R., & Wootton-Millward, L. (1993). Perceptions of group homogeneity during group formation and change. *Social Cognition, 11,* 126–149.

Cronbach, L. J. (1955). Processes affecting scores on "understanding of others" and "assumed similarity." *Psychological Bulletin, 52,* 177–193.

Dollard, J., Doob, L., Miller, N. E., Mowrer, O., & Sears, R. (1939). *Frustration and aggression.* New Haven, CT: Yale University Press.

Ellemers, N. (1993). The influence of socio-structural variables on identity management strategies. In W. Stroebe & M. Hewstone (Eds.), *European review of social psychology* (Vol. 4, pp. 27–57). Chichester, England: Wiley.

Fiske, S. T. (1993). Controlling other people: The impact of power on stereotyping. *American Psychologist, 48,* 621–628.

Funder, D. C. (1987). Errors and mistakes: Evaluating the accuracy of social judgment. *Psychological Bulletin, 101,* 75–90.

Hamilton, D. L., & Trolier, T. K. (1986). Stereotypes and stereotyping: An overview of the cognitive approach. In J. F. Dovidio & S. L. Gaertner (Eds.), *Prejudice, discrimination, and racism* (pp. 127–163). Orlando, FL: Academic Press.

Judd, C. M., & Park, B. (1993). Definition and assessment of accuracy in social stereotypes. *Psychological Review, 100,* 109–128.

Judd, C. M., Ryan, C. S., & Park, B. (1991). Accuracy in the judgments of in-group and out-group variability. *Journal of Personality and Social Psychology, 61,* 366–379.

Levine, J. M., & Moreland, R. L. (1994). Group socialization: Theory and research. In W. Stroebe & M. Hewstone (Eds.), *European review of social psychology* (Vol. 5, pp. 305–336). Chichester, England: Wiley.

Linville, P. W., Fischer, G. W., & Salovey, P. (1989). Perceived distributions of characteristics of in-group and out-group members: Empirical evidence and a computer simulation. *Journal of Personality and Social Psychology, 57,* 165–188.

McCauley, C., & Stitt, C. L. (1978). An individual and quantitative measure of stereotypes. *Journal of Personality and Social Psychology, 36,* 929–940.

Mullen, B. (1991). Group composition, salience, and cognitive representations: The phenomenology of being in a group. *Journal of Experimental Social Psychology, 27,* 297–323.

Park, B., & Judd, C. M. (1990). Measures and models of perceived group variability. *Journal of Personality and Social Psychology, 59,* 173–191.

Park, B., & Rothbart, M. (1982). Perception of out-group homogeneity and levels of social categorization: Memory for the subordinate attributes of in-group and out-group members. *Journal of Personality and Social Psychology, 42,* 1051–1068.

Ryan, C. S., Judd, C. M., & Park, B. (1993). *Effects of racial stereotypes on judgments of individuals: The moderating role of perceived group variability.* Unpublished manuscript, University of Pittsburgh.

Ryan, C. S., Park, B., & Judd, C. M. (in press). Assessing stereotype accuracy: Implications for understanding the stereotyping process. To appear in N. Macrae, M. Hewstone, & C. Stangor (Eds.), *Foundations of stereotypes and stereotyping.* New York: Guilford Press.

Sherif, M., & Sherif, C. W. (1953). *Groups in harmony and tension.* New York: Harper.

Simon, B. (1992). The perception of ingroup and outgroup homogeneity: Reintroducing the intergroup context. In W. Stroebe & M. Hewstone (Eds.), *European review of social psychology* (Vol. 3, pp. 1–30). Chichester, England: Wiley.

Simon, B., & Brown, R. (1987). Perceived intragroup homogeneity in minority–majority contexts. *Journal of Personality and Social Psychology, 53,* 703–711.

Swim, J. K. (1994). Perceived versus meta-analytic effect sizes: An assessment of the accuracy of gender stereotypes. *Journal of Personality and Social Psychology, 66,* 21–36.

Tajfel, H., & Turner, J. C. (1986). The social identity theory of intergroup behavior. In S. Worchel & W. G. Austin (Eds.), *Psychology of intergroup relations* (pp. 7–24). Chicago: Nelson-Hall.

Turner, J. C., Hogg, M. A., Oakes, P. J., Reicher, S. D., & Wetherell, M. S. (1987). *Rediscovering the social group: A self-categorization theory.* Oxford, England: Basil Blackwell.

9

Are Stereotypes Exaggerated?
A Sampling of Racial, Gender,
Academic, Occupational, and
Political Stereotypes

Clark R. McCauley

I begin with a brief review of classic and modern suggestions that stereotypes are likely to be exaggerations of whatever real differences may exist between groups. The review distinguishes two versions of the exaggeration hypothesis that are based entirely on cognitive psychology, *perceptual contrast* and *cognitive-processing limitations*, from more motivationally based accounts that predict exaggeration arising out of scapegoating or group conflict. Then I examine what I judge to be the strongest and best-known studies supporting the exaggeration hypothesis, as well as some studies of my own that do not support it. Finally, I evaluate the present status of the exaggeration hypothesis and suggest that the small and occasional exaggeration effects so far reported argue against any general cognitive mechanism of exaggeration. Future research may be able to show more powerful and consistent exaggeration effects in the context of intergroup hostility and conflict, that is, under circumstances in which motivational mechanisms of exaggeration would be salient.

I am grateful to Lee J. Jussim, Yueh-Ting Lee, and Linda Albright for helpful comments on a draft of this chapter. Correspondence concerning this chapter may be sent to Clark R. McCauley, Department of Psychology, Bryn Mawr College, Bryn Mawr, Pennsylvania 19010 (phone: 610–526–5017; email: cmccaule@cc.brynmawr.edu).

THE EXAGGERATION HYPOTHESIS

Few have been so bold as to suggest that all of our perceptions of group characteristics are incorrect. We act every day on such perceptions, and we do not usually suffer the social equivalent of walking into a door. Standing next to the bus driver, we are more likely to ask about traffic patterns than about the latest foreign film. On the highway, we try to squeeze into the exit lane in front of the man driving a 10-year-old station wagon rather than trying to pull in on the man driving a new Corvette. Looking for the school janitor, we are more likely to approach a young man in overalls than a young woman in overalls. This kind of discrimination on the basis of group differences can go wrong, but most of us probably feel that we are doing ourselves and others a favor when we respond to whatever cues and regularities our social environment affords us.

As described earlier in this volume, however, social scientists since Katz and Braly (1933) have been concerned that much of what we believe about groups and group differences is seriously flawed (Ottati & Lee, chapter 1). Errors in perception of group characteristics may be particularly dangerous to the extent that the perception supports prejudice and hostility toward an outgroup. What kind of error should we be concerned about? Early and late, the favorite answer has been that even when a stereotype is not altogether false, it is likely to be an exaggeration of the prevalence of stereotyped characteristics in the target group.

Katz and Braly

The exaggeration hypothesis got its start when Katz and Braly (1933) described stereotypes as oversimplified generalizations. A stereotype is overgeneralized to the extent that too many members of the stereotyped group are seen as possessing stereotyped characteristics. A stereotype is oversimplified to the extent that the correlation between group membership and possession of stereotyped characteristics is seen as greater than it really is: The stereotyped characteristics are seen as too rare outside the stereotyped group, as well as too common within. The extreme of overgeneralization and oversimplification is reached when the correlation between group membership and stereotyped characteristics is seen as perfect, for example, "All Germans are efficient, and no non-German is efficient."

Allport

Allport (1954) followed Katz and Braly in making "overgeneralization" the definition of a stereotype:

> Whether favorable or unfavorable, a stereotype is an exaggerated belief associated with a category. Its function is to justify (rationalize) our conduct in relation to that category. . . . A stereotype need not be altogether false. If we think of the Irish as more prone to alcoholism than, say, Jews, we are making a correct judgment in terms of probability. Yet if, as some say, "Jews don't drink," or "the Irish are whiskey-soaked" we are manifestly exaggerating the facts, and building up an unjustified stereotype. We can distinguish between a valid generalization and a stereotype only if we have solid data concerning the existence of (the probability of) true group differences. (Allport, 1954, pp. 191–192)

Note that Allport is ready to consider both positive and negative stereotypes (see Figure 1 in chapter 1, this volume) and ready also to consider motivational sources of stereotyping involved in justifying and rationalizing behavior toward the stereotyped group. Many years were to pass before stereotype research took up Allport's challenge to test the validity of probabilistic generalizations (see Ottati & Lee, chapter 2, this volume).

LeVine and Campbell

Although they sympathized with much of Allport's view of stereotypes, LeVine and Campbell (1972) stepped back from defining stereotypes as exaggerations. They examined anthropological evidence indicating that across many human societies, urban and rural dwellers have consistent mutual stereotypes, as do temperate and equatorial peoples. The reliability of these stereotypes makes it difficult to dismiss them as totally invalid, and indeed anthropology as a discipline must stand against any claim that there are not real differences between human groups.

Thus, LeVine and Campbell (1972) were led to recognize that stereo-types need not be 100% generalizations and that at least some stereotype content must have a basis in reality. But they followed the earlier litera-ture in asserting that stereotypes are generally inaccurate; their argument was that even stereotypes with a grain of truth will generally be exagger-ated. The same mechanisms of perception that sharpen differences across boundaries, that make light grey look lighter and dark grey look darker across a contour line, could be counted on to sharpen group differences. LeVine and Campbell (1972) seem themselves surprised at the strength of the prediction that emerged from their analysis: "It would seem from the standpoint of both perception and learning theory that this effect should hold true for all observers, not just prejudiced ones" (p. 170).

This is a very general form of the exaggeration hypothesis, which does not need to invoke any of the motivational or affective constructs often associated with stereotypes. As noted by LeVine and Campbell (1972), the perceptual-contrast version of the exaggeration hypothesis predicts stereo-type exaggeration of differences between any two groups, even if the per-son stereotyping has no stake or interest in either group. For LeVine and Campbell, the exaggeration hypothesis is as basic as sensation–perception psychology.

Expectancy Biases in Information Processing

More modern support for the exaggeration hypothesis comes from ex-perimental research on cognition and social cognition that uses an infor-mation-processing framework. In particular, this research has emphasized the ways in which our processing of information about others can be bi-ased toward confirming our expectations (Fiske & Neuberg, 1990). We may seek out or attend more to confirming evidence (Higgins & Bargh, 1987) or recall expectancy-confirming examples better (Stangor & Ford, 1992). There are, however, conditions under which expectancy-confirmation bias is not found (Stangor & McMillan, 1992), and it is not clear from the laboratory experiments how much of everyday social per-ception may be infected with this bias (see Jussim & Eccles, chapter 10, this volume). Nevertheless, the many laboratory demonstrations of expectancy bias in social perception have created a presumption that the phenomenon may be important outside the laboratory.

The implication of an expectancy-confirmation bias for stereotyping is that in relation to members of a stereotyped group who do not fit our expectations, we will notice and recall better the members of the group who have the stereotyped characteristics. The result should be that we exaggerate the homogeneity within the stereotyped group and underestimate the degree to which stereotype characteristics occur outside the stereotyped group (Judd & Park, 1993, p. 112). Like LeVine and Campbell's perceptual-contrast version, the information-processing version of the exaggeration hypothesis is founded in low-level cognitive processes. The function or explanation of expectancy-confirming biases is generally understood to be economizing of information-processing resources; it is supposed to be more work to process the unexpected. Here, the modern literature echoes Lippmann (1922), who saw stereotypes as simplified pictures in our head that save us from the staggering complexity of the world outside.

It is worth emphasizing that Allport's understanding of the exaggeration hypothesis includes motivational sources of exaggeration that are not included in either the perceptual-contrast or the information-processing versions of the hypothesis. According to Allport (1954, chapter 2), exaggeration of group differences occurs not only for reasons of cognitive economy and simplicity but also to rationalize group antipathy that may have its origins in group conflict or intrapsychic conflict (scapegoating). Stangor and Ford (1992) present a succinct summary of scapegoating and other motivational models of prejudice and exaggeration, including repressed hostility, self-esteem maintenance, and group identification.

To sum up, this section has traced a brief history of the idea that stereotypes are exaggerations, an idea that has been popular from the beginning of stereotype research. Allport defined stereotypes as exaggerated and saw this exaggeration as the result of both cognitive and motivational mechanisms. LeVine and Campbell predicted stereotype exaggeration as a derivation from sensation–perception psychology. Recent research in social cognition predicts stereotype exaggeration as the outcome of expectancy-confirmation biases in information processing. The next section examines empirical evidence in favor of this overdetermined and variously-plausible hypothesis.

I do not attempt here an exhaustive review of studies that have been interpreted as showing exaggeration of group differences; rather, I examine the studies I believe are the strongest and most cited in this regard. And I do not attempt to deal with studies on the related issue of whether outgroups or ingroups may be consistently seen as more homogenous than they really are (Simon & Pettigrew, 1990); as described in chapter 1 under Outgroup Homogeneity, research on this issue is in a state of creative ferment that does not yet offer any clear conclusion.

EVIDENCE SUPPORTING THE EXAGGERATION HYPOTHESIS

Black Versus White Test Performance

In support of their perceptual-contrast hypothesis, LeVine and Campbell cited a study by Clarke and Campbell (1955) and a study by Campbell (1956). The latter showed exaggeration of the perceived difference between groups of nonsense syllables and will not be considered here.

The study by Clarke and Campbell (1955) had Black students and White students (7th to 10th graders in integrated classes) predict the test score each classmate would get on an upcoming test. Each student received a standard score that represented his or her position in the class distribution of mean predicted scores and another standard score that represented his or her position in the class distribution of actual test scores. Both Black and White students estimated that Black students would do worse, on average, than White students; White students, but not Black students, exaggerated how much worse Black students would do.

This study offers some support for the exaggeration hypothesis, but the support is not strong. The degree of exaggeration was not great for White students (mean exaggeration of 0.19 standard score units). And no exaggeration effect was found for predictions by Black students, who, according to the perceptual-contrast hypothesis, should also have exaggerated the difference between Black and White performance. Substantial evidence of accuracy was also found: White predictions correlated .56 with performance of Black classmates; Black predictions of Black classmates correlated .47 with actual performance.

There is another sense in which the Clarke and Campbell study is not strong evidence of stereotype exaggeration: Properly speaking, this is not a study of stereotype accuracy. The study did not include any direct measure of stereotype belief, such as the percentage of Black students predicted to perform worse than the average White student. Rather, it was a study of judgments made about individual members of a stereotyped group— an issue of considerable controversy since Locksley, Borgida, Brekke, and Hepburn (1980) first suggested that stereotype beliefs are ignored in judging members of stereotyped groups when individuating information is available (see Funder, chapter 6, and Jussim & Eccles, chapter 10, this volume).

Hawk Versus Dove Opinions

Beginning with the classic study by Hovland, Harvey, and Sherif (1957), there has grown up a sizable literature suggesting that we tend to exaggerate the difference between our own opinions and the opinions of those we oppose (but see Zimbardo & Ebbesen, 1969, pp. 54–55, for another interpretation of Hovland et al. results). The contrast effect in social judgment is usually demonstrated by asking subjects to put opinion statements into categories representing different degrees of favorableness/ unfavorableness toward an attitude object. Subjects positive toward fraternities, for instance, may rate a profraternity statement as +2, whereas subjects negative toward fraternities may rate the same statement as +3. The weakness of this kind of demonstration is that it does not offer a criterion against which to measure exaggeration. Perhaps the difference between pro and anti judges is only a difference in the meaning of the words defining the scale categories.

Dawes, Singer, and Lemons (1972) recognized this problem and offered an ingenious way around it. They recruited students who were "hawks" and "doves" with regard to the Vietnam War and asked them to write opinion statements that the typical dove on campus would endorse as well as statements that the typical hawk on campus would endorse. Then they recruited a second group of hawks and doves, asked the hawks to agree or disagree with hawk statements written by hawks and doves, and asked doves to agree or disagree with dove statements written by hawks and doves. Hawks rejected more hawk statements written by doves than hawk statements written by hawks, and doves rejected more dove statements written by hawks than dove statements written by doves. Both hawks and doves rejected statements mostly on the grounds that they were too extreme.

These results indicate exaggeration relative to a behavioral criterion: the statements actually accepted by hawks and doves. The first-recruited hawks and doves erred systematically in estimating what their typical opponent would endorse; hawks wrote typical dove statements that tended to be more extreme than the average hawk would endorse, and doves wrote typical hawk statements that tended to be more extreme than the average hawk would endorse. The degree of exaggeration was, however, neither large nor consistent. Hawks rejected as too extreme 16 of 40 statements written by doves and 11 of 40 statements written by hawks; doves rejected as too extreme 9 of 40 statements written by hawks and 8 of 40 statements written by doves. Thus, doves significantly exaggerated the extremity of the typical hawk, but hawks showed only a weak tendency to exaggerate the extremity of the typical dove.

Dawes et al. (1972) recognized two possible explanations of their results. One is the information-processing version of exaggeration theory: We disregard information indicating moderation or neutrality because this information is more difficult to assimilate. The other possible explanation, attributed by Dawes et al. to Manis (1961), is motivational: Exaggerating the position of our opponents reduces the force of their arguments. The first explanation is purely cognitive; the second is motivational and strategic. If the first explanation is correct, then exaggeration of opponents' positions should be as likely on the issue of preferring black bread to white bread as on an issue of war and peace. A test of this prediction does not seem ever to have been attempted.

Male Versus Female Personality Traits

Two different studies reported by Martin (1987) are often cited as having shown stereotype exaggerations of real group differences. Martin's first study asked undergraduate students to estimate the percentage of North American men and North American women with 10 masculine and 10 feminine traits drawn from the Bem Sex-Role Inventory. Criterion percentages were obtained from male and female adult visitors to the University of British Columbia open house day, who circled true or false for themselves for each of the same 20 traits. The student data showed 19 traits with significant stereotypes, that is, the estimated percentage of North American men having the trait differed significantly from the estimated percentage of North American women having the trait. For 18 of the 19 stereotyped traits, the perceived difference between men and women was greater than the criterion difference.

The results of Martin's (1987) first study certainly suggest that stereotypes are generally (18 of 19 traits) exaggerated, but as Martin recognized, the sample of visitors to the university open house may not be representative of the target of students' estimates: North American men and women. Martin's second study aimed to improve the match between the stereotype target definition and the definition of the criterion group.

Undergraduate student volunteers were asked to estimate percentages of male and female university students having each of 16 male and 16 female traits drawn from Spence's Personal Attributes Questionnaire. Criterion percentages were obtained by asking the same students whether each of the 32 traits was true of themselves. The estimates showed significant stereotyping for all 32 traits, that is, the estimated percentage of male students with the trait significantly differed from the estimated percentage of female students with the trait. For 19 of the 32 stereotyped traits, the perceived difference between men and women was greater than the criterion difference. However, for 10 of the 32 stereotyped traits, the perceived difference between men and women was smaller than the criterion difference. A sign test of the tendency to exaggerate versus the tendency to underestimate did not reach conventional levels of significance (22 of 32 differences exaggerated, $z = 1.48$).

Thus, Martin's (1987) second study found students making substantial errors in gender stereotyping with traits, but the tendency for errors in the direction of exaggeration was not strong. Judging by the results of the second study, exaggeration is a relatively weak source of stereotype errors.

Both of Martin's studies are problematic in another way. Martin's criterion data were obtained by asking men and women to attribute evaluatively loaded words such as *aggressive* and *warm* to themselves. Respondents may not know or may not want to admit, even to themselves, that they are aggressive or that they are not warm. Furthermore, trait words such as *aggressive* may mean something different when applied to a woman than when applied to a man (Nelson, Biernat, & Manis, 1990; see Biernat, chapter 4, this volume). It is possible, then, that the differences Martin observed between perception and self-report may be some artifact of using trait words as the focus of gender stereotyping.

Business Versus Engineering Student Traits and Attitudes

In their notably complex and sophisticated study of exaggeration in ingroup and outgroup perceptions, Judd, Ryan, and Park (1991) compared mutual perceptions and self-reports of University of Colorado business majors and engineering majors. A random sample of students in each of the two majors responded to a questionnaire asking about four traits and four attitude statements. Two traits and two statements were stereotypic of business majors (seen as significantly more likely for business than for engineering majors) and two traits and two statements were stereotypic of engineering majors (seen as more likely for engineering majors than for business majors). Students estimated the percentage of business and engineering majors who had a given trait or would endorse a given statement and then reported for themselves whether each trait described them and whether they agreed with each statement. (Estimates of ingroup dispersion were also included in the questionnaire, but these gave results similar to the results for percentage estimates and are not considered here.)

For each trait and each statement, the percentage of self-endorsement by the random sample of business and engineering majors provided the criterion for the corresponding estimated percentages. A discrepancy between estimated and criterion percentages was assigned a positive sign if it represented stereotype exaggeration: estimated percentage too high on a trait or statement stereotypic of the target group (e.g., business majors as extraverted or engineers as reserved) or estimated percentage too low on a trait or statement counterstereotypic of the target group (e.g., business majors as reserved or engineers as extraverted). Collapsing over traits and statements, Judd et al. (1991, Table 7) reported negligible exaggeration of estimates for business majors by business majors, 8–10 percentage points' exaggeration of estimates for business majors by engineering majors and for engineering majors by engineering majors, and 18 percentage points' exaggeration of estimates for engineering majors by business majors.

These results indicate consistent stereotypic exaggeration for outgroup estimates (estimates for engineering students by business students and estimates for business students by engineering students), but inconsistent stereotypic exaggeration for ingroup estimates (no exaggeration for estimates of business students by business students). Judd et al. (1991) qualified these results by reporting briefly that stereotypic exaggeration was less for statements than for traits, although greater stereotypic exaggeration for outgroup than for ingroup estimates was still reliable for traits. Judd et al. went on to note that the difference in results for traits and statements may be attributable to more accurate self-reports for attitude than for personality traits.

These are probably the strongest results in the literature supporting the exaggeration hypothesis, but as Judd et al. (1991) pointed out in their conclusion, they cannot support an unqualified version of the hypothesis. If there are any stereotypes that are not exaggerated, as the ingroup estimates for business students were not exaggerated in this experiment, then exaggeration cannot be a defining characteristic of stereotypes. Note also that stereotypic exaggeration was not very strong except for the business majors' estimates for engineers (average exaggeration of 18 percentage points). Exaggeration of 10 percentage points or less can be interesting from the point of view of theory testing, but the impact of this level of exaggeration on judgments of members of the stereotyped group may be hard to measure.

EVIDENCE AGAINST THE
EXAGGERATION HYPOTHESIS

Black American Versus All American Census Statistics

One of the earliest studies to look for exaggeration of group differences found underestimation instead. McCauley and Stitt (1978) asked five groups of White subjects to estimate the percentage of Black Americans and the percentage of all Americans with each of seven characteristics (e.g., "completed high school" or "illegitimate"; see Table 1). Criterion percentages for these characteristics were available from the U.S. census. Stereotyping of Black Americans was measured as the extent to which percentage estimates were different for Black Americans than for all Americans.

The results were originally published in terms of mean ratios of percentage of Black Americans divided by corresponding percentage of all Americans, but here the same data are presented in terms of mean difference in the percentage of Blacks and all Americans having each characteristic. (Psychometrically, the diagnostic-ratio measure and the percentage-difference measure tell pretty much the same story; the difference measure is preferable for its relative simplicity in calculation and interpretation. See McCauley & Thangavelu, 1991.)

Table 1 shows that the five different groups of subjects produced generally similar estimates of Black versus all American percentage differences, similar stereotypes, for each characteristic. Perceived differences for each characteristic were almost always (34 of 35 differences) in the same direction as differences taken from the U.S. census. The first characteristic in Table 1, "completed high school," was seen as substantially less likely for Black Americans than for all Americans (i.e., counterstereotypic for Blacks). The remaining six characteristics were seen as more likely for Blacks (stereotypic for Blacks).

Entries with the superscript a in Table 1 are the 10 perceived dif-

Table 1

Criterion Differences and Mean Estimated Differences Between Black Americans and All Americans (Percentage of Black Americans − Percentage of All Americans)

Characteristics	Criterion	High school	College	Union	Choir	MSW students
n		10	17	12	10	13
1. Completed high school	−21	−22	−18	−18	−23	−22
2. Illegitimate	23	14	5[a]	12[a]	16	10[a]
3. Unemployed last month	7	9	5	9	16	7
4. Victim of violent crime	2	−5	6	7	7	8
5. Family on welfare	18	22	8[a]	6[a]	15	6[a]
6. Family with 4+ children	7	13	6	9	7	7
7. Female head of family	21	10[a]	11[a]	8[a]	8[a]	12

NOTE: Criterion data from U.S. census. MSW = master of social work
[a]Mean estimated difference differs from criterion difference by ≥10 percentage points.

ferences that are substantially in error (perceived Black American vs. all American difference at least 10 percentage points away from census difference). All 10 of the substantial errors were in the direction of underestimating the difference between Black Americans and all Americans.

Overall, the results in Table 1 indicate considerable accuracy. Correlation between mean estimated percentage differences (stereotypes) and corresponding criterion percentage differences was high (rs .85 to .90 for the five groups of subjects). Perceived difference departed substantially from census difference for 10 of 35 comparisons, but the errors were all underestimates rather than exaggerations.

This picture of accuracy with some underestimation of real differences might be misleading if, at the same time, percentage estimates for Black Americans were consistently exaggerated on characteristics stereotypic of Blacks. For example, estimates of the percentage of Black families headed by a female might be exaggerated (e.g., 50% vs. census 33%) even if the estimates of the Black versus the all American difference were underestimates. This result could occur if estimates of the percentage of all American families with a female head were, for some reason, even more exaggerated (e.g., 40% vs. census 12%, perceived difference then 10 percentage points vs. census difference of 21 percentage points).

To examine this possibility, Table 2 presents for each characteristic the mean percentage estimates for Black Americans and all Americans and the corresponding census percentages. All five groups of subjects tended to overestimate the percentage of Black Americans who had completed high school, although exaggeration of a counterstereotypic trait would predict underestimation. For the remaining six characteristics, which tended to be seen as more likely for Black Americans than all Americans, stereotypic exaggeration would predict exaggeration of estimates for Black Americans and underestimation of estimates for all Americans. For these six characteristics, 21 of 30 mean estimates for Black Americans were numerically greater than their corresponding criterion percentages; 30 of 30 mean estimates for all Americans were numerically greater than corresponding criterion percentages. These results indicate a general tendency toward overestimation, no matter what the target group; they do not show stereotypic exaggeration.

Taken together, Tables 1 and 2 indicate that diverse groups of subjects agree in estimating differences between Black Americans and all Americans that (a) are sensitive to real differences (high correlations with criterion differences), (b) are underestimates of real differences, and (c) are based on target estimates for Black and all American percentages that are generally overestimated rather than stereotypically exaggerated. Judd and Park (1993, p. 123) suggested that Black subjects might show the same pattern of underestimation of real differences as the five groups of White subjects in McCauley and Stitt (1978), but this surmise has not yet been substantiated.

Table 2

Criterion Percentages and Mean Estimated Percentages for Black Americans and All Americans

Characteristics	Criterion		High school		College		Union		Choir		MSW students	
	Black	All	Black	All	Black	All	Black	All	Black	All	Black	All
n			10		17		12		10		13	
1. Completed high school	39	60	48	70	52	71	43	61	50	73	40	62
2. Illegitimate	34	11	37	24	18	13	31	19	38	23	23	13
3. Unemployed last month	15	8	21	12	13	8	20	12	35	19	23	16
4. Victim of violent crime	5	4	29	34	17	11	16	9	27	20	20	12
5. Family on welfare	23	5	42	20	23	15	24	18	35	20	20	14
6. Family with 4+ children	15	8	50	38	29	24	33	24	44	37	34	27
7. Female head of family	33	12	25	15	33	21	41	33	39	31	33	21

NOTE: Criterion data from U.S. census. MSW = master of social work.

Male Versus Female Representation in Occupations

Many occupations are gender stereotyped, that is, perceived to be dispro-
portionately male or female. An unstereotyped occupation is one in which
the representation of males and females is seen as 50–50. In two studies,
McCauley and colleagues (McCauley & Thangavelu, 1991; McCauley,
Thangavelu, & Rozin, 1988) asked varied groups of subjects (high school
students, college students, and rail commuters) to estimate the proportion
of males or females in a number of gender-stereotyped occupations. Occupations stereotyped as "male" included doctor, lawyer, judge, college
teacher, scientist, laborer, police, bank official, mechanic, and bus driver.
Occupations stereotyped as "female" included sales clerk, secretary, school-
teacher, phone operator, and social worker.

The results of these two studies are available in detail in their published versions and will not be repeated here. For present purposes, it is
necessary to note only that these studies do not show any evidence of
stereotypic exaggeration. Across occupations, group mean percentage estimates and even individual subject's percentage estimates correlated with
criterion percentages at $r = .90$ or higher. Subjects' estimates were substantially in error for many occupations, but the direction of error was, in
nearly every case, toward underestimation of the census difference between
male and female representation in the occupation.

Business Student Versus Arts and Sciences Student
Behaviors and Preferences

An unpublished study by McCauley and Rozin (1989) used much the same
paradigm already described for Judd et al. (1991). Students in introductory psychology responded to a questionnaire presenting 20 descriptions,
for each description circled yes or no in regard to whether the description
fit them, and then estimated the percentage of Wharton (business school)
undergraduates who fit the description and the percentage of arts and sciences (A&S) undergraduates who fit the description. Approximately one
quarter of freshmen, both Wharton and A&S, at the University of Pennsylvania take introductory psychology, and McCauley and Rozin took the

self-reports from this broadly popular class as approximating criterion percentages that could be compared to the corresponding percentage estimates.

The first result of interest was the very strong agreement of Wharton and A&S subjects in their estimates of both Wharton and A&S percentages. For only 2 of 40 comparisons (20 descriptions for each of two target groups) did mean estimate by A&S students differ from mean estimate by Wharton students by as much as 10 percentage points. When Wharton students were the target, Wharton and A&S students' mean estimates differed by an average of 4.8 percentage points, and the correlation of Wharton and A&S mean estimates across the 20 descriptions was $r = .93$. When A&S students were the target, the corresponding figures were 4.1 percentage points, and $r = .85$. The similarity of mean estimates from Wharton and A&S students led McCauley and Rozin to collapse across subject group to evaluate the accuracy of the shared stereotype of Wharton and A&S students.

For Wharton and A&S subjects together, then, there were 12 descriptions with substantial stereotypes (at least 10 percentage points difference between mean estimated percentages of Wharton and A&S students fitting the description). These 12 stereotype descriptions are presented in Table 3. Columns 1 and 2 present the criterion percentages of Wharton and A&S students reporting that a description fit them, and column 5 presents the criterion difference between these two percentages (column 1 percentage − column 2 percentage). Columns 3 and 4 present, for Wharton and A&S subjects together, the mean estimated percentage of Wharton and A&S students who fit the description. Column 6 presents the mean estimated difference between these two percentages (column 3 − column 4), that is, the stereotype difference for each description.

Stereotype accuracy can be assessed by comparing columns 5 and 6. Ten of the 12 stereotyped differences were very accurate: in the same direction as, and within 4 percentage points of, their corresponding criterion differences. One description ("aware how much money others' clothing costs") showed substantial error of underestimation: The perceived difference was 12 percentage points, and the criterion difference was 28

Table 3

Self-Reports and Perceptions of Wharton and A&S Undergraduates

Description	% Wharton agreeing	% A&S agreeing	Mean estimated % Wharton	Mean estimated % A&S	Criterion Wharton − A&S	Mean stereotype Wharton − A&S
n	46	107	153	153		
1. Often wear preppie clothes	43	25	58	42	18	16
2. Favored Reagan over Mondale in 1984	65	41	72	46	24	26
3. Willing to move far from family and friends for job promotion	66	50	71	52	16	19
4. Expect to earn more than $50,000/year within 5 years of receiving AB/BS	70	31	76	41	39	35
5. Parents' income more than $100,000 in 1984	42	31	54	42	11	12

6. Feel that who you know is as important as what you know	59	62	69	50	−3	19
7. Male	59	46	62	52	13	10
8. Prefer a clean and orderly desk	78	67	61	50	11	11
9. Father employed with a large corporation	26	15	58	43	11	15
10. Think most Americans get pretty much what they deserve out of life	62	41	63	44	21	19
11. Would never take a poetry course	61	32	67	39	29	28
12. Aware how much others' clothing costs	67	39	62	50	28	12

NOTE: A&S = arts and sciences, AB = bachelor of arts degree, BS = bachelor of science degree.

percentage points. One description ("feel that who you know is as important as what you know") showed a stereotype that was simply incorrect: Wharton students were seen as 19 percentage points more likely than A&S students to agree with the description, but the criterion difference was a negligible 3 percentage points in the reverse direction.

Columns 5 and 6 do not show any general bias toward exaggerating real group differences; 11 stereotype differences were in the same direction as criterion differences, but for only 4 of the 11 were the perceived differences in the direction of exaggeration of the criterion differences. These results do not support the hypothesis that stereotypes consistently exaggerate real group differences.

Again the question can be raised as to whether there is stereotypic exaggeration in the estimates of the percentages of Wharton and A&S students who fit the descriptions. Mean estimated percentage of Wharton students who fit the stereotyped descriptions (column 3) can be compared with the corresponding criterion percentages (column 1). Ten of 12 estimated percentages were numerically greater than their corresponding criterion percentages, that is, 10 of 12 were in the direction of exaggeration. Mean estimated percentage of A&S students who fit the descriptions (column 4) could similarly be compared with corresponding criterion percentages (column 2). Because the descriptions stereotypic for Wharton students were counterstereotypic for A&S students, stereotypic exaggeration implies an estimate smaller than the criterion percentage. Only 2 of 12 estimated percentages was numerically smaller than its corresponding criterion percentage; that is, 2 of 12 was in the direction of stereotypic exaggeration.

Taken together, the estimates for Wharton targets and the estimates for A&S targets tended to err in the direction of stereotypic exaggeration in only 12 of 24 comparisons. These results again did not show any consistent bias toward stereotypic exaggeration.

Of course, it is possible that a strictly random sample of Wharton and A&S students might have produced different results than these obtained using introductory psychology students to approximate the criterion percentages. One might expect, however, that better criterion data would increase, rather than decrease, the surprising level of stereotype accuracy obtained in this study.

Male Versus Female Behaviors and Preferences

An unpublished study by McCauley and Hains (1991) followed the same paradigm of the study by McCauley and Rozin (1989). Students in introductory psychology at Westchester University responded to a questionnaire presenting 20 descriptions; for each description, circled yes or no regarding whether the description fit them; and then estimated the percentage of male and female undergraduates at their institution who fit the description. To avoid the problems of inaccuracy and variation in meaning that can affect self-report of trait descriptions, the 20 descriptions in this study were of behaviors and preferences rather than traits.

Male and female subjects were very close in their perceptions of male–female differences on the 20 descriptions. McCauley and Hains (1991) collapsed across subject group to evaluate the accuracy of the shared stereotype of gender differences.

For male and female subjects together, there were 11 descriptions with substantial gender stereotyping (at least 10 percentage points difference between mean estimated percentage of males and females fitting the description). These 11 stereotype descriptions are presented in Table 4, with criterion and estimated percentages and percentage differences appearing in the same columns as in Table 3. Nine of the descriptions were stereotypic for males and counterstereotypic for females; two ("would like to lose weight"; "own a hair dryer") were counterstereotypic for males and stereotypic for females.

Stereotype accuracy again can be assessed by comparing columns 5 and 6. All 11 mean estimated differences were in the same direction as their corresponding criterion differences, and 9 of the 11 perceived differences were within 8 percentage points of their criterion differences (8 of 11 within 4 percentage points). Two descriptions ("own a hair dryer"; "more than 5 ft, 5 in. tall") show substantial underestimates of real group differences. These results offer no support for the hypothesis that stereotypes consistently exaggerate real group differences.

Table 4

Self-Reports and Perceptions of Westchester Undergraduate Males and Females

Description	% males agreeing	% females agreeing	Mean estimated % males	Mean estimated % females	Criterion M–F agreeing	Mean stereotype M–F estimated
n	29	45	74	74		
1. Drink more than two beers in an average week at college	71	60	78	67	11	11
2. Watched sports on TV within the last week	76	40	81	46	36	35
3. Would like to lose weight	38	80	37	79	−42	−42
4. Like team sports more than individual sports	71	61	76	62	10	14

5. Own a hair dryer	52	92	62	94	−44	−32
6. More than 5 ft, 5 in. tall	100	44	80	51	56	29
7. Major in science or engineering	14	7	38	26	7	12
8. Hit someone in anger in the last year	45	27	57	31	18	26
9. Have driven a car faster than 75 miles per hour	86	64	77	55	22	22
10. Went to watch a college team at least once this semester	69	60	66	55	9	11
11. Have swatted a fly with bare hand	76	44	69	40	32	29

NOTE: M = male, F = female.

237

Again the question can be raised as to whether there is stereotypic exaggeration in the estimates of the percentages of male and female students who fit the descriptions. Mean estimated percentage of male students who fit the stereotyped descriptions (column 3) can be compared with the corresponding criterion percentages (column 1). Stereotypic exaggeration (estimated percentage tending higher than criterion for the 9 male stereotypic descriptions and tending lower for the 2 male counterstereotypic descriptions) occurred for 6 of the 11 descriptions. Similarly, comparison of estimated and criterion female percentages (columns 4 and 2) shows stereotypic exaggeration (estimated percentage tending to be higher than criterion for the 2 female stereotypic descriptions and tending to be lower than criterion for the 9 female counterstereotypic descriptions) for 4 of the 11 descriptions.

Taken together, the estimates for males and females tended to err in the direction of stereotypic exaggeration in 10 of 22 comparisons. These results again did not show any consistent bias toward stereotypic exaggeration.

As with the previous study, it is possible that a strictly random sample of male and female undergraduates at Westchester might have produced different results than these obtained using an ad hoc sample of introductory psychology students to approximate male and female criterion percentages. As before, however, one might expect that better criterion data would increase rather than decrease the high level of stereotype accuracy obtained in this study.

CONCLUSION

In everyday speech, a *stereotype* is a caricature of group characteristics, a perception that exaggerates the differences between the stereotyped group and others. This is an old idea; it goes back to Lippmann's (1922) use of the term to refer to the simple pictures in our heads that save us from the complexity of the world outside. Many psychologists, including such influential figures as Katz and Braly (1933) and Allport (1954), defined stereotypes as incorrect generalizations that attribute stereotyped characteristics to 100% of the members of the stereotyped group. More modern conceptualizations of stereotypes recognize that Lippmann's picture metaphor is misleading; a picture represents characteristics in all-or-none fashion, but few if any research subjects see stereotypes as 100% generalizations about the stereotyped group.

The modern understanding of stereotypes is that they are probabilistic perceptions of group differences. Many of those who subscribe to this conceptualization of stereotypes have nevertheless been reluctant to give up the idea that there is something systematically wrong with stereotypes and have focused on exaggeration as the common flaw. Stereotype exaggeration is variously ascribed to perceptual psychology (contrast across a group boundary), to information-processing psychology (bias toward confirming expectancies), and to various forms of motivational psychology (scapegoating, maintaining self-esteem through ingroup identification).

In contrast to its long prominence in the literature, the idea that stereotypes are exaggerations has had surprisingly little and relatively recent empirical investigation. The most salient evidence for the exaggeration hypothesis is not particularly strong: Exaggeration has been found for White estimates of Black test performance, but not for White estimates of White performance; for dove estimates of typical hawk opinions, but not for hawk estimates of typical dove opinions; and for personality traits more than for attitude statements as stereotypic of business and engineering majors. The size of stereotypic exaggeration seldom exceeds 10 percentage points difference between criterion and estimated percentages.

There is also considerable evidence against the exaggeration hypothesis. Estimated differences between Black Americans and all Americans are smaller than criterion differences, and estimated differences in the proportion of males and females in gender-stereotyped occupations are underestimates of criterion differences. Likewise, business students and arts and sciences students err as often toward underestimating as toward exaggerating differences between their two groups, and male and female students err as often toward underestimating as toward exaggerating gender differences in preferences and behaviors.

In summary, the evidence available does not support the hypothesis of a large and consistent exaggeration effect in group stereotyping. Significant exaggeration does occur, but so does significant underestimation of group differences. There are some indications that exaggeration is more likely to occur in stereotyping of outgroups than in stereotyping of ingroups (Judd et al., 1991), but this tendency is not easily understood in terms of purely cognitive mechanisms.

Indeed, the strongest conclusion from the present review is that purely cognitive mechanisms of stereotype exaggeration are inadequate to explain the pattern of results. If stereotypic exaggeration is a function of perceptual mechanisms of contrast across a group boundary, then exaggeration should be a powerful and consistent result in perception of different groups, no matter what their relationship. Similarly, if stereotypic exaggeration is a function of economizing scarce information-processing resources, then exaggeration should again be a powerful and consistent result in perception of any two groups with real differences. The weak and contingent exaggeration effects actually reported argue strongly that neither of these cognitive mechanisms can be very strong.

It is still too soon to throw out the exaggeration hypothesis, however. Exaggeration of stereotypic characteristics may be a powerful tendency in perceptions of a group seen as an enemy. U.S. perceptions of the Japanese in World War II, for example, certainly suggest the possibility of caricature and stereotypic exaggeration in perceptions of an enemy group. Thus, motivational mechanisms for stereotype exaggeration may be more powerful than the purely cognitive mechanisms featured in current literature. This possibility is not easily evaluated on the basis of available research, none of which contain any indication that the stereotyping group felt real hostility toward the stereotyped group.

In the absence of strong evidence for the exaggeration hypothesis, it is tempting to ask why the hypothesis has been so appealing to so many psychologists. The beginnings of an answer may be suggested on the basis of recent research on the accuracy of perceptions of others' stereotypes. Rettew, Billman, and Davis (1993) measured stereotypes of males versus females, of business students versus arts and sciences students, and of Southern versus Californian students. They asked their subjects not only for their own stereotypes of these group differences, but for their subjects' perceptions of the outgroup stereotypes of these differences (e.g., asked male subjects to estimate the male–female difference perceived by the typical female). The consistent result was that subjects saw others' stereotypes as larger than their own.

These results suggest that stereotypes of stereotypes may be consistently exaggerated, perhaps more strongly and more consistently exaggerated than are stereotypes of real group differences. Perhaps psychologists are like subjects in the Rettew et al. (1993) experiment in believing that others' stereotypes are larger than their own.

REFERENCES

Allport, G. W. (1954). *The nature of prejudice.* Cambridge, MA: Addison-Wesley.

Campbell, D. T. (1956). Enhancement of contrast as composite habit. *Journal of Abnormal and Social Psychology, 53,* 350–355.

Clarke, R. B., & Campbell, D. T. (1955). A demonstration of bias in estimates of Negro ability. *Journal of Abnormal and Social Psychology, 51,* 585–588.

Dawes, R. M., Singer, D., & Lemons, F. (1972). An experimental analysis of the contrast effect and its implications for intergroup communication and the indirect assessment of attitude. *Journal of Personality and Social Psychology, 21,* 281–295.

Fiske, S. T., & Neuberg, S. L. (1990). A continuum of impression formation, from category-based to individuating processes: Influences of information and motivation on attention and interpretation. In M. P. Zanna (Ed.), *Advances in experimental social psychology* (Vol. 23, pp. 1–74). New York: Academic Press.

Higgins, E. T., & Bargh, J. A. (1987). Social cognition and social perception. *Annual Review of Psychology, 38,* 369–425.

Hovland, C. L., Harvey, O. J., & Sherif, M. (1957). Assimilation and contrast effects in reaction to communication and attitude change. *Journal of Abnormal and Social Psychology, 55,* 244–252.

Judd, C., & Park, B. (1993). Definition and assessment of accuracy in social stereotypes. *Psychological Review, 100,* 109–128.

Judd, C., Ryan, C., & Park, B. (1991). Accuracy in the judgment of in-group and outgroup variability. *Journal of Personality and Social Psychology, 61,* 366–379.

Katz, D., & Braly, K. W. (1933). Racial stereotypes of one hundred college students. *Journal of Abnormal and Social Psychology, 28,* 280–290.

LeVine, R. A., & Campbell, D. T. (1972). *Ethnocentrism*. New York: Wiley.

Lippmann, W. (1922). *Public opinion*. New York: Harcourt, Brace.

Locksley, A., Borgida, E., Brekke, N., & Hepburn, C. (1980). Sex stereotypes and social judgment. *Journal of Personality and Social Psychology, 39*, 821–831.

Manis, M. (1961). The interpretation of opinion statements as a function of recipient attitude and source prestige. *Journal of Abnormal and Social Psychology, 63*, 82–86.

Martin, C. L. (1987). A ratio measure of sex stereotyping. *Journal of Personality and Social Psychology, 52*, 489–499.

McCauley, C., & Hains, L. (1991). *Gender stereotyping of college students' preferences and behaviors*. Unpublished manuscript.

McCauley, C., & Rozin, P. (1989, April). *Mutual stereotyping of business and liberal arts students: A study of stereotype accuracy*. Paper presented at the annual meeting of the Eastern Psychological Association, Washington, DC.

McCauley, C., & Stitt, C. L. (1978). An individual and quantitative measure of stereotypes. *Journal of Personality and Social Psychology, 36*, 929–940.

McCauley, C., Stitt, C. L., & Segal, M. (1980). Stereotyping: From prejudice to prediction. *Psychological Bulletin, 87*, 195–208.

McCauley, C., & Thangavelu, K. (1991). Individual differences in strength of sex-occupation stereotyping: Reliability, validity, and some correlates. *Social Psychology Quarterly, 54*, 267–279.

McCauley, C., Thangavelu, K., & Rozin, P. (1988). Sex stereotyping of occupations in relation to television representations and census facts. *Basic and Applied Social Psychology, 9*, 197–212.

Nelson, T. E., Biernat, M. R., & Manis, M. (1990). Everyday base rates (sex stereotypes): Potent and resilient. *Journal of Personality and Social Psychology, 59*, 664–675.

Rettew, D. C., Billman, D., & Davis, R. A. (1993). Inaccurate perceptions of the amount others stereotype: Estimates about stereotypes of one's own group and other groups. *Basic and Applied Social Psychology, 14*, 121–142.

Simon, B., & Pettigrew, T. F. (1990). Social identity and perceived group homogeneity: Evidence for the ingroup homogeneity effect. *European Journal of Social Psychology, 20*, 269–286.

Stangor, C., & Ford, T. E. (1992). Accuracy and expectancy-confirming processing orientations and the development of stereotypes and prejudice. In W. Stroebe

& M. Hewstone (Eds.), *European review of social psychology* (Vol. 3, pp. 57–89). New York: Wiley.

Stangor, C., & McMillan, D. (1992). Memory for expectancy-consistent and expectancy-inconsistent information: A review of the social and social developmental literatures. *Psychological Bulletin, 111,* 42–61.

Zimbardo, P., & Ebbesen, E. B. (1969). *Influencing attitudes and changing behavior.* Reading, MA: Addison-Wesley.

10

Are Teacher Expectations Biased by Students' Gender, Social Class, or Ethnicity?

Lee J. Jussim and Jacquelynne Eccles

For some time now, social science perspectives on stereotypes have generally been divided between those emphasizing error, bias, and inaccuracy (e.g., American Psychological Association [APA], 1991; Fiske & Taylor, 1991; Jones, 1990; Marger, 1991; Miller & Turnbull, 1986) and those arguing that the error/bias/inaccuracy issue is a largely unanswered empirical question (Campbell, 1967; Judd & Park, 1993; Jussim, 1990, 1991; Jussim, McCauley, & Lee, chapter 1, this volume; McCauley, Stitt, & Segal, 1980). There are many ways in which stereotypes may go awry. First, they may lead people to errors and biases in their beliefs about social groups. Those beliefs may be factually incorrect, they may exaggerate real differences, or they may lead people to perceive outgroups as all alike. Although these issues are extremely important, they are not the focus of this chapter.

We gratefully acknowledge the valuable suggestions regarding this research provided by attendees of the 1994 Conference on Stereotype Accuracy, especially those of Richard Ashmore, Clark R. McCauley, and Victor Ottati. Preparation of this chapter was supported in part by National Institute on Child Health and Human Development Grant 1 R29 HD28401-01A1 to Lee J. Jussim. Correspondence regarding this chapter may be sent to Lee Jussim at Department of Psychology, Rutgers University, New Brunswick, New Jersey 08903 (phone: 908–932–2070; fax: 908–932–0036).

Presumably, however, erroneous stereotypes are a social problem primarily if they lead to biases and discrimination (if some people hold inaccurate social beliefs, but do not act any differently than others who hold accurate social beliefs, inaccuracy is not a problem). Inaccuracy becomes a problem when perceivers treat or evaluate one group differently than another as a result of that inaccuracy. Furthermore, many social psychologists believe both that stereotypes are frequently inaccurate and that they lead to all sorts of biases—consequently, they are frequently accused of being the cognitive culprits in prejudice and discrimination (e.g., Fiske & Taylor, 1991; Hamilton, Sherman, & Ruvolo, 1990). Others, however, have argued that the empirical evidence supporting the conclusion that stereotypes are generally inaccurate and lead to biases and discrimination is actually sparse, weak, and equivocal (see reviews by Jussim, 1990, 1991; Jussim et al., chapter 1, this volume; McCauley et al., 1980). Therefore, this chapter focuses on the role of stereotypes in leading to errors and biases in a context of critical importance for issues of justice, fairness, and equality of opportunity: education. Specifically, this chapter addresses whether teachers' stereotypes lead them to evaluate students from different sex, social class, and ethnic groups differently, when they do not deserve to be evaluated differently. This question goes to the heart of some of the alleged problems with stereotypes.

PROCESS AND CONTENT IN RESEARCH ON STEREOTYPES

The overwhelming majority of social psychological research on stereotypes has been experimental laboratory studies. This research has several important merits. Tightly controlled studies aptly highlight some of the social and psychological processes relating stereotypes to person perception (e.g., Bodenhausen, 1988; Darley & Gross, 1983; Fiske & Neuberg, 1990; Krueger & Rothbart, 1988; Linville, 1982; Locksley, Borgida, Brekke, & Hepburn, 1980).

The experimental laboratory studies, however, also suffer several important limitations. They often use artificial or impoverished social stimuli (see, e.g., studies cited in APA, 1991, and reviews by Funder, chapter 6, this volume; Jussim, 1990, 1991, 1993). Perceivers often do not engage in face-to-face interactions with targets at all; they make judgments based on written descriptions of targets, slides, videotapes, and so on. Even when they do actually engage in a face-to-face interaction, it is usually with a stranger, for a period of an hour or less. And, of course, the laboratory studies primarily use college students as research subjects.

All of these factors may limit the generalizability of the findings from the experimental laboratory studies. However, the laboratory studies also suffer an extremely important conceptual or theoretical limitation. Studies that focus exclusively on identifying social–cognitive *processes* involved in stereotyping are completely incapable of drawing inferences about the accuracy of the *content* of stereotypes. For example, showing that categorization leads people to evaluate one group differently than they evaluate another group provides no information about whether the evaluation of either group is correct. Therefore, the implications of much of social psychology's knowledge base for understanding the accuracy of social stereotypes under naturalistic conditions are not clear.

Identifying accuracy or inaccuracy in the content and use of social stereotypes can be accomplished only when (a) the targets are real people with real attributes (as opposed to artificially created social stimuli), (b) there is some means of measuring those attributes (a criterion), and (c) perceivers' judgments are compared with the criterion.

The research described in this chapter was performed to help begin redressing this limitation to research on stereotypes by studying naturally occurring person perception and by comparing those perceptions to clear criteria. The first study addressed accuracy by comparing teacher perceptions of performance, talent, and effort differences among students from differing sex, socioeconomic, or ethnic groups to actual differences among those students. The second study examined the processes leading to accuracy and inaccuracy in teachers' perceptions of students from the differing groups.

TEACHER EXPECTATIONS

There are few contexts more important for investigating stereotypes than teachers' expectations for their students. Ever since Rosenthal and Jacobson's (1968) seminal and controversial (e.g., Elashoff & Snow, 1971) Pygmalion study, writers in both scholarly journals and the popular press have implicated teacher expectations as a major perpetrator of injustices and inequalities based on ethnicity, social class, and sex (see Wineburg, 1987, for a review). In this chapter, we present evidence suggesting that such claims present a greatly oversimplified picture of the role of teacher expectations in perpetuating social inequalities. This evidence will convey two main points. First, teachers generally perceive only small differences among social groups (e.g., ethnic groups, social class groups, and sex groups), that is, stereotypes do not seem to be a powerful influence on their expectations. Second, many of the differences that they do perceive are reasonably accurate; many (though not all) of the differences they perceive among different groups correspond to preexisting objective differences among those groups.

Perhaps the most comprehensive analysis to date of the role of stereotypes in the development of teacher expectations remains Dusek and Joseph's (1983) meta-analysis, which showed that teachers perceived moderate differences between students based on social class ($r = .23$) and little difference based on student sex or ethnicity ($rs = .04$ to $.10$). However, the relevance of these findings to naturally occurring teacher–student interactions is not clear. Most studies included in Dusek and Joseph's meta-analysis were experiments that suffered from two important limitations: (a) Targets were fictitious manipulations (they were not real students), and (b) although perceivers had access to some information about students, they generally had no opportunity to interact with students or observe their achievement over an extended period (as do real teachers interacting in real classrooms with real students). Therefore, whether in-service teachers perceive differences among students comparable to those obtained in Dusek and Joseph's (1983) meta-analysis is unknown.

STUDY 1

Three Main Research Questions

Study 1 addressed three main questions: (a) Do teachers perceive sex, social class, or ethnic differences in performance, talent, and effort? (b) How accurate are the differences (or lack of differences) teachers perceive among students from different sex, social class, and ethnic groups? (c) Do sex, social class, and ethnic stereotypes lead to biases and errors in teachers' perceptions of students?

The strategy for addressing these questions was straightforward. First, we identified whether teachers perceived performance, talent, and effort differences among students from the different demographic groups. Next, we compared the differing groups on measures of performance, talent, and effort. We concluded that teachers were accurate when the size of the difference they perceived approximately corresponded to the size of the actual difference among students. Teachers' perceptions were inaccurate when the differences they perceived among students from the different groups substantially deviated from the actual differences. They could be inaccurate in either of two directions: (a) They might overestimate differences among groups (in the extreme, they might see a difference where none existed), or (b) they might underestimate differences between groups (in the extreme, they might perceive no difference when one existed).

The Data

This study was based on the Michigan Study of Adolescent Life Transitions Project (Eccles, 1988), which assessed a variety of social, psychological, demographic, and achievement-related variables in a sample that included about 100 teachers and 2,600 students in sixth-grade math classes. Three teacher expectation variables were assessed in early October of sixth grade: teacher perceptions of students' performance, talent, and effort at math. Student motivation, which was also assessed in early October (just before the assessment of teacher perceptions), included self-concept of math ability and self-perceptions of effort and time spent on math homework. All measures were reliable and valid (for more detail, see Eccles, 1988; Eccles [Parsons], Adler, & Meece, 1984; Jussim, 1987, 1989; Jussim & Eccles, 1992; Parsons, 1980).

Final marks in fifth-grade math classes were the primary measure of performance. Scores on standardized achievement tests taken in late fifth or early sixth grade were the primary measure of talent. Although both measures are imperfect, we believe that they provide reasonable criteria with which to compare teacher perceptions. Grades are imperfect because they may reflect not only performance, but also neatness, assignment completion, cooperativeness, and teacher bias. Standardized tests are imperfect because in addition to underlying competencies, they may also reflect motivation, illness, and so on. Despite these imperfections, grades primarily represent the quality of students' performance over the course of the school year. If this were not true, the correlation between grades and standardized test scores (which are not influenced by neatness, cooperativeness, or teacher bias) would not be so high (e.g., Jussim, 1987; Jussim & Eccles, 1992). Also, standardized tests are intended to assess students' enduring competencies, knowledge, and skills, and in general, they are usually quite successful at doing so (e.g., Anastasi, 1982).

Results

Student Sex

These analyses were based on 942 girls (coded as 1) and 847 boys (coded as 2). This was the subsample that had valid data on all variables necessary for analyses involving student sex. Did teachers perceive differences between boys and girls? They did, albeit small ones. Teachers perceived girls as performing slightly more highly ($r = -.08$, $p < .001$) and as trying harder ($r = -.16$, $p < .001$). They perceived no difference in boys' and girls' talent ($r = .02$).

Were these perceptions accurate? For performance and talent, the answer is yes. Girls had performed slightly higher than did boys in fifth-grade math classes ($r = -.07$, $p < .01$), a real but small difference that corresponded closely to the real but small perceived difference in performance.

Similarly, there was no sex difference in standardized test scores ($r = .00$), which corresponded with teachers' perceptions of no talent difference.

There was no evidence in these data that teacher perceptions of sex differences in effort were accurate. Boys and girls reported exerting the same amounts of effort ($r = .00$) and spending the same amount of time on homework ($r = -.03$). Self-concept of ability was considered a motivational variable because of its crucial role in leading to effort and persistence, according to several motivational theories (e.g., Bandura, 1977; Eccles & Wigfield, 1985; Weiner, 1979). However, boys actually had slightly higher self-concepts of math ability than did girls ($r = .09$, $p < .001$).

Were teachers biased by students' sex? For performance and talent, the answer is no; for effort, the answer is yes. Were teachers biased against girls? No; if anything, they seemed biased in favor of girls. They evaluated girls as trying harder than boys, even though boys and girls claimed to be working equally hard and even though boys had higher self-concepts of ability.

Social Class

These analyses assessed whether teachers perceived differences among students from differing socioeconomic backgrounds. To address this question, we obtained the multiple correlation of parental education and family income with each of the three teacher-perception variables. Parental education (for 98% of the students, this was the mother's education) and family income information was available for 1,066 students.

Did teachers perceive social class differences in performance and talent? They did. Teachers perceived students from higher social class backgrounds as performing more highly ($R = .21$) and as more talented ($R = 26$, both $ps < .01$). Were there real social class differences? There were. Parental income and education correlated with fifth-grade final grades ($R = .27$) and previous standardized achievement test scores ($R = .31$, both $ps < .001$).

Did teachers perceive social class differences in effort? They did. Teachers saw students from higher social class backgrounds as trying harder ($R = .18$, $p < .01$). Were there real social class differences in effort? Although there were no social class differences in self-reported effort or time spent on homework (both $Rs < .05$, ns), students from higher social class backgrounds had higher self-concepts of math ability ($R = .15$, $p < .01$). Thus, teacher perceptions of effort corresponded reasonably well with student social class differences in self-concept of ability.

Overall, therefore, these results provided little evidence that teachers were biased by students' social class. There was no evidence at all that teachers were biased against students from lower socioeconomic backgrounds.

Ethnicity

These analyses focused on teacher perceptions of African American students and White students. There were too few students from other ethnic backgrounds to warrant performing analyses.

Did teachers perceive differences between African American students and White students? Answering this question turns out to be more difficult than it may seem, primarily because the continuing patterns of residential segregation in the United States were largely reflected in these data. Specifically, 10 school districts had predominantly White students. None had fewer than 88% White students, and as a group, 95% of the students in these 10 districts were White.

One district was integrated (63% White, 34% African American, and 3% other). One district included predominantly (93%) African American students. Because of these differences between districts, we performed two separate sets of analyses. The first set of analyses examined teacher perceptions and student differences among the White students in the White segregated districts, the African American students in the White segregated districts, and the African American students in the African American segregated districts. There were only four White students in the African American segregated district. Because this number is too small to permit meaningful analyses, data on this group were not included in any of the results we report below. The second set of analyses examined teacher perceptions of and student differences between the African American students and White students in the integrated district.

We report means, rather than correlations for analyses focusing on the segregated districts, to keep clear differences between teacher perceptions of African American students in the segregated White versus segregated African American districts. Also, because there were virtually no White students in the segregated African American district, it would be impossible to compute correlations involving ethnicity in that district. Because of the large sample size, very small and trivial differences among groups sometimes yielded statistically significant F values. Therefore, when results reach statistical significance, we also report the effect size (*etas*), and we used Scheffé's method (which is conservative) for testing post hoc comparisons among groups.

This first set of analyses actually combine two different sets of comparisons. Ethnic differences within the White segregated districts involve teacher ratings of different students in their classes. The questions here were, "In the White segregated district, do teachers perceive ethnic differences? And how well do their perceptions correspond to actual ethnic differences?" However, comparisons involving the segregated African American students involve *between-districts* comparisons. The questions here were, "Do teachers in the segregated African-American district view their students differently than teachers view African-American and White students in the White segregated district? And are there differences between students in the segregated African-American district and either the White or African-American students in the segregated White district?" Although these questions are quite different from one another, both are important. Therefore, the first set of analyses addressed these questions.

The segregated districts. In the segregated districts, none of the differences in teachers' perceptions of African American versus White students were statistically significant (all $Fs < 2.5$, all $ps > .05$). Teachers perceived little difference in the performance, talent, and effort between African American students and White students.

Were teacher perceptions of no performance or talent differences justified? The differences between the African American and White students in the segregated districts were significant for both standardized test scores, $F(2, 2034) = 35.75$, $p < .001$, $=.18$, and final grades, $F(2, 1947) = 11.88$, $p < .001$, $\eta = .11$. Table 1 contains the mean previous grades and standardized test scores for students in the segregated districts and shows that

<table>
<tr><th colspan="4" style="text-align:center">Table 1</th></tr>
</table>

Were There Ethnic Differences in Achievement in the Segregated Districts of Study 1?

Measure	White students in White districts	African American students in White districts	African American students in the African American district
Standardized test scores	61_a	52_a	38_b
n	1,907	39	91
Fifth grade final marks	$B-/B_a$	$C+/B-_{a,b}$	$C+_b$
n	1,865	26	59

NOTE: Standardized test scores listed in percentile ranks. Across rows, means that share at least one subscript are not significantly different at $p < .05$.

teacher perceptions were partially justified. In the segregated White districts, although there was a slight tendency for the White students to perform more highly than did African American students, neither the standardized test score differences nor the grade differences were statistically significant (all $ts < 1.4$, all $ps > .1$). Therefore, teachers were justified in perceiving few differences between African American students and White students in the White segregated districts.

However, Table 1 also shows that the African American students in the segregated African American district performed significantly more poorly in terms of both standardized test scores and previous grades than did White students (both $ts > 3$, both $ps < .01$). Therefore, teachers were not justified in evaluating the performance of the African American students in the segregated African American district as favorably as teachers judged the performance of the White students in the segregated White districts.

Teachers were also reasonably justified in perceiving no differences in the effort exerted by the different groups of students. The differences among students on the three motivation variables reached statistical significance for time spent on homework, $F(2, 2383) = 4.68$, $p < .01$; self-concept of math ability, $F(2, 2383) = 4.58$, $p < .02$; and marginal significance for self-perceptions of effort, $F(2, 2388) = 2.81$, $p < .07$. However, only one of the post hoc comparisons was significant: African American students in the segregated African American district had higher self-concepts of math ability than had the White students in the White segregated district ($t = 2.11, p < .05$). Furthermore, all of the *etas* were below .07, indicating that although statistically significant, the differences were minor.

The integrated district. Did teachers perceive the 22 African American students differently than they perceived the 40 White students in the integrated district? They did. Teachers perceived White students as performing more highly ($r = -.27, p < .05$), as more talented ($r = -.26, p < .05$), and as exerting more effort, although this last difference did not reach statistical significance ($r = -.20, p = .12$).

Were these perceptions justified? The African American students did have lower fifth-grade marks than did White students in this district (C/C+ vs. B−, $r = -.21$). However, because not all of the students in sixth grade attended this district in fifth grade, this difference was based on only 32 White students and 14 African American students, and it was not statistically significant ($p = .16$). It was, however, of about the same magnitude as the differences that teachers perceived. Unfortunately, no standardized test had been given in this district in fifth grade.

Did teacher perceptions of effort differences correspond to ethnic differences in the motivation variables? African American students and White students in this district all claimed to be exerting about the same amount of effort and spending about the same amount of time on homework; all had similar self-concepts of ability (all $rs < .07$, all $ps > .6$). Thus, there was a slight, but nonsignificant, tendency for teachers to perceive White students as trying harder, and no evidence in the student effort and motivation variables to suggest any ethnic difference in effort.

Discussion

Teacher Expectations and Stereotypes: Preliminary Conclusions

Some answers to the three questions guiding this first study are now available. Did teachers perceive differences between boys and girls, middle-class

255

and lower-class students, and African American and White students? They did. They perceived girls as performing slightly higher and as trying harder than boys, but they also evaluated their natural talent at math as similar. Teachers also viewed the performance, talent, and effort of middle-class students more favorably than those of lower-class students.

The results regarding ethnicity were mixed. Teachers perceived no differences among African American students and White students in the segregated districts. In the integrated districts, however, they evaluated the White students more favorably.

How accurate were the differences and similarities that teachers perceived? For the most part, they were accurate. For all three demographic groups, teachers' perceptions of students' performance or talent generally corresponded quite closely to the actual differences or similarities in those groups' previous grades and standardized test scores. There was only one exception to this pattern: Teachers rated African American students in the predominantly African American district as favorably as other students, when, in fact, both their grades and standardized test scores were not as high as those of other students.

The pattern for teacher perceptions of effort was more mixed, providing evidence of both accuracy and inaccuracy. Teachers believed that girls tried harder than boys, but there was no difference between the sexes on the effort measures, and boys felt they had more math ability than girls felt they had. Thus, there was no evidence of accuracy here. In contrast, however, teacher beliefs that middle-class students tried harder than did lower-class students corresponded closely to student social class differences in self-concept of math ability. This belief, therefore, seems to have been reasonably accurate. Similarly, in both the integrated and segregated school districts, the teachers perceived few differences in the effort of African American versus White students. These perceptions were also reasonably accurate; few differences emerged on either the effort measures or on self-concept of ability.

Were teachers biased by student sex, class, or ethnicity? Sometimes it seemed that they were. However, there was no evidence that teachers were biased against girls, students from lower-class backgrounds, or African American students. Instead, teacher perceptions of effort were biased in favor of girls, and their perceptions of performance and talent were biased in favor of the African American students in the predominantly African American district. They also perceived slightly smaller social class differences than really existed. Even these biases, however, were relatively modest. Overall, therefore, these data provide little evidence of pervasive or powerful biases based on sex, social class, or ethnicity.

Why Was There So Little Evidence of Bias?

Social desirability. Perhaps teachers attempted to appear socially desirable in providing favorable evaluations of girls and African American students. This seems unlikely for several methodological and conceptual reasons. First, teachers were simply asked to evaluate the students in their classes; the role of student demographics was never mentioned. Thus, issues involving stereotypes should not have been particularly salient. Second, if the social desirability explanation were true for ethnicity, there should have been more reverse bias in classes where teachers had both African American students and White students than in classes where there were only African American students. This is because interethnic comparisons should be far more salient in the mixed classes. In fact, however, the pattern we obtained was the opposite: There was no evidence of reverse bias in the mixed classes, whereas there was some bias in the segregated African American classes.

The main reverse bias for sex involved effort: Teachers perceived girls as trying harder than boys. Other analyses based on these same data, however, showed that teachers take their effort perceptions quite seriously; teachers provide higher grades to students believed to be trying harder (Jussim, 1989; Jussim & Eccles, 1992). This does not seem to be the behavior of teachers simply trying to act in a socially desirable manner. Furthermore, even the current data could be construed as providing at least a hint of bias against girls. That is, even though girls were perceived as performing more highly than boys, they were seen as "merely" equally talented, but as trying harder.

Another version of the social desirability explanation suggests that teachers may be more reluctant to rely on stereotypes than they were 20 or 30 years ago. That is, modern teacher training may often include discussion of self-fulfilling prophecy in general, or at least the original Rosenthal and Jacobson (1968) study, thereby reducing teachers' susceptibility to basing their expectations on erroneous, superficial information. In fact, however, there is no evidence that teachers' beliefs in demographic differences have changed much over the past 30 years (see Jussim, Madon, & Chatman, 1994, for a review); and self-fulfilling prophecies effect sizes have remained remarkably stable since the original Rosenthal and Jacobson study (see Jussim & Eccles, 1995, for a review).

Change of standards. Perhaps, however, the slight positive bias in favor of African American students in the segregated district resulted from teachers using differing standards for their students than were used in the other districts. When evaluating students on a subjective rating scale and when faced with overall lower levels of performance, perhaps a teacher's subjective rating of a student as meriting a 3 in performance in the segregated African American district reflects a somewhat lower level of actual performance than a 3 typically reflects in the White segregated districts (see, e.g., Biernat & Manis, 1994). Thus, even one of the results that looked like bias, teachers rating the students in the segregated African American district as highly as teachers rated students in the segregated White districts, may be more apparent than real.

They held no stereotypes. The simplest explanation for the lack of bias is that teachers held no negative stereotypes about girls, students from lower social class backgrounds, or African American students. If they held no stereotype, then there would be no stereotype to bias their perceptions. Unfortunately, this possibility cannot be tested directly, because teachers' social stereotypes were not assessed.

However, this explanation seems highly implausible for at least two reasons. First, nearly all of the teachers in the current study would need to have no such stereotypes. If even a substantial minority held (and used) stereotypes, there still should have been some evidence of bias. Furthermore, abundant research in the social sciences attests to the widespread existence and importance of these stereotypes (e.g., APA, 1991; Darley & Gross, 1983; Dusek & Joseph, 1983; Fiske & Taylor, 1991; Jones, 1990;

Marger, 1991). Thus, the likelihood that this sample of teachers was unique in that virtually none held stereotypes seems vanishingly small.

Second, some researchers have argued that one does not need even to subscribe to a stereotype for that stereotype to influence social perception (Devine, 1989; Sedikides & Skowronski, 1991). Mere knowledge of a cultural stereotype (regardless of whether one accepts it oneself), they argue, is sometimes sufficient to produce biases. Thus, one would need to argue not only that nearly our entire sample of teachers did not subscribe to stereotypes, but that they were all oblivious to them. This, too, seems highly implausible.

Teachers did not use their stereotypes. Another explanation could be that teachers did hold stereotypes regarding these groups, but did not use them in evaluating students. Research in education and social psychology suggests considerable plausibility for this explanation. Research on classrooms has consistently demonstrated considerable accuracy in teacher perceptions of students (Jussim, 1989; Jussim & Eccles, 1992; West & Anderson, 1976; Williams, 1976; see Brophy, 1983; Brophy & Good, 1974; Jussim, 1991, for reviews). Teachers generally judge students far more on the basis of their achievement and motivation than on teachers' own social stereotypes. And teachers are not the least bit unique. Whether individual targets are men and women, upper class and lower class, African American and White perceivers generally judge them far more on the basis of their personal characteristics than on their membership in these social groups. This occurs both in laboratory studies and in naturalistic studies (see Jussim, 1990, 1993, for reviews), and this possibility was directly tested in Study 2.

Teachers used accurate stereotypes. Another explanation could be that teachers do hold stereotypes regarding these groups, and they did, at least partially, rely on those stereotypes when judging students. Then why was there so little evidence of bias? If teachers relied on accurate stereotypes, they would have little or no tendency to exaggerate differences among the groups of students. This possibility could be tested with these data, and such a test is provided in the next study.

STUDY 2

Were Teachers Relying on Accurate Stereotypes?

Study 1 showed that teachers' perceptions of differences between students in the various groups were mostly accurate. In Study 2, additional analyses using the same data and teacher–student samples as in Study 1 were performed to compare the "teachers did not use their stereotypes" and "teachers used accurate stereotypes" alternative explanations for the lack of bias in Study 1. The question addressed in Study 2 was, Did relying on an accurate stereotype facilitate accuracy in teacher perceptions? Addressing this question requires answering two subquestions: (a) Did teachers rely on stereotypes when judging students, and (b) if so, did relying on stereotypes enhance or undermine their accuracy? Thus, whereas Study 1 focused exclusively on issues of content (e.g., were teacher perceptions of students from different groups accurate?), Study 2 focused on issues of process.

How can one discover if teachers relied on stereotypes when stereotypes were not assessed? One can do so indirectly, using the methods first developed in experimental social psychological laboratory studies of stereotypes and person perception. The prototypical and classic studies in this area involved no assessment of stereotypes. Instead, social psychological studies of the role of stereotypes in person perception typically manipulate targets' social group membership, hold constant or manipulate information about targets' personal characteristics, and assess whether perceivers judge targets from one group differently than targets from another group (e.g., Bodenhausen, 1988; Darley & Gross, 1983; Fiske & Neuberg, 1990; Krueger & Rothbart, 1988; Linville, 1982; Locksley et al., 1980; see reviews by Darley & Fazio, 1980; Fiske & Taylor, 1991; Hamilton et al., 1990; Jussim, 1990). If perceivers judge targets from different groups differently (holding constant targets' behavior or attributes), perceivers are assumed to be relying on their stereotypes when judging targets.

This is the strategy we used for identifying whether teachers relied on stereotypes in evaluating their students. Analyses assessed whether teachers perceived differences based on student sex, class, or ethnicity, when holding constant statistically students' achievement and motivation. Specifically, we performed a series of regressions in which students' performance and motivation, and their social group memberships, predicted teacher perceptions. Operationally, therefore, the "relied on stereotypes" hypothesis was that teacher perceptions would be based on student group membership, even after controlling for student performance and motivation.

Results

Sex Stereotypes

Three regressions were performed, in which student sex, previous grades, standardized test scores, self-concept of math ability, time spent on homework, and self-perceptions of effort predicted each of the three teacher-perception variables. The main questions here were (a) Would student sex predict teacher perceptions, independent of the other variables, (b) if so, did the student sex effect enhance or undermine accuracy, and (c) to what extent did teachers rely on their sex stereotypes versus individuating information (previous achievement and motivation)?

Table 2 summarizes the results from these analyses. These results showed that teachers seemed to be relying on an accurate stereotype when judging students' performance. The *beta* relating student sex to teacher perceptions of performance was −.09, which closely corresponded to the small sex differences in grades of −.07 (found in Study 1). Although teachers also judged students on the basis of their performance, doing so was not the main source of the correlation between teacher perceptions and student sex. The effect of student sex on teacher perceptions (−.09) accounted for most of the correlation between sex and teacher perceptions (−.07). This means that teachers apparently stereotyped girls as performing at a higher level than boys, independent of the actual sex differences in performance. However, the extent to which they did so corresponded reasonably well with the actual small sex difference in performance.

Results for teacher perceptions of talent provided no evidence of

	Table 2

Did Teachers Rely on Students' Sex, Independent of Students' Achievement and Motivation in Study 2?

	Teacher's perception		
Predictor	Performance	Talent	Effort
Student sex	−.09*	.02	−.16*
Fifth-grade final marks	.23*	.21*	.22*
Standardized test scores	.36*	.42*	.25*
Self-concept of math ability	.22*	.18*	.15*
Effort self-perceptions	.05*	.00	.11*
Time spent on homework	−.06*	−.05*	−.02
R^2	.47*	.47*	.32*

NOTE: All entries are standardized regression coefficients. $N = 1,789$ (942 girls; 847 boys).
*$p < .01.89$ (942 girls and 847 boys)

teachers relying on a stereotype. The *beta* relating student sex to teacher perceptions of talent was .02 (*ns*), corresponding closely to a .00 correlation of student sex with standardized test scores.

Results for teacher perceptions of effort suggested reliance on an inaccurate stereotype. The *beta* relating student sex to teacher perceptions of effort was −.16 ($p < .001$), even though the correlations of student sex with self-concept of ability, time spent on homework, and self-perceptions of effort were .09, −.03, and .00, respectively. Teachers apparently erroneously stereotype girls as trying harder, oblivious to boys' higher motivation (as indicated by self-concept of ability) and the similarities between boys' and girls' effort.

Which was a more powerful influence on teacher perceptions, sex stereotypes or individuating information? Table 2 clearly shows that all three teacher perceptions were based far more on students' grades, standardized test scores, and self-concept of ability than they were based on student sex.

Social Class Stereotypes

Analyses were identical to those examining teachers' sex stereotypes, except that instead of student sex, parental education and income were included in the equations predicting teacher perceptions of performance, talent, and effort. Results are presented in Table 3.

These analyses provided no evidence that teachers relied on social class stereotypes. The R^2 increment associated with adding parental income and education to the regression equations never exceeded .05 and was never statistically significant (all $Fs < 2.3$, all $ps > .1$). Of the six possible individual relations between income and education and the three teacher-perception variables, only one was statistically significant (education predicted teacher perceptions of talent, $p < .05$), but the *beta* was very small (.05). Apparently, the accuracy of teacher perceptions of social class differences in performance, talent, and effort occurred because teachers evaluated students on the basis of their achievement and motivation—factors that correlated with social class.

Table 3

Did Teachers Rely on Students' Social Class, Independent of Students' Achievement and Motivation in Study 2?

	Teacher's perception		
Predictor	Performance	Talent	Effort
Parental income	−.02	.00	.00
Parental education	.02	.05*	.02
Fifth-grade final marks	.26**	.21**	.27**
Standardized test scores	.35**	.42**	.21**
Self-concept of math ability	.20**	.16**	.11**
Effort self-perceptions	.09**	.03	.13**
Time spent on homework	−.06*	−.05*	−.03
R^2	.48**	.48**	.30**

NOTE: All entries are standardized regression coefficients. $N = 1,066$.
*$p < .05$.   **$p < .01$.

Which was a more powerful influence on teacher perceptions, social class stereotypes or individuating information? Table 3 clearly shows that teachers almost always based their perceptions more (and often much more) on the individuating information (previous achievement and motivation) than on student social class as indicated by parental income and education.

Ethnic Stereotypes

For these analyses, students' ethnicity, grades, self-concept of ability, effort, and time spent on homework predicted teacher perceptions. Standardized test scores were not used as predictors because in the integrated districts, students had not taken a standardized test in fifth or early sixth grade. Therefore, using standardized test scores as a predictor would have had the undesirable effect of excluding these students from the analyses. These analyses included 1,873 White students and 96 African American students. Results are presented in Table 4.

Table 4

Did Teachers Rely on Students' Ethnicity, Independent of Students' Achievement and Motivation in Study 2?

| | Teacher's perception | | |
Predictor	Performance	Talent	Effort
Student ethnicity	.00	.03	.06*
Fifth-grade final marks	.41*	.42*	.36*
Self-concept of math ability	.32*	.29*	.21*
Effort self-perceptions	.02	−.02	.10*
Time spent on homework	−.06*	−.06*	−.03
R^2	.38	.36	.26

NOTE: All entries are standardized regression coefficients. $N = 1,969$ (1,873 White students and 96 African American students).
*$p < .01$.

These analyses provided little evidence that teachers relied on ethnic stereotypes. Student ethnicity had no significant effect on teacher perceptions of performance ($\beta = .00$, *ns*) and talent ($\beta = .03$). Ethnicity did, however, have a small effect on teacher perceptions of effort ($\beta = .06$, $p < .01$), indicating a slight tendency to see African American students as trying harder.

Which was a more powerful influence on teacher perceptions, ethnic stereotypes or individuating information? Table 4 clearly shows that all three teacher perceptions were based far more on students' grades, standardized test scores, and self-concept of ability than they were based on student ethnicity.

Discussion

Study 2 provided some clear insights into why the results of Study 1 showed such minimal evidence of bias. With a few notable exceptions (discussed below), teachers seemed to be basing their perceptions of students on those students' actual performance and motivation. Neither student social class nor ethnicity influenced teacher perceptions, after controlling for students' actual achievement and motivation. Similarly, student sex had no influence on teacher perceptions of talent, after controlling for students' actual achievement and motivation.

These results clearly rule out one possible explanation for the results showing accuracy in Study 1. Those results did not occur because teachers were relying on an accurate stereotype. Instead, these Study 2 results showed that teachers judged students almost exclusively on the basis of their actual performance and motivation. Thus, either teachers were oblivious to sex, class, and ethnic stereotypes, or they did not apply their stereotypes when evaluating their students.

The likelihood that teachers were oblivious to three of the major stereotypes in American culture seems vanishingly small. The cumulative wisdom of years of social psychological research on stereotypes points to the second explanation, that teachers did not apply their stereotypes. Abundant research in the laboratory and field shows that perceivers generally evaluate targets far more on the basis of targets' personal characteristics than on targets' membership in social groups (Jussim, 1990, 1991,

1993, for reviews). In general, the more individuating information perceivers have, the less they rely on stereotypes (Eagly, Ashmore, Makhijani, & Longo, 1991; Krueger & Rothbart, 1988; Locksley et al. 1980). Of course, teachers interacting with students over the first month of the school year generally have considerably more (and probably more objective) individuating information about students than do subjects in even the most ecologically valid laboratory experiment. Thus, it should come as no surprise that, in general, teachers did not rely much on their stereotypes when evaluating students.

There were a few exceptions to this pattern. In the case of student sex, teachers did indeed seem to be relying on an accurate stereotype regarding performance: Teachers apparently evaluated students' performance on the basis of their sex, independent of their actual achievement. However, the extent to which they did so corresponded reasonably well with actual prior sex differences in achievement. It is important to highlight just what this means. Because even an accurate stereotype does not apply equally well to all members of the stereotyped group, it seems likely that teachers misperceived some boys and girls. However, it also means that there was no tendency to systematically over- or underestimate the performance of girls.

In contrast, however, teachers seemed to be relying on an inaccurate stereotype in evaluating boys' and girls' effort. Teachers' more favorable impressions of girls' effort probably occur because, on average, girls are often more cooperative and pleasant than are boys and because teachers prefer more cooperative and pleasant students (e.g., Brophy & Good, 1974; Bye, 1994; Wentzel, 1989). The results regarding effort are consistent with a growing body of literature showing that school is often a hostile place for boys. For example, at least some teachers believe that boys suffer from inferior verbal skills—and this belief may become self-fulfilling (Palardy, 1969). Similarly, boys are referred for psychological evaluations far more than are girls, even when the teachers themselves do not rate boys as any more aggressive or in need of psychological services than girls (Bye, 1994). Similarly, one usually finds far more boys than girls in special education classes (Bye, 1994; Ravitch, 1993). And boys often receive lower grades than do girls, even when their performances on standardized achievement tests are similar (Kimball, 1989).

The finding that teachers seemed to be relying on sex stereotypes more than ethnic or social class stereotypes is broadly consistent with other research suggesting something uniquely powerful about sex stereotypes. Specifically, after 25 years of research, there is currently excellent converging evidence from both laboratory and field studies in a variety of contexts, showing that sex stereotypes are often self-fulfilling. In contrast, the evidence regarding the self-fulfilling effects of ethnic or social class stereotypes is either extremely limited or nonexistent. Precisely identifying why sex stereotypes may be unique remains an important question for future research.

CONCLUSION

Given the extent to which sexism, classism, and racism supposedly pervade American society, at first glance, the results of this study may appear surprising indeed. There was no evidence of teachers being biased against girls, students from lower-class backgrounds, or African American students. When teachers evaluated the students from one group more favorably than students from another group, those perceptions usually corresponded reasonably well to reality. The few biases and errors teachers seem to have committed were in the direction of evaluating students from traditionally disfavored groups more favorably than they deserved (girls' effort; in the African American, segregated district, performance and talent), or of seeing a slightly smaller difference than really existed (social class differences in performance and talent).

Of course, the current studies are mute on the question of the genesis of those real differences among groups. Furthermore, we are not claiming that stereotypes, prejudice, and discrimination do not exist or that they are unimportant. Perhaps sexism, classism, and racism contributed to the real differences among students. Nonetheless, claims about the power of stereotypes are rarely based on scientific, empirical data collected under naturalistic conditions. The current studies redress this limitation and provide little evidence of powerful or pervasive biases produced by stereotypes.

Social problems associated with gender, social class, and race undoubtedly exist, and they are terribly important. But economics, cultural differences among groups, socialization, after-effects of a history of discrimination, and a host of other factors probably play major roles in those social problems. The role of individuals' stereotypes in creating those problems is less clear.

REFERENCES

American Psychological Association. (1991). In the Supreme Court of the United States: *Price Waterhouse v. Ann B. Hopkins: Amicus curiae brief for the American Psychological Association. American Psychologist*, 46, 1061–1070.

Anastasi, A. (1982). *Psychological testing.* New York: Macmillan.

Bandura, A. (1977). Self-efficacy: Toward a unifying theory of behavioral change. *Psychological Bulletin*, 84, 191–215.

Biernat, M., & Manis, M. (1994). Shifting standards and stereotype-based judgments. *Journal of Personality and Social Psychology*, 66, 5–20.

Bodenhausen, G. V. (1988). Stereotypic biases in social decision making and memory: Testing process models of stereotype use. *Journal of Personality and Social Psychology*, 55, 726–737.

Brophy, J. (1983). Research on the self-fulfilling prophecy and teacher expectations. *Journal of Educational Psychology*, 75, 631–661.

Brophy, J., & Good, T. (1974). *Teacher–student relationships: Causes and consequences.* New York: Holt, Rinehart & Winston.

Bye, L. (1994). *Referral of elementary age students for social skill training: Student and teacher characteristics.* Unpublished doctoral dissertation, Rutgers University, New Brunswick, NJ.

Campbell, D. T. (1967). Stereotypes and the perception of group differences. *American Psychologist*, 22, 817–829.

Darley, J. M., & Fazio, R. H. (1980). Expectancy-confirmation processes arising in the social interaction sequence. *American Psychologist*, 35, 867–881.

Darley, J. M., & Gross, P. H. (1983). A hypothesis-confirming bias in labeling effects. *Journal of Personality and Social Psychology*, 44, 20–33.

Devine, P. (1989). Stereotypes and prejudice: Their automatic and controlled components. *Journal of Personality and Social Psychology, 56*, 5–18.

Dusek, J., & Joseph, G. (1983). The bases of teacher expectancies: A meta-analysis. *Journal of Educational Psychology, 75*, 327–346.

Eagly, A. H., Ashmore, R. D., Makhijani, M. G., & Longo, L. C. (1991). What is beautiful is good, but . . . : A meta-analysis of research on the physical attractiveness stereotype. *Psychological Bulletin, 110*, 109–128.

Eccles, J. (1988). *Achievement beliefs and environment.* Final report to the National Institute of Child Health and Development. Ann Arbor: University of Michigan.

Eccles (Parsons), J., Adler, T., & Meece, J. L. (1984). Sex differences in achievement: A test of alternate theories. *Journal of Personality and Social Psychology, 46*, 26–43.

Eccles, J., & Wigfield, A. (1985). Teacher expectations and student motivation. In J. Dusek (Ed.), *Teacher expectancies* (pp. 185–226). Hillsdale, NJ: Erlbaum.

Elashoff, J. D., & Snow, R. E. (1971). *Pygmalion reconsidered.* Worthington, OH: Jones.

Fiske, S. T., & Neuberg, S. L. (1990). A continuum of impression formation, from category-based to individuating processes: Influences of information and motivation on attention and interpretation. *Advances in Experimental Social Psychology, 23*, 1–74.

Fiske, S. T., & Taylor, S. E. (1991). *Social cognition* (2nd ed.). Reading, MA: Addison-Wesley.

Hamilton, D. L., Sherman, S. J., & Ruvolo, C. M. (1990). Stereotype-based expectancies: Effects on information processing and social behavior. *Journal of Social Issues, 46*, 35–60.

Jones, E. E. (1990). *Interpersonal perception.* New York: W. H. Freeman.

Judd, C. M., & Park, B. (1993). Definition and assessment of accuracy in social stereotypes. *Psychological Review, 100*, 109–128.

Jussim, L. (1987). Interpersonal expectations in social interaction: Self-fulfilling prophecies, confirmatory biases, and accuracy (Doctoral dissertation, University of Michigan, 1987). *Dissertation Abstracts International, 48*, 1845B.

Jussim, L. (1989). Teacher expectations: Self-fulfilling prophecies, perceptual biases, and accuracy. *Journal of Personality and Social Psychology, 57*, 469–480.

Jussim, L. (1990). Social reality and social problems: The role of expectancies. *Journal of Social Issues, 46*, 9–34.

Jussim, L. (1991). Social perception and social reality: A reflection–construction model. *Psychological Review, 98*, 54–73.

Jussim, L. (1993). Accuracy in interpersonal expectations: A reflection–construction analysis of current and classic research. *Journal of Personality, 61*, 637–668.

Jussim, L., & Eccles, J. (1992). Teacher expectations: II. Reflection and construction of student achievement. *Journal of Personality and Social Psychology, 63,* 947–961.

Jussim, L., & Eccles, J. (1995). Naturalistic studies of interpersonal expectancies. *Review of Personality and Social Psychology, 15,* 74–108.

Jussim, L., Madon, S., & Chatman, C. (1994). Teacher expectations and student achievement: Self-fulfilling prophecies, biases, and accuracy. In L. Heath et al. (Eds.), *Applications of heuristics and biases to social issues* (pp. 303–334). New York: Plenum.

Kimball, M. M. (1989). A new perspective on women's math achievement. *Psychological Bulletin, 105,* 198–214.

Krueger, J., & Rothbart, M. (1988). Use of categorical and individuating information in making inferences about personality. *Journal of Personality and Social Psychology, 55,* 187–195.

Linville, P. (1982). The complexity–extremity effect and age-based stereotyping. *Journal of Personality and Social Psychology, 42,* 193–211.

Locksley, A., Borgida, E., Brekke, N., & Hepburn, C. (1980). Sex stereotypes and social judgment. *Journal of Personality and Social Psychology, 39,* 821–831.

Marger, M. N. (1991). *Race and ethnic relations* (2nd ed.). Belmont, CA: Wadsworth.

McCauley, C., Stitt, C. L., & Segal, M. (1980). Stereotyping: From prejudice to prediction. *Psychological Bulletin, 87,* 195–208.

Miller, D. T., & Turnbull, W. (1986). Expectancies and interpersonal processes. *Annual Review of Psychology, 37,* 233–256.

Palardy, J. (1969). What teachers believe—What students achieve. *Elementary School Journal, 69,* 370–374.

Parsons, J. E. (1980). *Final Report to the National Institute of Education.* Washington, DC: National Institute of Education. (ERIC Document Reproduction Service No. ED 186 477)

Ravitch, D. (1993, November 26). Gender bias in the schools? It isn't true. *Newsday,* p. 151.

Rosenthal, R., & Jacobson, L. (1968). *Pygmalion in the classroom: Teacher expectation and student intellectual development.* New York: Holt, Rinehart and Winston.

Sedikides, C., & Skowronski, J. J. (1991). The law of cognitive structure activation. *Psychological Inquiry, 2,* 169–184.

Weiner, B. (1979). A theory of motivation for some classroom experiences. *Journal of Educational Psychology, 71,* 3–25.

Wentzel, K. R. (1989). Adolescent classroom goals, standards for performance, and academic achievement: An interactionist perspective. *Journal of Educational Psychology, 81,* 131–142.

West, C., & Anderson, T. (1976). The question of preponderant causation in teacher expectancy research. *Review of Educational Research, 46,* 613–630.

Williams, T. (1976). Teacher prophecies and the inheritance of inequality. *Sociology of Education, 49,* 223–236.

Wineburg, S. S. (1987). The self-fulfillment of the self-fulfilling prophecy. *Educational Researcher, 16,* 28–37.

PART FOUR

Conclusion: Opposing Views

11

Content and Application Inaccuracy in Social Stereotyping

Charles Stangor

This book on stereotype accuracy and inaccuracy owes its existence, at least in part, to the recent turn in social psychological research toward a focus on the accuracy of person perception, following a hiatus of two decades, during which the study of errors and biases of human judgment has been paramount. The current change has been spearheaded by the publication of important review pieces on the accuracy of social judgment (Funder, 1987; Kruglanski, 1989), in tandem with the development of new approaches of assessing accuracy (Kenny & Albright, 1987).

Although we are currently enjoying a "second coming" of accuracy research within the span of only several decades in social psychology as a whole, such rapid change has decidedly not been true of work within the area of social stereotyping. By any account, the focus of stereotyping researchers has been consistent and steady, involving a persistent concern with the potential inaccuracy of stereotypes and the negative outcomes of stereotyping on the victims of the stereotyping process. The themes of inaccuracy and injustice have been part and parcel of the writings of all in-

Work on this chapter was supported in part by a grant from the Lilly Foundation and by a University of Maryland Graduate School fellowship. Correspondence concerning this chapter should be addressed to Charles Stangor, Department of Psychology, University of Maryland, College Park, Maryland 20742.

fluential scholars in the field, beginning with Lippman (1922), Katz and Braly (1933), and Allport (1954), and continuing with the work of Tajfel (1981) and the contemporary theorists (Brewer, 1988; Fiske & Neuberg, 1990; Hamilton, 1981).

Despite this historical focus on error, inaccuracy, and unfairness, the notion that stereotypes are, at least in part, accurate is now being taken seriously for the first time within social psychology. This shift was apparent not only in the meeting of the present congress on stereotype accuracy, but also in the publication of an important book from a highly influential group of stereotype researchers (Oakes, Haslam, & Turner, 1994). The prevailing theme of both conference and book is that stereotypes are, at least in part, accurate and constitute the "social reality" of the individual. Of course, such statements are not entirely novel, for they have existed for many years in the form of the kernel-of-truth hypothesis (Brigham, 1971; Eagly & Steffen, 1984; Vinacke, 1957), which states that most stereotypes are, at least in part, accurate. And although this basic truth has frequently been lost in the focus on error, most contemporary work on stereotyping is entirely based on the assumption that there are real group differences that are perceived in everyday life and then exaggerated and distorted through cognitive and motivational biases (cf. Stangor & Lange, 1994).

Changes in the approach to a field of inquiry, such as a switch from a focus on inaccuracy to a focus on accuracy, are usually either the outcome of a decline in the utility of the current scientific paradigm or are the result of changes in the political and social climate surrounding the researchers. Although it is possible that a waning utility of the "bias" approach to social knowledge has prompted the recent turn of events in studying stereotypes, it is also possible that the social context is, at least in part, the determining cause. Political events in the sixties brought social psychology, along with the United States as a whole, into an era of concern with political correctness. During this time, we became sensitive (and perhaps overly so) to the use of stereotypes in everyday life. Today, the social context has radically changed. "Backlash" politics has brought with it an open discussion of the realities of intergroup differences, the explicit inequality of affirmative action programs, and a concern with the impact of true cultural differences on the future of our society. Even if not a contributing causal factor, the contemporary social context certainly provides an appropriate climate for the renewed study of stereotype accuracy.

The historical tradition of social stereotyping research within social psychology is also a contributing factor to the possibility of a focus on stereotype accuracy. Stereotype research has operated in a sort of social vacuum, in which only certain types of questions have been addressed. Most important, we have proceeded as if studying stereotyping meant that we study the stereotyper. Our literature is filled with articles documenting the development, maintenance, use, and potential change of stereotypes within the stereotyper; yet, we have virtually ignored the question of how those who are the targets of stereotyping respond to being stereotyped or to the implications of stereotyping on their social lives (for some few exceptions, see recent work by Crocker & Major, 1989; Frable, Blackstone, & Scherbaum, 1990; Lord & Saenz, 1985). This focus on the stereotyper, rather than the stereotyped, has determined how the accuracy question is itself framed. Our traditions lead us to be more likely to ask whether it is accurate for a stereotyper to use his or her stereotypes than to ask whether the outcomes of stereotype use are accurate for, or fair to, the targets of stereotyping.

Although from an empirical and scientific point of view, there is much to be learned by reconsidering issues of stereotype accuracy, in doing so we must continually remember that this research is located in a social and political context. It is my hope not only that the current focus on stereotype accuracy will be beneficial in a scientific sense in terms of advancing our theorizing about stereotypes and stereotyping, but also that this work will lead to a more explicit consideration of the impact of stereotypes on the targets of stereotyping, a concern that has long been neglected within the field.

CONTENT AND APPLICATION INACCURACY IN STEREOTYPING

In this chapter, I draw a distinction between *content inaccuracy* and *application inaccuracy* in the area of social stereotyping. This distinction reflects the relationship between stereotypes (as cognitive representations of social groups and their members) and stereotyping (the use of this knowledge as a basis of responding to others; cf. Brewer, in press). I consider both factors that are likely to produce either accurate or inaccurate social stereotypes (content effects), as well as factors that may lead to inappropriate, unfair, or inaccurate use of such stereotypes in the judgments of others (application effects).

In the course of this review, I come to the conclusion that measuring the content accuracy (or inaccuracy) of social stereotypes is a venture that is premature, that will at best produce relatively limited payoffs, and that at worst may result in our unintentionally communicating to the society at large that stereotypes are by and large accurate and, thus, generally appropriate to use as a basis for judging others. Fundamentally, I believe that a focus on the content accuracy of stereotypes is premature because we do not yet have a well-established method for documenting those group differences themselves. I believe that cataloging the nature of group differences is an important first step in producing an adequate remedy for negative intergroup behavior. We need to know both how big existing group differences are and how to communicate the extent of those differences to people. And we need to develop appropriate methodologies for assessing those differences. Yet I also believe that the likelihood that we will be able to draw broad conclusions about the general or even the specific accuracy of the *perceptions* of those differences (social stereotypes) is small. And even if ultimately successful, cataloging the accuracy of those stereotypes is a project that will have little importance for the study of intergroup relations more broadly.

Although I am not sanguine about the goal of assessing the content accuracy of stereotypes, I believe that studying accuracy in their application (the process of stereotyping others) represents a very important line of inquiry and one that should be a prime focus of those interested in the stereotyping process. Of course, such an interest is not a new one. Indeed, the major part of stereotyping research over the past two decades has been focused on the question of when and how stereotypes are used as a basis of judgment (Brewer, in press; Fiske & Neuberg, 1990; Locksley, Borgida,

Brekke, & Hepburn, 1980). I believe that a focus on application rather than content has been due partly to the perception that application inaccuracy is an extremely important question with direct social relevance.

My conclusion that application accuracy is more important than content accuracy is based on my belief that stereotypes, as one type of social belief, are inherently neutral entities. Stereotypes, even when objectively inaccurate or overly negative, are neither "good" nor "bad." A person who holds the belief that most Jews are stingy may be factually incorrect and may be deceiving him- or herself, but holding this belief does not in itself represent a grave danger to Jews or to the society at large. On the other hand, the inappropriate use of stereotypic beliefs as a basis of responding to others, *even if those beliefs are entirely accurate*, is potentially damaging to the stereotyped individuals.

The distinction between content and application inaccuracy leads to the potential question of whether application effects should be considered as accuracy or whether *stereotype accuracy* refers only to the issue of content. Yet, I see no reason to consider one question more relevant to the accuracy issue than the other. Content accuracy and application accuracy represent two different issues, each of which can be studied in terms of potential accuracy or inaccuracy.

FACTORS LIKELY TO PRODUCE ACCURATE OR INACCURATE STEREOTYPES

Although I do not believe that studying the content accuracy of social stereotypes is a particularly fruitful endeavor, an analysis of the processes underlying stereotype development more generally may be useful for those interested in understanding when and why stereotypes are likely to be accurate or inaccurate. Stereotypes are frequently conceptualized as "tools" (Gilbert & Hixon, 1991; Macrae, Milne, & Bodenhausen, 1994) that individuals create to help them solve a variety of everyday social needs. If this utilitarian conceptualization of stereotypes has validity, then we may well expect that stereotypes that develop to fulfill different functions will have differential content accuracy. Although my analysis of the content accuracy issue is based on this assumption, I actually know of no research that has directly tested these predictions.

Some social stereotypes develop because they serve for the stereotyper the function of providing diagnostic information about social groups. In this case, stereotypes allow the individual to understand, predict, control, and "master" their social worlds. It is useful to know that lawyers are likely to be rich and nurses poor when one is choosing a marriage partner or even a date for the evening. This goal of creating social reality and "enriching" social perception forms the theme of Oakes et al.'s analysis of stereotypes (Oakes et al., 1994). There is existing evidence to support the idea that some stereotypes develop due to their diagnostic functions. For instance, Ford and Stangor (1992) found that traits that most highly distinguished among social groups became more stereotypic (in the sense of becoming strongly connected with the group representation in memory) in comparison with traits that were less differentiating. In this sense, more diagnostic information became stereotypic.

The finding that some stereotypes develop on the basis of their informational value does not, however, mean that all or even most stereotypes are accurate. For one, accuracy *motives* do not necessarily lead to accurate *beliefs* (cf. Kruglanski, 1989). Just as opponent processes in visual and auditory perception, which have developed because they serve the basic function of providing useful information about the environment, provide useful information by routinely exaggerating perceptual differences, adopting a goal of accurate group perceptions may result in exaggerations of perceived between-groups differences and minimizations of perceived within-group variability (Tajfel, 1970; Tajfel & Wilkes, 1963). Indeed, the basic process of cognitively representing groups (the mapping of a categorical dimension onto a continuous one) is well known to result in such perceptual biases (Eiser & Stroebe, 1972).

Furthermore, the goal of accurately summarizing the characteristics of social groups and differentiating among them is only one of the many motivations that stereotypes serve. An additional function is to simplify a complex social environment (Macrae, Milne, & Bodenhausen, 1994; Stangor & Ford, 1992). Stereotypes develop more strongly under cognitively demanding conditions, such as when the number of groups that individuals have to learn about increases or when individuals are distracted by a secondary task (Stangor & Duan, 1991). Parallel results have been found in the area of individual differences. Individuals with high "need for structure" (Neuberg & Newsom, 1993; Schaller, Boyd, Yohannes, & O'Brien, 1995) develop stronger stereotypes. It would be expected that stereotypes that develop to fulfill the function of cognitive parsimony would be particularly likely to be less variable and more extreme than their objective basis, for it is exactly such "simplified" beliefs that are most functional in simplifying the social world.

Perhaps the most basic function of stereotypes is that they provide positive feedback about the self and the ingroup. Stereotypes help create both individual and social self-esteem. Stereotypes that are developed to fulfill such needs will likely be not only distorted, but systematically biased in the sense that the perceived content of stereotypes about the ingroup will be more positive than the content of stereotypes ascribed to outgroups. Again, such biases have been well documented in the literature (cf. Brewer, 1979; Diehl, 1990; Howard & Rothbart, 1980) and develop even in "minimal" situations, where there is little need for self-enhancement.

Finally, stereotypes may function to justify existing attitudes or social situations (cf. Jost & Banaji, 1994). At the collective level, groups of individuals may develop collective beliefs that serve to justify or support the superiority of their own group over other groups (Stangor & Schaller, in press). As with self-enhancement motives, such justification functions lead individuals to focus on dimensions that favorably differentiate them from others.

In addition to potential inaccuracy that may result from the motivational functions of stereotypes reviewed above, there is also a host of cognitive mechanisms that may produce inaccurate group beliefs. The well-known *illusory correlation phenomenon* suggests that people are likely to develop overly negative beliefs about minority groups. And once such negative stereotypes begin to develop, they may be maintained through self-fulfilling prophecies, biased social memory (Fyock & Stangor, 1994), confirming information search, and biased exposure to members of the groups (cf. Hamilton, 1981; Macrae, Stangor, & Hewstone, in press).

Of course, none of the previous analysis can be taken to indicate that stereotypes are necessarily accurate or inaccurate. The studies demonstrating that underlying motivational needs influence stereotype development have only demonstrated that different motives increase or decrease the perceived extremity or variability of stereotypic beliefs. And if it is true that people routinely underestimate the actual distribution of stereotypes in the population (cf. McCauley, Stitt, & Segal, 1980), then when stereotypes are exaggerated through cognitive or motivational biases, they may actually turn out to be more accurate! My guess is that cognitive and motivational processes frequently result in objectively inaccurate beliefs, particularly because there are many motivational reasons to hold inaccurate group beliefs and there are few objective checks on the accuracy of these beliefs. Most perceivers simply do not know if their stereotypes are correct or incorrect and have no way of finding out. Furthermore, the ubiquitous processes of consistency resolution that occur in everyday life make it unlikely that individuals will frequently disconfirm their expectancies. In any case, I believe the study of the content accuracy of stereotypes can be informed by a consideration of their underlying functions. Stereotypes are likely to be differentially accurate, depending on the goal for which they have been developed. Similarly, there is likely to be variability in stereotype accuracy across individuals as a function of the underlying functions that their stereotypes serve for them.

ON THE LIMITATIONS OF STUDYING
CONTENT INACCURACY

Even if I thought it were desirable or important to catalog the accuracy of social stereotypes, I would be pessimistic about our ability to make definitive statements in this regard. This is because I believe the prognosis for developing unambiguous criteria on which to make such statements is small. The problem is that stereotypes often represent beliefs about the trait characteristics of a social group rather than beliefs about more objective criteria, such as group attitudes or behaviors. And the criteria for assessing the accuracy of trait beliefs are simply not clear. Consider two individuals who are in perfect agreement regarding behaviors that are evidenced by a group (i.e., "not holding a job" and "not spending much money"), and consider also the possibility that these beliefs are objectively accurate, as indexed by current unemployment rates or percentage of yearly income that is saved versus spent. And yet these two individuals may still differ dramatically in how they interpret these behaviors and, thus, differ substantially in the stereotypes they form about the group. One individual may interpret high rates of savings as "thrifty," whereas another may interpret the same behavior as "stingy" (see Maass & Arcuri, in press; Peabody, 1968). Indeed, it is expected that the same behavior will be differentially interpreted by different perceivers because these beliefs are inherently bound up in the host of motivational and social functions that stereotypes serve. Because an aggressive behavior does not necessarily denote an aggressive personality, a person who makes that inference is no more "right" or "wrong," no more "accurate" or "inaccurate," than a person who does not. Both people have perceived reality correctly and yet have developed very different interpretations of it (cf. Oakes et al., 1994, chapter 8).

There may be a solution to this dilemma, but I do not know what it is. I do know, however, that the approach taken by Oakes et al. (1994), namely, to argue that it is the phenomenological validity of the stereotype that represents its reality, will not work. To the perceiver, his or her group beliefs certainly appear to be accurate. If they did not, they would certainly be abandoned. The accuracy of a stereotype must be determined on an objective basis (see Judd & Park, 1993), but what criteria will form the basis of that determination when assessing beliefs about the trait characteristics of social groups is not yet clear.

There is still one more aspect of the content accuracy question that further complicates its study. This issue concerns the question of which categories become the basis on which stereotypes are developed. There are many potential features that can be used as a basis of categorization, and yet only a few become stereotypes. Race, sex, and age are commonly used social categories, whereas eye and hair color, height, and shoe size are not. Yet, we do not know whether category dimensions that are highly stereotyped are more informative about personality than are the dimensions that are not highly stereotyped. Thus, people may not develop stereotypes on the basis of their accuracy, but rather on the basis of important sociopolitical variables, such as sex, race, age, and social class. Any complete study of content inaccuracy must address not only the accuracy of beliefs about existing categories, but also the issue of whether those categories are themselves the most useful and accurate. As discussed in the next section, one form of application inaccuracy involves the persistent overuse of a given set of social categories.

DETERMINANTS OF APPLICATION ACCURACY

I argued in the previous section that there is nothing inherently wrong with possessing stereotypes, even if they are negative and inaccurate. But I believe that there is also nothing inherently wrong with using them; social categorization and social stereotyping are inherently neutral processes. Stereotypes, as social tools, are sometimes highly efficient. Consider a case in which all a perceiver knows about a target is a social category membership (that the target is female). If this perceiver's beliefs about the traits of women in general are at least partially accurate, then it seems reasonable for him or her to use that belief as a basis of judgment, in lieu of making a decision on the basis of no information at all. Thus, it is not the tools themselves that are bad, nor is the appropriate application of the tools incorrect. But although the appropriate tool can be highly useful if applied in an appropriate manner, even a normally useful tool can produce disastrous results when misapplied.

It is the potential misuse of social stereotypes as perceptual tools, and the negative consequences of such misuse, that has fueled the interest of researchers within social psychology. Social psychologists realize that it *matters* when stereotypes are misused. It matters when an employer hires a man rather than a woman for a given job because he believes that men are inherently more suited for it. It matters when girls are told that they should take English rather than mathematics in high school. It matters when a Black family is excluded from the possibility of owning a house in a nice neighborhood because a real estate agent believes that they will have too many children and not take care of the property. In this sense, the critical issues of stereotyping go beyond the question of whether the perceiver, on average, is accurate in his or her perceptions, to the potential negative outcomes that can occur when targets are inappropriately stereotyped.

The potential negative outcomes of the misuse of stereotypes are, of course, most serious when the applied stereotypes are negative. But stereotyping can also be inappropriate and unfair when the stereotypes are positive. When a Black person is characterized with such positive stereotypes as "athletic" or "musical," this process may be perceived as presumptuous and unfair. Furthermore, such stereotyping may limit the individual's opportunities to demonstrate that he or she possesses skills or qualities that are different from those of other Blacks.

Stereotypes can be considered to have been misapplied when they are used as a basis of judgment while ignoring or underusing other potentially available information that is more diagnostic about the person being judged. The most common type of misapplication occurs when people rely on their stereotypes to judge others in lieu of using behavioral information. For instance, in one relevant field study, Glick, Zion, and Nelson (1988) found that male interviewees were more likely to be interviewed or hired for a sales manager job and that female interviewees were more likely to be interviewed or hired for a dental receptionist/secretary position, even though information provided in the resumés of the applicants was identical.

Stereotypes can also be misused, not when an individual uses social categories rather than individuating information as a basis for a response, but rather when one specific category or set of categories is used repeatedly as a basis of judgment rather than other more diagnostic categories. Such misapplication of stereotypes occurs, for instance, in prejudiced perceivers, who categorize on the basis of race rather than on the basis of other appropriate categories, or for misogynists, who categorize on the basis of sex. Empirical research supports the contention that prejudiced perceivers are more likely to categorize by race than on the basis of other competing categories (cf. Allport & Kramer, 1946; Stangor, Lynch, Duan, & Glass, 1992).

Although the studies cited above suggest that stereotypes are sometimes used as a basis of judgment instead of other more diagnostic information, it is not possible to draw the strong conclusion from these data that any application of stereotypes is inappropriate, whereas any application of individuating information is appropriate. Conceptually, there is little difference between the information that a social category can provide and the information that a behavioral category can provide. Each type of information has the potential to be accurate or inaccurate.

Indeed, there are times when taking into consideration the category membership of an individual can have highly positive consequences. Consider, for instance, the potential positive outcomes that can accrue when unique advice is given to a minority undergraduate student that helps him or her develop social support networks to cope with the prejudice and racism that he or she may experience during college. Many colleges and universities have added minority-advising offices to provide this information to students. Yet, would it not be even more appropriate to base responses to these individuals on their personal situation, rather than on categorical information? Although many Blacks may lack social support at the university setting and may require remedial work, not all do, nor do all desire this support. Social categories are not the most appropriate basis of information simply because they provide some relevant information. It is virtually always possible to find other personal variables that are even more diagnostic and relevant. Although going beyond categorization requires making the "hard choice" (Fiske, 1989), it is the right thing to do in almost every case.

CONCLUSION

My review of the current state of empirical and theoretical approaches to the issue of stereotype accuracy has led me to question the utility of an approach that is based primarily on assessing the content accuracy of social stereotypes. Although it is the theme of this book that there is merit to assessing group differences and the perceptions of those differences, I do not believe that this approach will be highly productive in terms of producing a better understanding of the causes or consequences of stereotyping. And I believe this study could also have negative social consequences if readers of our research interpret our conclusions to indicate that stereotypes are by and large accurate and, thus, generally appropriate to use. Furthermore, I believe that a focus on content may distract us from other, more important, questions regarding issues of stereotypes and stereotyping.

A focus on the application of stereotypes makes it clear to me that the issue of content of the stereotype itself is entirely irrelevant to an understanding of the stereotyping process. This is because stereotypes are never true of every group member. Thus, using a stereotype, regardless of its accuracy, is potentially inaccurate and unfair. When a man denies an opportunity for employment to a woman because he believes that "women are not assertive," without attempting to assess whether the individual candidate in question is or is not assertive, it is entirely irrelevant (and especially so from the point of view of the applicant) whether 24% or 94% of women actually are assertive! *All* that matters is the assertiveness of the candidate herself.

One could consider the problem a different way by imagining a simple thought experiment: What would be learned by categorizing all beliefs about all social groups as either accurate or inaccurate? Would this knowledge inform us that it is appropriate to use one set of stereotypes, but not another? Or would it provide a convenient rationalization for the use of stereotypes in all situations? The implications of conceptualizing stereotype accuracy go far beyond that of scientific investigation, and we must consider these ramifications carefully. Imagine a legal case in which an employer denied employment to a qualified woman on the basis of his belief that women are too emotional to hold a management position. Yet, what would be different about this situation if it had previously been determined, on the basis of careful scientific study, that women are indeed more emotional, on average, than men and that this employer's beliefs about those differences are entirely accurate? This information is irrelevant to the judgment of this particular woman. Yet, it is not difficult to imagine that it would be used to justify the type of decision that the employer made.

Of course, one could argue that *all* information can potentially be misused and, thus, question why my concern is with the misuse of stereotypes rather than the misuse of other potentially inaccurate information. Social psychologists have historically been concerned about the use of stereotypes when these beliefs are based on *ascribed* rather than *achieved* characteristics. Ascribed characteristics are those that are attained by birth or by accident and that are out of the control of the individual. Achieved characteristics are those that are freely chosen by the individual. I would be less concerned when an employer assumes a conservative outlook for a person who identifies herself or himself as a Republican or assumes an evil personality for an individual who is an acknowledged member of the Ku Klux Klan. When an individual freely chooses a category membership, he or she is well aware of the potential stereotypes that may follow this decision. Yet, stereotyping on the basis of ascribed social group membership, such as race, sex, age, religion, and body type, has the potential for more serious outcomes on the targets of these judgments, because these categories are not actively chosen by the individual and, thus, the potential negative stereotyping is out of the person's own control.

Although the practice of using beliefs about social groups to judge others can be harmful when the stereotypes are individual beliefs, the negative outcomes of stereotyping are dramatically increased when many people within a society share these beliefs (Stangor & Schaller, in press). It matters less if one employer believes that Blacks are not fit for managerial positions. It matters much more when that belief is shared by many different employers. Thus, although both individual and collective stereotypes can be harmful, the latter are more serious. And the implications of collective group beliefs on individuals have not heretofore been adequately studied within social psychology.

As scientists concerned with improving the social condition, we must be wary of arguments that can be used to justify the use of stereotypes. While it may be tempting to argue that a person's beliefs that most Blacks are stupid, lazy, and aggressive represents a "social reality" and, thus, that these beliefs enrich, inform, and enhance his or her social perception, we cannot allow a bigot to continue to use his or her stereotypes, even if those beliefs seem to them to be accurate. Allowing this would be to ignore the potential damage that can result when stereotypes are misapplied. This argument is not the same as saying that it is only other people's beliefs that are incorrect (see Oakes, Haslam, & Turner, p. 206). All stereotypes, if inappropriately applied, are unfair to the targets of judgment.

There are certainly social, political, and economic causes of group inequalities that do not involve stereotyping. And it is possible that we have overestimated the role of stereotypes as determinants of inequities in our society. Certainly, not all people who hold stereotypes practice discrimination, nor is all discrimination the result of stereotypes. Yet the role of individual and collective perceptions, such as social stereotypes, as determinants of group relationships has been well documented in the social psychological literature, and research has clearly shown that stereotypes have powerful, and frequently unintended, influence on social behavior (Macrae et al., in press).

Arguments that stereotypes are by and large accurate are premature. It is tempting, from a purely scientific point of view, to argue that stereotypes are just other pieces of social information that should be used to the extent that they provide diagnostic information about a target. Yet the cost of misusing these beliefs is potentially high, and most important, these costs are not equally distributed between the perceiver and the receiver of the judgment. It is relatively easy for individuals with power and status to convince themselves that their social beliefs are accurate and that their use is appropriate. But it is the stigmatized and the powerless for whom the inappropriate use of stereotypes really matters. The misuse of stereotypes can have grave consequences for the victims of stereotyping; thus, it behooves every one of us to think twice or even three times before using category memberships as a basis of thinking about others.

REFERENCES

Allport, G. W. (1954). *The nature of prejudice.* Reading, MA: Addison-Wesley.

Allport, G. W., & Kramer, B. W. (1946). Some roots of prejudice. *Journal of Psychology, 22,* 9–39.

Brewer, M. B. (1979). In-group bias in the minimal intergroup situation: A cognitive–motivational analysis. *Psychological Bulletin, 86,* 307–324.

Brewer, M. B. (1988). A dual process model of impression formation. In T. K. Srull & R. S. Wyer (Eds.), *Advances in social cognition* (Vol. 1, pp. 177–183). Hillsdale, NJ: Erlbaum.

Brewer, M. B. (in press). When stereotypes lead to stereotyping: The use of stereotypes in person perception. In C. N. Macrae, C. Stangor, & M. Hewstone (Eds.), *Foundations of stereotypes and stereotyping.* New York: Guilford Press.

Brigham, J. C. (1971). Ethnic stereotypes. *Psychological Bulletin, 76,* 15–38.

Crocker, J., & Major, B. (1989). Social stigma and self-esteem: The self-protective properties of stigma. *Psychological Review, 96,* 608–630.

Diehl, M. (1990). The minimal group paradigm: Theoretical explanations and empirical findings. In M. Hewstone & W. Stroebe (Eds.), *European review of social psychology* (Vol. 1, pp. 263–292). Chichester, England: Wiley.

Eagly, A. H., & Steffen, V. J. (1984). Gender stereotypes stem from the distribution of women and men into social roles. *Journal of Personality and Social Psychology, 46,* 735–754.

Eiser, R. J., & Stroebe, W. (1972). *Categorization and social judgment.* New York: Academic Press.

Fiske, S. T. (1989). Examining the role of intent: Toward understanding its role in stereotyping and prejudice. In J. S. Uleman & J. A. Bargh (Eds.), *Unintended thought* (pp. 253–286). New York: Guilford Press.

Fiske, S. T., & Neuberg, S. L. (1990). A continuum of impression formation, from category based to individuating processes: Influences of information and motivation on attention and interpretation. *Advances in Experimental Social Psychology, 23,* 1–74.

Ford, T. E., & Stangor, C. (1992). The role of diagnosticity in stereotype formation: Perceiving group means and variances. *Journal of Personality and Social Psychology, 63,* 356–367.

Frable, D. E. S., Blackstone, T., & Scherbaum, C. (1990). Marginal and mindful: Deviants in social interaction. *Journal of Personality and Social Psychology, 59,* 140–149.

Funder, D. (1987). Errors and mistakes: Evaluating the accuracy of social judgment. *Psychological Bulletin, 101*, 75–90.

Fyock, J., & Stangor, C. (1994). The role of memory biases in stereotype maintenance. *British Journal of Social Psychology, 33*, 331–344.

Gilbert, D. T., & Hixon, J. G. (1991). The trouble of thinking: Activation and application of stereotypic beliefs. *Journal of Personality and Social Psychology, 60*, 509–517.

Glick, P., Zion, C., & Nelson, C. (1988). What mediates sex discrimination in hiring decisions? *Journal of Personality and Social Psychology, 55*, 178–186.

Hamilton, D. L. (Ed.). (1981). *Cognitive processes in stereotyping and intergroup behavior.* Hillsdale, NJ: Erlbaum.

Howard, J. W., & Rothbart, M. (1980). Social categorization and memory for in-group and out-group behavior. *Journal of Personality and Social Psychology, 38*, 301– 310.

Jost, J. T., & Banaji, M. R. (1994). The role of stereotyping in system-justification and the production of false consciousness. *British Journal of Social Psychology, 33*, 1–27.

Judd, C. M., & Park, B. (1993). Definition and assessment of accuracy in social stereotypes. *Psychological Review, 100*, 109–128.

Katz, D., & Braly, K. W. (1933). Racial stereotypes of one hundred college students. *Journal of Abnormal and Social Psychology, 28*, 280–290.

Kenny, D. A., & Albright, L. (1987). Accuracy in interpersonal perception: A social relations analysis. *Psychological Bulletin, 102*, 390–402.

Kruglanski, A. W. (1989). The psychology of being "right": On the problem of accuracy in social perception and cognition. *Psychological Bulletin, 106*, 395–409.

Lippmann, W. (1922). *Public opinion.* New York: Harcourt & Brace.

Locksley, A., Borgida, E., Brekke, N., & Hepburn, C. (1980). Sex stereotypes and judgments of individuals. *Journal of Personality and Social Psychology, 39*, 821–831.

Lord, C., & Saenz, D. (1985). Memory deficits and memory surfeits: Differential cognitive consequences of tokenism for tokens and observers. *Journal of Personality and Social Psychology, 49*, 918–926.

Maass, A., & Arcuri, L. (in press). Language and stereotyping. In C. N. Macrae, C. Stangor, & M. Hewstone (Eds.), *Foundations of stereotypes and stereotyping.* New York: Guilford Press.

Macrae, C. N., Milne, A. B., & Bodenhausen, G. V. (1994). Stereotypes as energy-saving devices: A peek inside the cognitive toolbox. *Journal of Personality and Social Psychology, 66*, 37–47.

Macrae, C. N., Stangor, C., & Hewstone, M. (Eds.). (in press). *Foundations of stereotypes and stereotyping.* New York: Guilford Press.

McCauley, C., Stitt, C. L., & Segal, M. (1980). Stereotyping: From prejudice to prediction. *Psychological Bulletin, 87,* 195–208.

Neuberg, S. L., & Newsom, J. T. (1993). Personal need for structure: Individual differences in the desire for simple structure. *Journal of Personality and Social Psychology, 65,* 113–131.

Oakes, P. J., Haslam, S. A., & Turner, J. C. (1994). *Stereotyping and social reality.* Oxford, England: Basil Blackwell.

Peabody, D. (1968). Group judgments in the Philippines: Evaluative and descriptive aspects. *Journal of Personality and Social Psychology, 10,* 290–300.

Schaller, M., Boyd, C., Yohannes, J., & O'Brien, M. (1995). The prejudiced personality revisited: Personal need for structure and the formation of erroneous group stereotypes. *Journal of Personality and Social Psychology, 68,* 544–555.

Stangor, C., & Duan, C. (1991). Effects of multiple task demands upon memory for information about social groups. *Journal of Experimental Social Psychology, 27,* 357–378.

Stangor, C., & Ford, T. E. (1992). Accuracy and expectancy-confirming processing orientations and the development of stereotypes and prejudice. *European Review of Social Psychology, 3,* 57–89.

Stangor, C., & Lange, J. (1994). Cognitive representations of social groups: Advances in conceptualizing stereotypes and stereotyping. *Advances in Experimental Social Psychology, 26,* 357–416.

Stangor, C., Lynch, L., Duan, C., & Glass, B. (1992). Categorization of individuals on the basis of multiple social features. *Journal of Personality and Social Psychology, 62,* 207–281.

Stangor, C., & Schaller, M. (in press). Stereotypes as individual and collective representations. In C. N. Macrae, C. Stangor, & M. Hewstone (Eds.), *Foundations of stereotypes and stereotyping.* New York: Guilford Press.

Tajfel, H. (1970). Experiments in intergroup discrimination. *Scientific American, 223,* 96–102.

Tajfel, H. (1981). Social stereotypes and social groups. In J. C. Turner & H. Giles (Eds.), *Intergroup behavior* (pp. 144–167). Chicago: University of Chicago Press.

Tajfel, H., & Wilkes, A. L. (1963). Classification and quantitative judgment. *British Journal of Psychology, 54,* 101–114.

Vinacke, W. E. (1957). Stereotypes as social concepts. *Journal of Social Psychology, 46,* 229–243.

12

Stereotype Accuracy: Toward Appreciating Group Differences

Clark R. McCauley, Lee J. Jussim, and Yueh-Ting Lee

The contributions to this volume indicate that empirical research on stereotype accuracy is not only possible, but burgeoning. In this final chapter, we draw on previous chapters to offer a number of emerging conclusions about stereotype accuracy. These conclusions contradict easy assumptions about stereotype inaccuracy and bias and lead to several suggestions about directions for future stereotype research.

EMERGING CONCLUSIONS ABOUT STEREOTYPE ACCURACY

Stereotype Accuracy Is More Than Trait Accuracy

Group stereotypes include beliefs about many different kinds of characteristics (Ashmore & Longo, chapter 3, this volume). In addition to personality-trait attributions, the stereotypes represented in this volume include beliefs about appearance, behavior, attitudes, preferences, skills,

Correspondence concerning this chapter should be addressed to Clark R. McCauley, Department of Psychology, Bryn Mawr College, Bryn Mawr, Pennsylvania 19010.

occupations, and census statistics. It is by no means clear that personality-trait stereotypes are the most important or central determinants of evaluation of stereotyped groups; Struch and Schwartz (1989), for instance, found that perceived differences in group values were more important in this sense than perceived differences in group traits. There is also evidence that cultures differ in the extent to which behavior is explained in terms of individual dispositions such as personality traits; Miller (1984) found Indians much less likely than Americans to use dispositional terms.

We suspect that the continuing emphasis on personality-trait attributions in stereotype research is a historical accident of the "typical trait" measures introduced in the first empirical study of stereotypes (Katz & Braly, 1933). If so, this accident is in the process of being repaired as research in social perception begins to recognize that stereotypes, as theoretical constructs, are much richer and more complex than traits (e.g., Deaux & Lewis, 1984; Fiske, 1993, on "stereotypes as complex portraits" p. 165). The contributions to the present volume suggest that research on stereotype accuracy is leading social psychology toward exploration of the world of social perception that lies beyond our well-tended garden of trait terms.

Assessing Stereotype Accuracy Is Not Simple

Conceptually, study of stereotype accuracy is a simple business: Compare beliefs about groups and group differences with relevant criteria. Beneath this simplicity, however, lurk some complex issues (Cronbach, 1955; Judd & Park, 1993). All of the contributions to this volume recognize this complexity in one way or another, but Ashmore and Longo (chapter 3) are perhaps most explicit in drawing attention to a number of important problems. There is, as already noted, the problem of determining the full range of stereotype content. There is the problem of dealing with structure: Some beliefs about a group may be more central to the stereotype than others (Solomon Asch, call your office). There is the problem of meaning: The same attribute may have different connotations for different observers. There is the problem of what stereotype to study: Assessing the accuracy of a general "beautiful is good" stereotype cannot be very rewarding if what we use everyday are subtype stereotypes of "handsome man" and "beautiful woman." There is the problem of individual differences in stereotyping: The accuracy of "personal" stereotypes may be different from the averaged "social" stereotype.

Finally, there is the criterion problem. Use of self-reports from the stereotyped group assumes that self-reports are accurate, which, of course, is not necessarily true. The accuracy of different kinds of self-report is itself an empirical question. Self-descriptions, especially regarding personality traits or behaviors loaded with social desirability, are notoriously subject to self-serving and self-enhancing biases. Thus, a discrepancy between stereotype and self-description means that at least one group is incorrect, but whether it is the stereotype or the self-report that is in error cannot be determined simply from the existence of the discrepancy. The stereotype that links campus fraternities with excessive drinking, for instance, may not be incorrect simply because fraternity members deny drinking to excess.

A more subtle version of the criterion problem is the difficulty of obtaining criterion measures that correspond exactly to the stereotype beliefs. Beliefs about group differences in the use of welfare may not correspond exactly to the census definition of Aid for Dependent Children (AFDC; see McCauley, chapter 9, this volume). Belief that a beautiful woman is more likely to be sociable may correspond to a criterion measure of amount of social activity engaged in rather than to a measure of motivation for social activity (Ashmore & Longo, chapter 3, this volume).

A potentially important version of the correspondence problem may arise when the criterion for stereotype beliefs is the self-report of members of the stereotyped group. Stereotype beliefs are usually measured by asking respondents to estimate what percentage of a stereotyped group *have* a particular characteristic (trait, opinion, preference . . . ; see Ryan, chapter 8, and McCauley, chapter 9, this volume). Perhaps respondents might more fairly be asked to estimate what percentage of the stereotyped group *would say they have* a particular characteristic. This problem was raised to the editors by Dana Bramel (personal communication). The significance of this problem cannot be assessed without empirical research to determine whether or when these two kinds of questions produce different assessments of stereotype accuracy.

Assessing Stereotype Accuracy Is Particularly Difficult for Trait Stereotypes

The special difficulty in assessing accuracy for personality-trait stereotyping is to secure a good criterion measure. The difficulty has three parts.

First, a trait is an abstraction or inference from observed behavior, a theoretical construct, about which there has been considerable controversy in the personality literature. Doubts have been raised as to whether individuals show enough cross-situational consistency in behavior to make trait terms scientifically useful (but see Funder, chapter 6, this volume).

Second, as pointed out by LeVine and Campbell (1972; see also Ashmore & Longo, chapter 3, and Ottati & Lee, chapter 2, this volume), most trait words are a complex amalgam of description and evaluation. Disagreement over trait attributions can, therefore, arise from disagreement over evaluation, concealing substantial agreement at the level of description. "I am thrifty, he is profligate; I am generous, he is stingy." Furthermore, the evaluative component of trait words can make self-report of traits a problematic criterion; not everyone is ready to recognize him- or herself as aggressive, ambitious, ignorant, or lazy.

Third, personality traits are perhaps the most prominent examples of the class of stereotype attributions that suffer from "shifting standards" of reference, as described by Biernat (chapter 4, this volume). *Tall* for a woman does not mean the same number of inches as *tall* for a man. Although not addressed by Biernat, standards may shift qualitatively as well as quantitatively. An aggressive man, for instance, is probably understood to be physically aggressive, whereas an aggressive woman may be only pushy.

The difficulty of getting a good criterion for personality-trait stereotypes has probably been responsible for the trend, noted above, toward research on stereotype characteristics other than traits. This trend is likely to continue.

Stereotypes Can Be Inaccurate, but They Can Also Be Quite Accurate

The common denominator of the contributions to the present volume is the suggestion that group stereotypes and perceptions of members of stereotyped groups can be quite accurate. This suggestion emerges from historical review of stereotype research (Ottati & Lee, chapter 2), from conceptualization of stereotypes as base-rate predictions (Funder, chapter 6) or ecological correlations (Baron, chapter 5), from practical experience with cross-cultural interaction (Lee & Duenas, chapter 7), and from various kinds of data (Ashmore & Longo, chapter 3; Biernat, chapter 4; Ryan, chapter 8; McCauley, chapter 9; and Jussim, & Eccles, chapter 10). There is likewise no doubt that stereotypes can be very inaccurate, including both exaggeration of real differences (Ryan, chapter 8) and perception of group difference where there is none (McCauley, chapter 9), although the errors found are not typically very large.

One important limitation of the data on stereotype accuracy is that, thus far, the stereotypes assessed have been for groups where perceivers and perceived have a great deal of contact. Stereotypes of Black Americans versus White Americans, males versus females, beautiful people versus plain people, and business students versus engineering or arts students on the same campus—these all involve mutual perceptions of familiar and frequently interacting groups. There is reason to believe that contact can make stereotypes more accurate.

In particular, the contact hypothesis (Allport, 1954) suggests that contact that is personal, equal status, cooperative, and institutionally encouraged will reduce intergroup hostility and negative stereotyping. Although Stephan's (1985) review of research relevant to the hypothesis has raised the number of qualifying conditions to 13 (with suggestion of more qualifications to come), Allport's 4 conditions remain central.

Often cited in support of the contact hypothesis is the Robbers Cave experiment (Sherif & Sherif, 1969), in which group conflict led to hostility and negative stereotyping, but cooperative contact—equal-status, personal, and authority-supported contact—dissolved the group distinctions. This result is sometimes overinterpreted to suggest that the right kind of contact can dissolve real group differences, but note that Sherif and Sherif started their experiment with two groups of boys as similar as they could make them. Their carefully arranged cooperative contact eliminated mutual hostility and negative stereotyping between two groups who did not, in fact, differ. Thus, a reasonable conclusion from Sherif and Sherif's experiment is that the right kind of contact can reduce inaccurate stereotypes.

With this understanding of the contact hypothesis, we can say that it predicts that the mutual stereotyping of the kinds of groups so far studied should be relatively accurate. Males and females, business and engineering students, beautiful people and plain people, and even Black and White American students have considerable experience of interaction under conditions approximating the requirements of the contact hypothesis. It is, therefore, not surprising that their mutual stereotyping is often quite accurate. Whether stereotype accuracy would be as good for more distant or more hostile groups must remain a question for future research.

Note that even if more contact is associated with more accuracy, there remains an important uncertainty about the mediation of this relationship. Is it accumulating personal contact with individual members of another group that teaches accurate beliefs about the characteristics of the outgroup? This has been a tempting assumption in the literature on group contact and is in keeping with the emphasis on interpersonal as opposed to intergroup contact as one of the conditions required for contact to improve intergroup relations. But there remains the possibility that even in the midst of many interpersonal contacts with members of another group, stereotype beliefs may be largely learned from other members of one's own group.

The latter possibility is at least suggested by Sherif and Sherif in calling for more research on the origins of intergroup attitudes:

> In essence, Hartley (1936, 1944) showed that the individual's attitudes towards other groups stem primarily from contacts within his reference group, rather than from personal experiences with the outgroup in question. The powerful role of group reference was documented again in Pars Ram's UNESCO study (1955) showing that

intensity of personal suffering in intergroup conflict is not directly related to the strength of hostility toward the group seen as the cause of the suffering. (Sherif & Sherif, 1965, pp. 171–172)

Stereotypes, too, may be more a matter of group reference than of personal experience, even when personal experience is plentiful. More intergroup contact may make the group reference, the social stereotype, more accurate, and acculturation into the social stereotype may then make the individual's beliefs more accurate.

Whatever the nature of the relation between contact and accuracy, degree of intergroup contact is only one of many factors that may affect stereotype accuracy. In chapter 8, Ryan points to group identification as another possible moderator of stereotype accuracy. These are signposts in a direction that needs further investigation; as Ryan suggests, we should be interested in developing predictions about when and how stereotypes are likely to be more or less accurate. This kind of moderator research may prove as difficult as it is important, and we suspect that progress will depend on accumulation of more examples of accurate and inaccurate stereotypes. That is, the relatively few and recent studies of stereotype accuracy probably do not yet provide an adequate grounding of fact on which to raise or test powerful hypotheses about the moderators of stereotype accuracy.

Stereotypes Do Not Generally Exaggerate Real Group Differences

The idea that stereotypes are exaggerations of real group differences (Campbell, 1967) has been very popular in social psychology. As influential a figure as Allport (1954) went so far as to define stereotypes as all-or-none beliefs about a group. With the advent of a more probabilistic definition of stereotype belief (McCauley, Stitt, & Segal, 1980), stereotype exaggeration became an attractive hypothesis. An important part of its attraction is that it offers an answer to the question, What is wrong with stereotypes? As noted in the Introduction (chapters 1 and 2), this question was easy to answer when stereotypes were seen as all-or-none beliefs, but no longer easy to answer once stereotypes were understood as probabilistic expectations (but see Stangor, chapter 11, this volume).

The exaggeration hypothesis is also attractive because it is the confluence of a number of plausible theories. Exaggeration can be predicted as a species of perceptual-contrast effect, as a simplification that helps reduce demands on limited human information-processing resources, or as a result of motivations for self-esteem embedded in group identification or group conflict.

Despite its popularity and its plausibility, the hypothesis that stereotypes generally or consistently exaggerate real group differences is not supported by the accumulating evidence (McCauley, chapter 9, this volume). There is no doubt that stereotypes sometimes exaggerate group differences, but also no doubt that stereotypes sometimes underestimate these differences. The purely cognitive versions of the exaggeration hypothesis, which predict exaggeration as a function of general mechanisms of perceptual contrast or information processing, are not consistent with the small and sometime nature of the exaggerations so far reported. More motivational versions of the exaggeration hypothesis remain to be tested; research assessing the accuracy of mutual stereotyping for groups in conflict is, so far, notably rare. Ryan (chapter 8, this volume) makes a beginning in this direction in studying mutual stereotyping of Republicans and Democrats, and of Black undergraduates and White undergraduates, although these groups may be more rivalrous than hostile.

Stereotypes Do Not Necessarily Lead to Inaccuracy in Judgments About Individual Members of Stereotyped Group

The effect of stereotypes on judgments about members of stereotyped groups is quite different, depending on which of two cases is at issue.

The first case involves reaction to one or many members of a stereotyped group when nothing else but group membership is known about the target (e.g., attitude toward a halfway house for addicts in one's neighborhood, vote on government benefits for defined minorities, decision of taxi driver whether to pick up a lone Black male at midnight in a bad neighborhood). In this case, the stereotype of the group is likely to dominate the evaluation of the stereotyped target (as, normatively, it should; Funder, chapter 6, this volume).

The second case concerns evaluation of an individual target about whom there is information beyond group membership, information about previous behavior or experience or personal characteristics other than membership in a stereotyped group. In this case, there is considerable evidence that stereotypes do not get in the way of the impact of "individuating evidence" (Jussim & Eccles, chapter 10, this volume) and even some lingering doubt about whether stereotypes may be underutilized in the presence of individuating information (Funder, chapter 6, this volume).

Jussim and Eccles (chapter 10, this volume) make the important point that laboratory studies of social judgment are valuable for demonstrating mechanisms by which categorical expectations in general and stereotypes in particular can bias judgment, but that only study of judgments outside the laboratory can tell us about the extent to which these mechanisms do bias everyday judgment. In a rare study of everyday judgment, Jussim and Eccles found that teachers' judgments about their students showed little impact of race, gender, or socioeconomic status stereotyping. Rather, teachers' judgments seem to be determined by objective student differences in performance.

The generalization of this point is perhaps even more important. Empirical research on accuracy and inaccuracy in stereotypes affords an opportunity to address more directly many long-standing problems of intergroup relations. Social psychologists aspire to ameliorate the group conflicts—between ethnic, religious, and socioeconomic groups—that often spill into violence, but our journals do not reflect much firsthand knowledge of these groups. Because issues of accuracy are primarily content issues rather than process issues, a concern for accuracy and inaccuracy in social stereotypes will have the beneficial effect of coaxing social psychologists out of their ivory tower laboratories and into the field, where real people perceive and interact with other real people and groups. By studying the accuracy of everyday social perceptions and judgments (as opposed to studying mechanisms of perception and judgment of college students perceiving or interacting with confederates or with constructed targets appearing on paper, in slides, or on videotape), social psychologists will have a chance not only to test the practical significance of their cognitive-process theories, but to enrich their research with specific knowledge of current social problems of intergroup relations.

The Relation Between Stereotype Accuracy and Attitude Toward the Stereotyped Group Is Complex

More accuracy does not necessarily mean less prejudice. Some inaccurate stereotypes attribute positive characteristics to a group; some accurate stereotypes attribute negative characteristics to a group (Ottati & Lee, chapter 2, McCauley, chapter 9, and Jussim & Eccles, chapter 10, this volume).

Compounding this complexity is the problem of defining prejudice. We view current usage of the word *prejudice* much as Brigham (1971) viewed usage of the word *stereotype* 25 years ago. He aptly noted that *stereotype* was generally used as an accusation that one held unjustified beliefs about an ethnic group. He went on to define a stereotype as "a generalization made about an ethnic group . . . considered to be unjustified by an observer" (Brigham, 1971, p. 31). The explicit subjectivity of this definition made it scientifically untenable; Brigham's review deserves considerable credit for helping push social psychologists away from defining stereotypes as inaccurate.

Similarly, the word *prejudice* is currently used to mean "a negative attitude considered to be unjustified by an observer." Again, this usage is too subjective for scientific use. It may also obscure the importance of real cultural differences in intergroup relations (Ichheiser, 1948). We believe that nothing would be lost and considerable clarity gained by dropping all reference to prejudice in favor of studying the origins and consequences of negative attitudes. Olson and Zanna (1993) tacitly did just this in their recent review of attitude research. Rather than examining the relation between stereotypes and prejudice, then, we prefer to examine the relation between stereotype accuracy and attitude toward the stereotyped group.

Fishbein's model of attitude (Ajzen & Fishbein, 1980) seems to be a leading contender for representing the relation between stereotypes, accurate or inaccurate, and attitude toward the stereotyped group (Eagly & Mladinic, 1989; Stangor, Sullivan, & Ford, 1992). This model can deal with results such as reported by Lee and Duenas (chapter 7, this volume), where the Chinese and Americans agree that the Chinese are more inhibited, but disagree about whether being inhibited is bad or good. In principle, every stereotype characteristic needs to be evaluated by the stereotyper to ascertain the attitudinal implication of the belief. Is it good or bad to be willing to move far from family and friends for a big promotion? Is it good or bad to have driven a car more than 75 miles an hour? The Ajzen and Fishbein model translates stereotype beliefs into attitude toward the stereotyped group by aggregating the evaluative implications of the salient beliefs.

There Is More to Stereotypes Than Beliefs About Group Characteristics and Group Differences

The Ajzen and Fishbein (1980) model of attitude, and any model that treats stereotypes as collections of beliefs about group characteristics, will take us only part of the way toward understanding the role of stereotypes in intergroup relations. Baron (chapter 5, this volume) reminds us that stereotypes function for action and that accuracy measured as efficient action in the social world may be quite different from accuracy measured as static agreement between belief and criterion. Lee and Duenas (chapter 7, this volume) make a similar point in drawing our attention to a growing industry that tries to teach more accurate cultural stereotypes to actors in multinational and multicultural settings: Accuracy in mutual stereotyping may be helpful, but is not sufficient to bring different cultures to cooperative action.

Consider two observers who agree that Black Americans are more likely to be receiving AFDC (welfare) than are other Americans. They have the same stereotype belief, that is, they agree on the size of the correlation between race and receiving AFDC. They also agree that receiving AFDC is not a desirable characteristic; that is, they agree on the evaluation of the stereotyped characteristic. But they have different theories of origin. One believes that this difference between Black Americans and other Americans is a result of different genes; the other believes that it is a result of different history, culture, politics, or economics (cf. Baron, chapter 5, this volume, on "constraints"). Their stereotypes are not the same, and their actions toward Black Americans are likely to be very different.

Jones et al. (1984) raise substantially the same issue in discussing reactions to stigmatized groups. Attitude toward a member of one of these groups depends on the observer's construction of how the stigmatized person came to be different from others: by accident, ignorance, culpable error, or choice. Attitude and behavior toward a blind person, an alcoholic, or a schizophrenic is, thus, a moral judgment that depends on the observer's understanding of the origin of the victim's difference from others rather than on a simple evaluation of the characteristics of the difference.

It follows from these examples that study of stereotype beliefs—about an ethnic group, a stigmatized group, or any other kind of group—should include study of the theories of origin that are part of our stereotypes (see also Stangor & Lange, 1994, p. 398).

This conclusion follows equally from the recognition that stereotypes are concepts; a stereotype is our representation of a category of persons. Cognitive psychologists (Keil, 1989; Murphy & Medin, 1985) have had to recognize that our representations of natural-kind categories are more than concatenations of correlated characteristics. A cat is more than the combination of fur, claws, purr, mouse hunting, and so forth. The concept of "cat" includes some theory about the essence of cat and the origins of being a cat. The cognitive psychologists, thus, point in the same direction as the chapters by Baron (5) and by Lee and Duenas (7): To understand evaluation and action in relation to group differences, we will have to expand our conception of stereotypes to include beliefs about the origins of these differences.

WHAT IS WRONG WITH STUDYING STEREOTYPE ACCURACY?

In the Introduction (chapters 1 and 2), we reviewed, and found wanting, both the classic charges against stereotypes and the more sophisticated charges made by LeVine and Campbell (1972). Here we take up a modern case against stereotypes, in which the accuracy of stereotypes is unknowable or irrelevant and the focus is on the error and injustice associated with using even accurate stereotypes. In chapter 11, "Content and Application Inaccuracy in Social Stereotyping," Stangor stands strongly against the interest in stereotype accuracy that is the theme of every other contribution to this volume. His concerns are typical of those felt by many social psychologists and deserve to be taken seriously.

First we want to acknowledge how much common ground there is in Stangor's view of stereotype research and our own. He recognizes that there are important differences between groups, that at least some of these differences are perceived with substantial accuracy, and that at least sometimes it is reasonable to use one's stereotype in judging a member of a stereotyped group. He makes the same distinction between accuracy of stereotype belief and accuracy of judgments of members of stereotyped groups (Stangor's "application accuracy"), which informs other chapters in this volume (see, especially, Jussim & Eccles [10]; Jussim, McCauley, & Lee [1]). He also calls for more attention to the effects of stereotyping on those stereotyped, and we agree that more work of this kind is desirable (Chapman & McCauley, 1993; Jussim, 1991).

Beyond this agreement, however, lie some serious differences. Stangor argues that studying the accuracy of stereotypic beliefs is scientifically unpromising and politically dangerous, but that studying the inaccuracy of stereotypic judgments is scientifically important and politically responsible. We will consider what we take to be Stangor's major contentions about these two kinds of accuracy research. We begin with his doubts about the value of studying the accuracy of stereotype beliefs.

Stereotypes are likely to be "exaggerated and distorted through cognitive and motivational biases" (Stangor, chapter 11, this volume, p. 276). Stangor accurately describes this as an assumption of most contemporary work on stereotyping. It does suggest that study of stereotype accuracy is a waste of time: Why study accuracy if distortion is the rule and accuracy the exception? As with earlier assumptions about stereotype inaccuracy, we interpret this as a hypothesis in need of empirical support.

In suggesting the likelihood of cognitive bias, Stangor reviews the arguments from perceptual contrast and information-processing limitations that suggest that stereotype perceptions should be exaggerations of real differences (see McCauley, chapter 9, this volume). As already noted, however, the accumulating evidence does not indicate any general tendency for stereotypes to be exaggerated.

In suggesting the likelihood of motivational bias, Stangor begins with the startling claim that *"perhaps the most basic function of stereotypes is that they provide positive feedback about the self and the ingroup"* (Stangor, chapter 11, this volume, p. 281). Certainly, there is evidence that social comparison tends to focus more on dimensions that favor the subject, but we are aware of no evidence even purporting to show that the self-esteem function of belief is more important than the reality function. If, less extremely, Stangor means to hypothesize that self-esteem is a powerful force for distortion in intergroup perception, then we believe it should be interesting and important to get beyond laboratory study of minimal groups to test this hypothesis in relation to the accuracy of everyday stereotypes.

"Fundamentally, I believe that a focus on the content accuracy of stereotypes is premature because we do not yet have a well-established method for documenting those group differences themselves" (Stangor, chapter 11, this volume, p. 278). It is true that there is no gold standard for assessing real group differences, but the methods of sociology, political science, and anthropology are surely relevant. Social psychological methods are on display throughout this volume, particularly in the chapters by Ottati and Lee (2), Ryan (8), and McCauley (9). We invite readers to judge for themselves the status of these methods.

"The criteria for assessing the accuracy of trait beliefs are simply not clear" (Stangor, chapter 11, this volume, p. 283). Stangor is doubtful about our ability to develop unambiguous criteria against which to assess stereotype accuracy for personality-trait stereotypes. We have already expressed similar doubts above. With regard to the larger project of studying stereotype accuracy, however, the significance of this doubt depends entirely on how much of everyday stereotyping involves personality traits or, more

precisely, on how much of intergroup judgment and behavior depends on trait stereotyping as opposed to stereotyping of appearance, values, attitudes, behaviors, and all of the other characteristics that together make up group culture. Although research on this topic is rare, we concluded above that perceived group differences in personality are probably not the most important contributors to intergroup hostility.

"*Even if ultimately successful, cataloging the accuracy of those stereotypes is a project that will have little importance for the study of intergroup relations more broadly*" (Stangor, chapter 11, this volume, p. 278). Setting aside the pejorative implication of "cataloging," this doubt is difficult to understand in relation to Stangor's assertion a few sentences earlier: "*I believe that cataloging the nature of group differences is an important first step in producing an adequate remedy for negative intergroup behavior*" (p. 278).

More generally, we find it difficult to understand the cavalier way in which Stangor claims in several places that knowledge of stereotype accuracy is irrelevant for study of intergroup relations. This contention goes against the most basic assumption of research in social cognition: People respond not to the world as it is, but to the world as they perceive it.

In brief, Stangor's arguments that stereotype accuracy or inaccuracy is somewhere between unknowable and irrelevant do not seem to us very persuasive. We turn now to his concern with the dangers of using even an accurate stereotype.

"*Stereotypes can be considered to have been misapplied when they are used as a basis of judgment while ignoring or underusing other potentially available information that is more diagnostic about the person being judged*" (Stangor, chapter 11, this volume, p. 285). We agree entirely with this definition of how stereotypes can be misused. There is, however, no evidence to suggest that this kind of misuse is common or, indeed, that it occurs at all. First, we are not aware of any research comparing the impact of stereotype information (e.g., gender or race) and individuating information (e.g., behaviors or written resumé) that include measures of the perceived diagnostic value of these two kinds of information. That is, we are not aware of any research in which the investigators showed explicitly that what they called *individuating information* was seen by their subjects as more diagnostic than what they called *stereotype* or *base-rate information*. Second, we are not aware of any research that showed judges ignoring relevant individuating information in favor of stereotypic inference. Indeed, judges seem always to take account of variations in individuating information (see Jussim & Eccles, chapter 10, this volume, and Jussim, 1991, for review of research on this issue).

Stangor (chapter 11, this volume) cites only one study (Glick et al., 1988) to exemplify the misuse of stereotypes about which he is concerned. The study showed that male applicants were more likely to be interviewed or hired for a job as sales manager, whereas female applicants were more likely to be interviewed or hired for a job as receptionist/secretary. The resumés of male and female applicants were identical, implying that gender-occupational stereotypes must have entered into decisions about the job applicants. Unfortunately, this study did not vary the content of the resumé and so cannot tell us anything about whether individuating information was ignored. Nor can it tell us anything about the validity of the stereotype that links gender with successful performance in the two jobs studied.

In contrast, Jussim and Eccles (chapter 10, this volume) present a rare example of research examining the use of stereotypes in an everyday setting. They found, as described above, that teachers judged students mostly on individual differences in performance and showed only weak and occasional use of gender, socioeconomic status, and race stereotypes.

We conclude that misuse of stereotypes, by Stangor's own definition, remains to be demonstrated.

"Stereotypes are never true of every group member. Thus, using a stereotype, regardless of its accuracy, is potentially inaccurate and unfair" (Stangor, chapter 11, this volume, p. 287). This is a concern that extends to any probabilistic cue, that is, to any information that is less than perfectly diagnostic. Any probabilistic cue is potentially inaccurate. Using an accurate stereotype is not unfair, however, unless it is used when more diagnostic cues are ignored—as just discussed.

"Social psychologists have historically been concerned about the use of

stereotypes when these beliefs are based on ascribed rather than achieved characteristics" (Stangor, chapter 11, this volume, p. 288). Here, we believe that Stangor has enunciated most clearly the nature of his concern about the unfairness of using stereotypes in judging others. The unfairness is not that stereotypes are always negative, nor that they are always inaccurate, nor that they always lead to inaccurate judgments. Rather, the unfairness is that stereotypes will sometimes lead to inaccurate judgments of individuals for characteristics over which they have no control—sex, race, or age.

We share Stangor's unease about judging someone on the basis of an accident of birth, but this seems to us a moral rather than a scientific judgment. As Stangor recognizes elsewhere in his chapter, *"Conceptually, there is little difference between the information that a social category can provide and the information that a behavioral category can provide"* (p. 286). And, as Funder (chapter 6, this volume) makes clear, a judge aiming to maximize accuracy must weigh cues in relation to their diagnosticity; whether the cues are ascribed or achieved characteristics must be irrelevant.

Using an accurate stereotype, then, is just as fair as using any other cue of equal diagnosticity for the judgment required. To take Stangor's example, imagine two candidates for a management position who have the same qualifications except that one is male and the other female. Is gender relevant to the choice? Stangor says no. We say maybe yes—yes to the extent that gender is an accurate predictor of success on this job, beyond the extent to which success is predicted by other available information (such as might appear in a resumé). Whether the stereotype linking gender and success for this job is accurate is, to us, a vital issue in evaluating the selection procedure.

CONCLUSION

Thus, we find little support for Stangor's doubts about the value of studying stereotype accuracy and little support for his concerns about the unfairness of using even accurate stereotypes. Rather, we see Stangor as caught between the modern view of stereotypes and the old identification of stereotypes with prejudice. He is no longer ready to maintain that stereotypes are necessarily or even generally inaccurate, so he is moved to argue that accuracy is unknowable or unimportant in comparison with the dangers of misusing stereotypes. We are grateful to him for making explicit some of the concerns that many social scientists share, and we cannot better acknowledge his value as devil's advocate than by quoting the concluding sentences of his recent review of stereotype research:

> To what extent is stereotyping accurate versus (as more commonly assumed) biasing? Finding answers to these issues will not be easy given the difficulty of defining appropriate standards for assessing accuracy, but stereotype accuracy is a question that is not going to go away, and one that needs to be more frankly addressed. (Stangor & Lange, 1994, p. 406)

We believe that the contributions to this volume document and illustrate a multitude of pressing research problems involving stereotype accuracy. We hope that the volume may also stand against the too common tendency to identify research on stereotype accuracy with some kind of hostility against stereotyped groups.

A few years ago, one of us wrote a paper in which, at one point, he called for more research on the accuracy of stereotypes on the grounds that the assumption of inaccuracy seemed so important in social psychology. One reviewer responded very negatively to this aspect of the paper: "What should we be doing? Articles with titles like 'Are Blacks really lazy?' and 'Are Jews really cheap?'?"

This volume is our answer to that question.

REFERENCES

Ajzen, I., & Fishbein, M. (1980). *Understanding attitudes and predicting behavior.* Englewood Cliffs, NJ: Prentice Hall.

Allport, G. W. (1954). *The nature of prejudice.* Cambridge, MA: Addison-Wesley.

Brigham, J. C. (1971). Ethnic stereotypes. *Psychological Bulletin, 76,* 15–38.

Campbell, D. T. (1967). Stereotypes and the perception of group differences. *American Psychologist, 22,* 817–829.

Chapman, G.B., & McCauley, C. (1993). Early career achievements of National Science Foundation (NSF) graduate applicants: Looking for Pygmalion and Galatea effects on NSF winners. *Journal of Applied Psychology, 78*, 815–820.

Cronbach, L. J. (1955). Processes affecting scores on "understanding of others" and "assumed similarity." *Psychological Bulletin, 52*, 177–193.

Deaux, K., & Lewis, L. L. (1984). Structure of gender stereotypes: Interrelationships among components and gender label. *Journal of Personality and Social Psychology, 46*, 991–1004.

Eagly, A. H., & Mladinic, A. (1989). Gender stereotypes and attitudes toward women and men. *Personality and Social Psychology Bulletin, 15*, 543–558.

Fiske, S. (1993). Social cognition and social perception. *Annual Review of Psychology, 44*, 155–194.

Glick, P., Zion, C., & Nelson, C. (1988). What mediates sex discrimination in hiring decisions? *Journal of Personality and Social Psychology, 55*, 178–186.

Hartley (Horowitz), E. L. (1936). The development of attitudes toward the Negro. *Archives of Psychology, 28*, 178–186.

Hartley (Horowitz), E. L. (1944). Race attitudes. In O. Klineberg (Ed.), *Characteristics of the American Negro* (pp. 139–247). New York: Harper.

Ichheiser, G. (1948). Are our silent presuppositions about prejudice correct? [Letter to the editor]. *American Psychologist, 3*, 451.

Jones, E. E., Farina, A., Hastorf, A. H., Markus, H., Miller, D. T., & Scott, R. A. (1984). *Social stigma: The psychology of marked relationships.* New York: W. H. Freeman.

Judd, C. M., & Park, B. (1993). Definition and assessment of accuracy in social stereotypes. *Psychological Bulletin, 100*, 109–128.

Jussim, L. (1991). Social perception and social reality: A reflection–construction model. *Psychological Review, 98*, 54–73.

Katz, D., & Braly, K. (1933). Racial stereotypes of one hundred college students. *Journal of Abnormal and Social Psychology, 28*, 280–290.

Keil, F. C. (1989). *Concepts, kinds, and cognitive development.* Cambridge, MA: MIT Press.

Levine, R. A., & Campbell, D. T. (1972). *Ethnocentrism.* New York: Wiley.

McCauley, C., Stitt, C., & Segal, M. (1980). Stereotyping: From prejudice to prediction. *Psychological Bulletin, 87*, 195–208.

Miller, J. G. (1984). Culture and the development of everyday social explanation. *Journal of Personality and Social Psychology, 46*, 961–978.

Murphy, G. L., & Medin, D. L. (1985). The role of theories in conceptual coherence. *Psychological Review, 92*, 289–316.

Olson, J. M., & Zanna, M. P. (1993). Attitudes and attitude change. *Annual Review of Psychology, 44*, 117–154.

Ram, P. (1955). *A UNESCO study of social tensions in Aligarh, 1950–51*. Ahmedebad, India: New Order.

Sherif, M., & Sherif, C. W. (1965). Research on intergroup relations. In O. Klineberg & R. Christie (Eds.), *Perspectives in social psychology* (pp. 153–177). New York: Holt, Rinehart & Winston.

Sherif, M., & Sherif, C. W. (1969). *An outline of social psychology* (Rev. ed.). New York: Harper & Row.

Stangor, C., & Lange, J. E. (1994). Mental representations of social groups: Advances in understanding stereotypes and stereotyping. *Advances in Experimental Social Psychology, 26*, 357–416.

Stangor, C., Sullivan, L. A., & Ford, T. E. (1992). Affective and cognitive determinants of prejudice. *Social Cognition, 9*, 359–380.

Stephan, W. G. (1985). Intergroup relations. In G. Lindzey & E. Aronson (Eds.), *The handbook of social psychology* (Vol. 2, pp. 599–658). New York: Random House.

Struch, N., & Schwartz, S. H. (1989). Intergroup aggression: Its predictors and distinctness from in-group bias. *Journal of Personality and Social Psychology, 56*, 364–373.

Author Index

Numbers in italics refer to listings in the reference sections.

Subject Index

About the Editors

Yueh-Ting Lee received his PhD in personality and social psychology from the State University of New York at Stony Brook in 1991 and is currently assistant professor of psychology at Westfield State College, Westfield, Massachusetts. He has been teaching personality/social psychology and cross-cultural psychology and doing research on such issues as stereotypes, prejudice, interpersonal and intergroup/intercultural conflict and perception, social identity and beliefs, and personality differences both in mainland China and in the United States since 1985. Many of his articles have been published in national and international refereed journals. He has published a few books both in Chinese and in English.

Lee J. Jussim received his PhD from the University of Michigan and is currently associate professor of psychology at Rutgers University. His research addresses relations among social perception, self-perception, and social reality. This work includes research on self-fulfilling prophecies, bias, accuracy, stereotypes, and reactions to evaluations. He has won several awards for this research, including a 1993 Rutgers University Board of Trustees Fellowship for Scholarly Excellence, the 1991 Gordon Allport Award from the Society for the Psychological Study of Social Issues, and the 1988 Society for Experimental Social Psychology Dissertation Award. Much of his current research, which is on relations between teacher expectations and student achievement, is supported by a FIRST award from the National Institute of Child Health and Development.

Clark R. McCauley received his PhD in social psychology from the University of Pennsylvania in 1970. He is professor of psychology at Bryn Mawr College and adjunct professor of psychology at the University of

Pennsylvania. He has published broadly in social and testing psychology and serves on the editorial board of *Understanding Violence*, the Harry Frank Guggenheim Foundation's review of research on dominance, aggression, and violence.